Professional Blogging FOR DUMMIES®

by Susan Getgood

Foreword by Elisa Camahort Page,
Co-founder and COO, BlogHer, Inc.

WILEY

Wiley Publishing, Inc.

Professional Blogging For Dummies®

Published by
Wiley Publishing, Inc.
111 River Street
Hoboken, NJ 07030-5774

www.wiley.com

Copyright © 2010 by Wiley Publishing, Inc., Indianapolis, Indiana

Published by Wiley Publishing, Inc., Indianapolis, Indiana

Published simultaneously in Canada

For general information on our other products and services, please contact our Customer Care Department within the U.S. at 877-762-2974, outside the U.S. at 317-572-3993, or fax 317-572-4002.

For technical support, please visit www.wiley.com/techsupport.

Wiley also publishes its books in a variety of electronic formats. Some content that appears in print may not be available in electronic books.

Library of Congress Control Number: 2010930958

ISBN: 978-0-470-60179-2

Manufactured in the United States of America

10 9 8 7 6 5 4 3 2 1

WILEY

About the Author

Susan Getgood has been involved in online marketing since the early '90s, and watched the Web evolve from the first browsers to the interactive communities people participate in today. Since 2004, she has helped organizations integrate social media into their marketing strategies to meet their customers online, build their brands, and drive revenue.

Prior to founding her consulting practice, Susan held a variety of corporate marketing and management roles including Senior Vice President of Marketing at Internet software company SurfControl, General Manager of Cyber Patrol, and Director of Corporate Communications at The Learning Company.

Her professional marketing blog, where she writes about blogger outreach, social media, and marketing strategy, is Marketing Roadmaps (`http://get good.com/roadmaps`). She also writes a personal blog, Snapshot Chronicles (`http://snapshotchronicles.com`), and a family travel blog, Snapshot Chronicles Roadtrip (`http://snapshotchronicles.com/roadtrip`).

Susan was named a Fellow of the Society for New Communications Research in 2008, and speaks regularly at social media conferences like BlogHer, Mom 2.0, and New Comm Forum. She is a co-founder of blog ethics and education initiative, Blog with Integrity (`www.blogwithintegrity.com`), and was a contributing editor for BlogHer's Fall 2009/Winter 2010 Digital Parenting/Family Connections project.

She lives in a suburban setting that includes a big backyard full of birds, including two Downy Woodpeckers who are extremely possessive about their territory and have been known to chase off much larger birds. She has two cats who are very interested in making the acquaintance of the birds and spend much of the day plotting, a ten-year-old son whose role model is Chuck Bartowski, and several Scottish Terriers who are determined to trap a skunk of their very own under the deck, so they can play with it any time they want.

Susan loves to talk about blogging and social media, and looks forward to hearing from the readers of *Professional Blogging For Dummies*. You can contact her at `sgetgood@getgood.com` or on Twitter at `@sgetgood`. More information about her consulting and speaking services is available at `http://getgood.com`.

Dedication

To my mother Sandra and my son Douglas. Mum, because she's been my first reader my entire life. And Douglas, because he's the most important one.

Author's Acknowledgments

Thank you to everyone I know. Seriously, somehow, you had a part in the final product that is this book.

Particular thanks to my friends and colleagues who shared their expertise and experiences with me for the book:

Many thanks to Acquisitions Editor Amy Fandrei, Project Editor Kim Darosett, and the entire Wiley team for all your work in making this book happen, to Ellen Gerstein for introducing me to Amy at BlogHer '09, and to Yvonne DiVita, for your advice and feedback on the initial proposal. I wouldn't be the author of this book without all of you.

Finally, thank you to my family for your love and support. It means everything.

Throughout this book, I used real examples and case studies. Some stories became case studies, other information was used as background, but everyone's contribution was important:

Rita Arens: Surrender, Dorothy (surrenderdorothy.typepad.com)

Joanne Bamberger: PunditMom (punditmom.com)

Carla Birnberg: MizFitOnline (mizfitonline.com)

Janice Newell Bissex and Liz Weiss: Meal Makeover Moms (mealmakeover moms.com/kitchen)

Beth Blecherman: TechMamas (techmamas.com)

Ciaran Blumenfeld: Momfluential (momfluential.net)

Kristin Brandt: Manic Mommies (manicmommies.com)

Stefania Pomponi Butler: CityMama (citymama.typepad.com)

Megan Garnhum Capone: A Girl Must Shop (agirlmustshop.com)

Sarah Caron: Sarah's Cucina Bella (sarahscucinabella.com)

Kristen Chase: Motherhood Uncensored (motherhooduncensored.net)

Marie Cloutier: Boston Bibliophile (bostonbibliophile.com)

Kimberly Coleman: Mom in the City (mominthecity.com)

Allison Czarnecki: Petit Elefant (petitelefant.com)

Kevin Dugan: Bad Pitch Blog (badpitch.blogspot.com)

Danielle Friedland: That Danielle (daniellefriedland.com)

Tracey Gaughran-Perez: MamaPop (mamapop.com)

Jodi Grundig: Mom's Favorite Stuff (momsfavoritestuff.com)

Jaden Hair: Steamy Kitchen (steamykitchen.com)

Edward Hasbrouck: The Practical Nomad (www.hasbrouck.org/blog)

Chris Hogan: Off the Cuff (offthecuffdc.com)

Megan Jordan: Velveteen Mind (velveteenmind.com)

Mir Kamin: Want Not (wantnot.net)

Matt Kepnes: Nomadic Matt's Travel Site (nomadicmatt.com)

Christine Koh: Boston Mamas (bostonmamas.com)

Preston Koerner: Jetson Green (jetsongreen.com)

Debbie Lawrence: Lagniappe Marketing (lagniappemarketing.net)

Jeff McIntire-Strasburg: Sustainablog (sustainablog.org)

Jill Notkin: The Daily Grind of a Work at Home Mom (workathomemom.typepad.com/the_daily_grind_of_a_work)

Sherry and John Petersik: Young House Love (younghouselove.com)

Florinda Pendley Vasquez: The 3 R's Blog (3rsblog.com)

Kyran Pittman: Notes to Self (notestoself.us)

Devra Renner: Parentopia (parentopia.net/blog)

Debra Roby: A Stitch in Time (astitchintime.blogspot.com)

I'm also grateful to my professional colleagues who were gracious enough to share their expertise on specific topics:

Liza Barry-Kessler: Privacy Counsel LLC (privacycounsel.net) and Liza Was Here (lizawashere.com) (Chapter 3)

Chris Baskind: chrisbaskind.com (Chapter 9)

Toby Bloomberg: Diva Marketing (divamarketingblog.com) (Chapter 12)

Todd Defren: SHIFT Public Relations and blog PR-Squared (pr-squared.com) (Chapter 12)

Yvonne DiVita: Windsor Media Enterprises (wmebooks.com) and Lip-sticking (lipsticking.com) (Chapters 5 and 7)

Liz Gumbinner: Cool Mom Picks (coolmompicks.com) and Mom-101 (mom-101.com) (Chapter 6)

David Herrington: Active Oak, LLC (activeoak.com) (Chapters 4, 5, and 8)

Kami Watson Huyse: Communication Overtones (overtonecomm.blogspot.com) and Zoetica (zoeticamedia.com) (Chapter 12)

Jaelithe Judy: jaejudy.com (Chapter 11)

Kim Kramer: Berluti & McLaughlin, LLC (bermac-law.com) (Chapter 3)

Julie Marsh: Cool Mom Picks (coolmompicks.com) (Chapter 6)

Elisa Camahort Page: BlogHer (blogher.com) (Chapter 6)

Ike Pigott: Occam's Razr (occamsrazr.com) (Chapter 12)

Jim Prather: YouData (youdata.com) (Chapter 6)

Laura Tomasetti: 360 Public Relations (360prblog.com) (Chapter 12)

David Wescott: APCO Worldwide and blog It's Not a Lecture (itsnotalecture.blogspot.com) (Chapter 12)

Publisher's Acknowledgments

We're proud of this book; please send us your comments at http://dummies.custhelp.com. For other comments, please contact our Customer Care Department within the U.S. at 877-762-2974, outside the U.S. at 317-572-3993, or fax 317-572-4002.

Some of the people who helped bring this book to market include the following:

Acquisitions and Editorial

Project Editor: Kim Darosett

Acquisitions Editor: Amy Fandrei

Copy Editor: Jennifer Riggs

Technical Editor: Renee Wilmeth

Editorial Manager: Leah Cameron

Editorial Assistant: Amanda Graham

Sr. Editorial Assistant: Cherie Case

Cartoons: Rich Tennant
  (www.the5thwave.com)

Composition Services

Project Coordinator: Lynsey Stanford

Layout and Graphics: Tim Detrick

Proofreaders: John Greenough,
  Lauren Mandelbaum, Bonnie Mikkelson

Indexer: Sherry Massey

Publishing and Editorial for Technology Dummies

  Richard Swadley, Vice President and Executive Group Publisher

  Andy Cummings, Vice President and Publisher

  Mary Bednarek, Executive Acquisitions Director

  Mary C. Corder, Editorial Director

Publishing for Consumer Dummies

  Diane Graves Steele, Vice President and Publisher

Composition Services

  Debbie Stailey, Director of Composition Services

Contents at a Glance

Table of Contents

Foreword

*O*ver five years ago when I first met Susan Getgood, the term *professional blogging* might have seemed almost oxymoronic. Sure, there were a handful of bloggers who had been hired by forward-thinking companies to write nascent "corporate" blogs. There were a couple of blog networks that hired bloggers to churn out regular content. There were a couple of advertising and affiliate marketing options out there (most of them low-paying) through which a handful of very large individual bloggers made some actual money.

But the average blogger wasn't motivated by monetization. The average company wasn't thinking about how to engage with bloggers. And the average reader didn't consider their favorite bloggers to be professionals, let alone *brands*.

A lot has changed in five years.

Today, the vast majority of the largest businesses are active in some way with social media. They have blogs, Twitter accounts, and Facebook fan pages. They advertise on blogs and hire PR firms to conduct *blogger relations*.

Today, blogging and social media savvy is a highly sought-after job skill.

Today, the opportunities for bloggers have exploded.

What hasn't changed in these last five years is the fact that most bloggers are still motivated by passion and commitment. And the best professional bloggers have as much passion and commitment as the ardent hobbyist.

So, driven by passion and commitment, and presented with numerous, sometimes competing opportunities . . . how can bloggers make the most of their opportunities in the most sustainable, professional way possible?

Whether you're newly drawn to the blogosphere and its opportunities, or wanting to take your blogging to the next level, this book is a comprehensive guide to how to do just that.

A lot has changed in five years. These are exciting times, and I can't think of anyone better to give you great advice on joining the ranks of professional bloggers than Susan Getgood . . . a veteran marketer, long-time blogger, and leading voice on best practices for businesses and bloggers alike.

Elisa Camahort Page, co-founder and COO, BlogHer, Inc.

Introduction

● ●

*A*ccording to the Pew Research Center Internet & American Life Project, nearly 80 percent of U.S. adults use the Internet. These people use search engines to find information, consult review sites for product recommendations, make travel arrangements, and read blogs. With numbers as large as these, big business has embraced online marketing through blogs and social networks in a big way: More than 90 percent of the Fortune 500 companies use social media in some fashion and nearly 16 percent publish blogs.

On the other hand, small businesses and individuals have had difficulty tapping into this mother lode. Small businesses typically don't have big budgets to devote to experimental marketing programs. Every dollar matters, and the new online forms are largely unproven.

You may have heard stories about professional bloggers, such as Heather Armstrong (www.dooce.com) and Darren Rowse (www.problogger.com), who make a great living from their blogs. Maybe you have an idea you want to try or perhaps you built a successful hobby blog, but just don't know where to start to make the blog work as a business.

This book offers small businesses and individuals practical guidance for successfully using a blog in, for, and as a business. I can't make you a success or deliver a six-figure blogging income, but this book can point you in the right direction.

About This Book

You don't have to read this book from front to back, but you might want to. *Professional Blogging For Dummies* follows a chronological progression that mirrors the steps of building a professional blog.

I start with what you need to think about when you decide to do a blog, provide an overview of the different ways you can make money with your blog, and then move into a step-by-step guideline for building the blog. I conclude with tips for maximizing your blog's success with the right promotion, measurement, and content strategies.

Of course, each chapter also stands alone, so you can use this book as a reference. I divided chapters into sections to make it easy to find the specific information you need to accomplish a particular task.

The best part about the book? I chocked it full of real-life examples of people just like you who have built successful blogs and were gracious enough to share their experiences with me so that I could share them with you.

Foolish Assumptions

Every author writes for an audience. In fact, that's one of the things I cover in this book. And at some point, the author has to make a few assumptions about her readers. These are my main assumptions about you:

- ✔ You have a hobby, passion, or idea and think you want to start a professional blog. Maybe you have a hobby blog that you want to monetize.

- ✔ You have a computer with high-speed Internet access and know how to use your Web browser and a word-processing application.

- ✔ You may already read blogs and participate in social networks, such as Facebook and Twitter.

Conventions Used in This Book

I know that doing something the same way over and over again can get boring, but sometimes consistency is a good thing. For one thing, consistency makes stuff easier to understand. In this book, those consistent elements are *conventions:*

- ✔ When I type URLs within a paragraph, they look like this: www.wiley. com.

- ✔ When I want you to type something or give you steps to follow, they appear in **bold.**

- ✔ New terms appear in *italic* the first time they're used. Thank the copy editor!

How This Book Is Organized

This book is organized into five parts. If you're just getting started with your first blog, you probably want to read the chapters in order. If you already have an established blog and are just trying to understand how to monetize or promote it, Parts II and IV are the most important parts.

No matter what, be sure to read Chapter 3. That chapter has important information about the impact of the Federal Trade Commission's guidelines for endorsements and testimonials on professional blogs.

Part 1: Getting Started with the Business of Blogging

Part I examines blogging at the professional level and explains how a blog can help you promote your existing business or create a new blog-based business. Practical guidance includes setting objectives, identifying your audience, analyzing your competition, and defining a unique niche for your professional blogging effort. I also provide an overview of legal issues that impact your blog, including U.S. laws regarding copyright, online advertising, and privacy.

Part 11: Making Money with Your Blog

Part II is all about how to make money with your blog. Chapter 4 is an overview of the options, and the subsequent chapters delve into each area — sales, consulting, advertising, and paid posts — in detail. I include real-world examples throughout so you can hear from people just like you who have developed successful blogs.

Part 111: Building Your Blog, Step by Step

Part III covers the things you need to do before you can develop your blog, from how to choose your blog name, software, and Web hosting to making decisions about the design. This part also goes over the key milestones in developing (or redesigning) your blog, including a step-by-step checklist you can use to monitor your progress.

Part IV: Maximizing Your Blog's Success

After you build your blog, get the word out and start building your community of readers. Part IV covers blog promotion strategies, search engine optimization, working with marketers, and measurement. Because launching the blog is only the beginning, I offer some suggestions for how to grow your blog and keep it fresh.

Part V: The Part of Tens

Like all *For Dummies* books, this one has a Part of Tens. These chapters list ten common mistakes and how to avoid them, ten blogs you can benefit from simply by reading (I have), and ten tips for jump-starting your creativity. Some of the most important advice in the book is found here.

Professional Blogging For Dummies survey

In 2008, Technorati reported that the top reasons bloggers blog are to

- ✔ Speak their mind
- ✔ Share their expertise
- ✔ Connect with like-minded people
- ✔ Keep friends and family updated

And in 2009, Technorati probed into the financial side of blogging and reported that only 17 percent of bloggers derive their primary income from blogging, largely from advertising and affiliate marketing. (See `http://technorati.com/blogging/article/day-4-blogging-revenues-brands-and.`)

Not wanting to base my conclusions on Technorati alone, I conducted a little original research into the subject, using online survey tool SurveyMonkey (`www.surveymonkey.com`). My survey objective was simple: To give you a snapshot of what people just like you do with their blogs. The best way to use the data is as an indicator of general trends among bloggers.

To solicit respondents, I reached out through my blog, Facebook, and Twitter, clearly describing the survey as a survey of independent, individual, or small-business bloggers, to be used as data for this book. A number of my friends and colleagues also passed the word onto their fans and followers.

My conclusions: It's a smaller sample than a national polling organization would have, but it's sufficient to confirm the Technorati results — that a fairly small percentage of bloggers earn their livings from their blogs.

In conjunction with the in-depth case-study interviews in the book, the survey also paints a good picture of what's going on with blogging. You don't have to ask 139 bloggers what they're doing to measure results or promote their blogs. I did it for you.

To see the complete results from this survey, check out my blog Marketing Roadmaps (`http://getgood.com/roadmaps`).

e-Cheat Sheet

The e-Cheat Sheet (`www.dummies.com/cheatsheet/professional blogging`) pulls together important checklists, such as setting your professional blogging objectives, creating your editorial mission, and working on blog development.

Icons Used in This Book

To make your experience with this book even easier, I use various icons in the margins to indicate particular points of interest.

A lot of the content in *Professional Blogging For Dummies* is informative and requires you to do more digging into your situation before you can take action. However, sometimes I give you specific suggestions on how to do something more effectively. When I do, I mark that info with this Tip icon.

This icon is a friendly reminder of an important point you want to make sure that you keep in mind.

This icon is the equivalent of an exclamation point. I use this icon to alert you to things that aren't as obvious as perhaps they should be. Think of this icon as a Remember icon with a big red flag attached.

I use this icon when I get a bit more geeky than usual to highlight technical information or steps. If you already know how to do whatever the topic is or aren't as geeky as I am, please feel free to ignore it.

Where to Go from Here

Time to just dig in. If you're new to blogging, I highly recommend that you start at the beginning and at least read Part I before you start skipping around.

If you have a blog and are looking for advice on

- ✔ **Monetization:** Read Part II.
- ✔ **Redesigning your site:** Go to Part III.
- ✔ **Promoting your blog:** Check out Part IV.

You can find more tips on the e-Cheat Sheet at www.dummies.com/cheat sheet/professionalblogging. I also write about these topics on my own blog, Marketing Roadmaps (http://getgood.com/roadmaps).

I'd love to check out your blog! Drop me a note about your experiences at sgetgood@getgood.com (or on Twitter via @sgetgood). I especially want to hear about anything you want added to this book.

Part I
Getting Started with the Business of Blogging

The 5th Wave   By Rich Tennant

"Before the Internet, we were only bustin' chops locally. But now, with our blog we're bustin' chops all over the world."

In this part . . .

Part I starts with an examination of blogging at the professional level, and explains how a blog can help promote your existing business or create a new blog-based business.

I give practical guidance on setting your objectives, identifying your audience, and analyzing your competition so you can define a unique niche for your professional blogging effort.

And because you need to know U.S. laws regarding copyright, online advertising, and privacy, I cover those topics as well and recommend best practices for use with your blog.

Chapter 1

Examining Blogging at the Professional Level

*W*hen you do something professionally, it generally means getting paid, and professional blogging is no different. Whether you want to earn your living with your blog or simply enough to pay for the family vacation or a college education, you want to know how to make money with your professional blog. This book explains the different ways to monetize your blog so you can pick the ones that work best for you.

However, to be a successful professional blogger, you need to think about more than just the sources of revenue — advertising, paid posts, affiliate commissions, and so on. You need to think about your professional, business objectives and then develop a plan to meet them. That's the big difference between a personal or hobby blog and a professional blog.

Personal bloggers have stories and experiences they want to share and may fall into making a little money along the way, but it doesn't start out that way. Professional bloggers have a business objective for their blog, and they develop a plan to achieve it.

Can you be successful with a blog without a clear plan? Sure, but it isn't probable. For instance, TechCrunch is a blog that began by reviewing new Internet products and companies and has since grown into a network of technology sites about content and new media; however, hundreds of abandoned blogs never get past a few readers. Even a lucky accident doesn't stay successful without a long-term plan, especially now that the field is far more crowded.

This chapter gets you started with your professional blogging plan. I describe what professional bloggers do, go over the main reasons to start a professional blog, and give you some tips for setting your professional blogging objectives and getting started.

Knowing What Professional Bloggers Do

According to blog search engine Technorati's annual survey of the blogosphere, the top reasons that bloggers blog are to

- Speak their mind
- Share their expertise and experience
- Make money or do business

The principal difference between a personal, or hobby, blogger and a professional one is that the personal blogger has an interest in a subject, and the successful professional blogger has an interest, a professional objective, and a plan to achieve it. Usually, making money is part of the plan; for the most part, that's what I'm concerned with in this book.

However, I don't equate professional with commercial. Although making money is often a goal of the professional blogger, it isn't the only successful outcome. For example, swaying public opinion or building a support community for a health issue or charity is a successful professional outcome.

Regardless of whether you expect your blog to be a moneymaker, a marketing tool, or a means to promote a cause, a well-planned blog can help you achieve your goals. In blog search engine Technorati's 2009 survey, 71 percent of the bloggers surveyed said they're better known in their industry because of their blog, 63 percent said prospective clients have purchased products or services after reading their blog, and 56 percent believe that their blog helped their company be regarded as a thought leader (see Chapter 5 for more about what being a thought leader means).

Building Your Online Community: The Blogging Advantage

For the most part, the professional blogger writes to support or promote an organization or himself, or wants to develop a blog as a central element of an online business — and for good reason. Prospective customers are online in ever-increasing numbers. What if you already have a Web site? Why would you need a blog to reach all those prospective customers online?

On your Web site, you talk at your visitors. On a blog, however, you speak with them. A traditional Web site is like a monologue; you speak and hope someone is listening. If you have a Web site, it's probably all about you, and that's okay; it's your online brochure.

But your Web site isn't a community, and there's rarely any conversation.

A blog, on the other hand, is a conversation with your community — the readers, customers, and prospects who are interested in what you have to say or offer. In your blog, you write about, and link to, the ideas of others as well as your own. You also create space — or places for comments — for your readers to participate and to speak with you.

This conversation on the blog is what engages and establishes your online community. In the process, you build deeper relationships with your readers and customers and achieve greater awareness for you, your blog, and your brand.

Simplifying Web site management with blogging software

Apart from the conversational opportunities of the blog, a blog may be preferable for a simple technical reason if you don't already have a Web site. Blogging software is a lightweight content management system (CMS) that allows you to share content on the Web without the expertise needed to develop a full-scale Web site. Most blogging programs are much easier to use than Web development tools, which means you can manage a simple blog with relatively little tech support. As a result, you're more likely to update the blog frequently. Search engines love sites that are updated frequently.

Knowing what people do online

According to the Pew Research Center's September 2009 research, 77 percent of American adults use the Internet, up from 67 percent in 2005, 46 percent in 2000, and 14 percent in 1995.

And 73 percent of U.S. adults use the Internet in an average day, doing one or more online activities like

✔ Using a search engine to find information (50 percent)

✔ Looking for information about a hobby or interest (29 percent)

✔ Doing research for their jobs (23 percent)

✔ Looking for information about products and services (20 percent)

✔ Reading blogs (10 percent)

✔ Buying products (8 percent)

The latest versions of the most popular blogging platforms (I focus on TypePad, WordPress, and Google Blogger in this book) are also very flexible and support a wide variety of advanced functionality. Because of this, you can develop fairly robust sites with blogging software. This means you can add things, such as multiple sections, shopping carts, and discussion forums, and online users won't realize that you're using blogging software.

Establishing trust

You need to understand why blogs are increasingly seen as trustworthy.

It starts with a human voice. People trust other people, not faceless entities. When people speak with each other on a blog, they get the chance to know each other. This humanizes the organization in a way that can't be matched by any number of missions and manifestos.

Readers also approach blogs with an expectation of honesty and transparency. Combined with the human voice, this creates an accessible platform for your expertise.

Of course, you have to live up to the expectations, but assuming you do, your blog is an unparalleled tool for attracting customers, industry influencers, and advertisers. (In Part II of this book, I give you more information on how to attract those types of valuable readers.)

Extending networking opportunities with social media

Social media, such as blogs, Twitter, and Facebook, is hot. Traditional Web sites? Not so much. Starting a blog lets you bask in the social media glow. Your blog tells your customers that you get it and are on top of the latest trends. Now, those aren't good enough reasons to embrace social media on their own; consider them beneficial and unintended consequences.

The real reason you want to contribute to the social media buzz, loud though it may be, is the network effect. If you tell a compelling story to the right people, they'll share it with others, and each person who hears it shares it onward with her network. Messages delivered through social media, including blogs, spread faster and farther, and sometimes they even spread at accelerated rates, dubbed going viral. This speed is built into the form.

Linking to and building upon other people's ideas are core values of the blogosphere. Blogging software makes doing so easy, with no need to understand HyperText Markup Language (HTML), the programming language used to create Web sites.

The proliferation of social sharing tools that allow blog readers to organize their favorite content and pass it along to friends and colleagues makes it just that much easier to share, and share widely. The most popular tools include the following:

- ✔ **Widgets:** A *widget* is an onscreen tool that displays or allows access to content — blog posts or their titles, the weather, ads, and so on. A widget, shown in Figure 1-1, lets you easily share your content. Bloggers who are fans of your blog simply insert the code in their blog sidebar to give their readers a preview of your posts.

- ✔ **Social bookmarking sites:** A social bookmarking site, such as Delicious, lets you save, tag, and share bookmarks to sites. You can even display your Delicious selections on your blog sidebar.

- ✔ **Content aggregators:** Content aggregators like Digg (see Figure 1-2), kirtsy, and memeorandum are a good way to find the hot topics in a community. Content aggregators let you submit and vote on posts. The most popular topics are featured at the top of the rankings on the aggregator's Web site.

Figure 1-1:
This widget
displays
previews
of recent
posts.

Figure 1-2:
Aggregators
like Digg
distribute
blog posts
to a wider
audience.

WARNING!

Don't fall into the myth of *viral marketing*. Tell your story, make it a good one, and encourage your community to share the message. But never forget that the community, not you, decides whether a story is compelling enough to go viral. All you can do is create the potential.

Deciding Whether a Blog Is Right for You

Blogging is a lot of fun and offers many advantages, but it may not be the right solution for you. The following sections help you decide whether you're willing to make the long-term commitment and invest your time, effort, and money to develop a blog.

You like to write or are willing to hire someone else to do it for you

Do you like to write? If you do, a blog may be the right social media choice for you. If you don't, you have alternatives. You can hire someone to write the blog, explore other forms like podcasting or video, or focus your social media effort on social networks like Facebook and Twitter. I discuss your options in more detail in the nearby sidebar "Hiring consultants versus doing everything yourself."

Do yourself a favor: If you don't like to write, don't kid yourself that you'll miraculously come to love it. That rarely happens.

Hiring consultants versus doing everything yourself

Should you hire consultants to help you or try to do everything yourself? This question doesn't have a so-called "right" answer. Both approaches have their merits, and you can combine them, getting help when you need it and doing things yourself when you don't. Although this book makes it easier to do everything on your own, I discuss the options at different stages of your blog and plan development.

The most important question to ask is: Do you like to do a task, or is it a task you're happy to avoid? Are you really good at the task, or are you better off focusing your talents on what you really do well?

For example, I'm fairly capable with blogging software and HTML; however, I'm a marketing strategist, not a graphic artist. I always bring in designers to help me with logos, blog mastheads, and graphics.

If you don't like writing and decide to look into implementing podcasts or videos, you'll most likely use a blog to distribute your multimedia content, so most of the advice in this book is still relevant. However, you need to understand additional tools and techniques that are beyond the scope of this text. I recommend that you invest in a general introduction to podcasts or online video, such as *Podcasting For Dummies,* 2nd Edition, by Tee Morris, Chuck Tomasi, Evo Terra, and Kreg Steppe, and after you select your toolset, a book that covers your chosen tools. For example, I use Sound Forge to edit podcast files and rely heavily on an aftermarket book.

You have a point of view you want to share

Regardless of whether you write, record, or film your story, you need to have a point of view, or personality, for your blog. Back to the human voice: Brochures, like your Web site, are impartial and factual. They can use the impersonal third-person voice, and no one minds — not too much anyway.

Your readers expect your blog to go beyond that, to reveal some of the person(s) behind the organization. First-person and second-person voice are required. If that's something you feel comfortable and confident with, blogging might be a good option for you.

Also consider the following points:

✔ **Blogging takes time.** Ask whether you can devote the time and resources to developing, writing, and promoting the blog.

✔ **You need to say something interesting to capture an audience's attention.** Do you have something you want to say? I dig into how to fine-tune this into an editorial mission for your blog in Chapter 2, but before you even start, you need to have an idea about topics of mutual interest to you and your prospective customers.

When deciding what you want to write about, keep in mind that a contrarian position can be very effective. This isn't a license to be argumentative. No one likes a bully. But don't think that the only approach is to agree with prevailing opinion. A controversial point of view can be very successful.

Your customers and prospects read blogs

Also consider whether a blog is right for your business goals. Here are some points to ponder:

✔ **Your customers must be interested in reading blogs.** Are your customers and prospects online? Are they reading blogs? If you don't know, ask them.

✔ **What are your competitors doing (or not doing) in social media?** Do they have blogs? If they do, do they have an engaged readership, or is their blog merely a mirror of their Web site?

Exploring the Blog and Business Connection

In the following section, I outline three basic ways bloggers use blogs to achieve professional objectives:

- ✔ Starting a blog to promote a business
- ✔ Converting a hobby or personal blog into a revenue generator
- ✔ Creating a blog-based business, such as an online magazine or review site

Use these definitions and the real-world examples sprinkled throughout the chapter to home in on the situation that fits you best.

Using a blog to promote your business

Whether you sell a product or a service, your business relies on earning the confidence of your customers, their trust that your products will perform as promised, and their trust in your expert advice. Your blog helps you forge the personal relationships that lead to mutual trust.

When a blog promotes an existing business, the main sources of revenue are usually fees and product sales, not advertising.

Small businesses, particularly ones that sell online, use blogs to promote their products and services. In 2007, Jill Notkin started The Daily Grind of a Work at Home Mom blog (`http://workathomemom.typepad.com/the_daily_grind_of_a_work`) to support her online boutique of upscale baby products, Alex Casey Baby. As shown in Figure 1-3, most of her blog content isn't about her store, but the branding is always visible, and she sprinkles in the occasional post about her products and special discounts.

However, you don't have to be an online business to have a blog. In 2004, Butler Sheetmetal, a small, family-owned firm in the United Kingdom, started the award-winning blog The Tinbasher (`www.butlersheetmetal.com/tinbasherblog`), shown in Figure 1-4, and it's still going strong.

Figure 1-3:
For an online store, a blog is a great way to engage with prospective customers.

Figure 1-4:
Even if your product can't be sold or delivered online, a blog can be an effective way to connect with your customers.

Sometimes your product is you. Professional service firms, consultants, and authors use their blogs to showcase their expertise and promote their services. For example, on her blog Communication Overtones (www.overtonecomm.blogspot.com), public relations (PR) consultant Kami Watson Huyse writes about PR and social media strategy, and often uses stories drawn from her own business experience to illustrate her point, as shown in Figure 1-5.

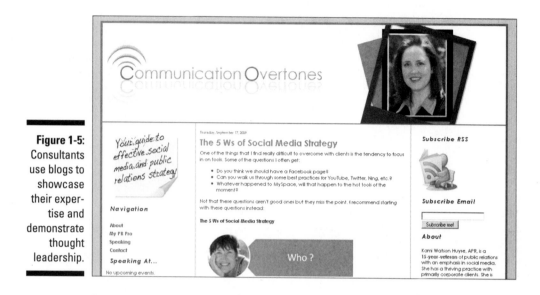

Figure 1-5:
Consultants use blogs to showcase their expertise and demonstrate thought leadership.

Carla Birnberg, a professional freelance writer who blogs about healthy living at MizFitOnline (www.mizfitonline.com), started her blog as a place for editors to read her work and to broaden her platform for a potential book. Read Carla's advice for new bloggers in the nearby sidebar, "Words of advice from bloggers who've been there."

Some other examples of consultants who use blogs to demonstrate thought leadership include

- ✔ **Seth Godin:** Well-known author and marketing pundit (http://seth godin.typepad.com)
- ✔ **Yvonne DiVita:** Entrepreneur and expert in marketing to women online (www.lipsticking.com)
- ✔ **Shel Holtz:** Organizational communications and podcasting expert (http://blog.holtz.com)

REMEMBER

Write in your authentic, first-person voice — "I" not "we" unless you have a multi-author blog. Avoid being too promotional.

Turning a hobby blog into a business

Going from hobby blog to a blog-based business is the most likely path for individual, or personal, bloggers. They start a blog to share their passion for a topic — everything from parenting to health issues to hobbies like crafting and bird watching. Their voice is honest, fresh, and informative. They build a following, and before long, the blog is a full-time unpaid job.

To convert a hobby blog to a business, you need a business plan and a monetization strategy. Generally, revenues come from a mix of streams, including advertising, affiliate commissions, product sales, consulting services, freelance writing, and speaking fees.

Words of advice from bloggers who've been there

Carla Birnberg writes about healthy living at MizFitOnline (www.mizfitonline.com). A professional freelance writer, she started the blog as a place for editors to read her work and broaden her platform for a potential book.

The most rewarding thing about blogging for her is helping people: *"I owned a personal training studio in the early '90s and have been passionate about fitness ever since. I love that MizFit allows me to give away all the information and knowledge I've accrued for free."*

Like many bloggers, her passion has led to other opportunities, including radio and a podcast, www.twofitchicks.org. Her tip for new bloggers:

"Read, read, read other blogs in your genre. Offer to do guest posts for them!"

Marie Cloutier started Boston Bibliophile (www.bostonbibliophile.com) to combine her personal hobby, reading, with her professional life as a librarian. She says:

"I was deep into job hunting and wanted to create something online that would reflect my personality and interests, and maybe help distinguish me from other people. At the same time, I hoped that by talking about the books I love, I would be able to connect with like-minded readers and share our love of literature."

Like many bloggers, she doesn't consider the blog to be a major contributor to her income but has gotten business opportunities as a result of it, including a yearlong contract job.

Her tip for new bloggers:

"Have some idea about what you want to accomplish with your blog and start slowly. You don't have to do it all at once."

Matt Kepnes, author of Nomadic Matt's Travel Site (www.nomadicmatt.com), wanted to become a professional travel writer and thought a blog would be a good way to build a portfolio. Instead, he's been able to turn his Web site into a job that permits him to travel the world full time. Most of his revenue comes from advertising and e-book sales, and the site gets about 100,000 visitors per month.

For Matt, the most rewarding thing about blogging is *"the ability to work from anywhere and meet people all over the world."* Read more about Nomadic Matt's Travel site in Chapter 2.

Blogger and freelance writer Mir Kamin is a self-described frugal shopper. She started her shopping blog Want Not (http://wantnot.net) to share the many deals she found online with her friends (see Figure 1-6). Her blog has since grown into a successful commercial enterprise and a full-time job.

Figure 1-6: Want Not is a hobby blog that made the transition to a full-time business.

Sherry and John Petersik started their home improvement blog Young House Love (www.younghouselove.com) as a way to share the story of their kitchen renovation with friends and family. Today, their initial labor of love (shown in Figure 1-7) is a full-time job for them both and includes a successful online shop, design consulting business, and column in a national do-it-yourself magazine.

Sometimes, your hobby blog bears fruit for your career. That's what happened to Megan Garnhum Capone, author of shopping blog A Girl Must Shop (www.agirlmustshop.com) and a professional graphic designer. A Girl Must Shop makes some money from advertising, affiliate commissions, and sponsored post opportunities, but the real success has been the career opportunities it has created for Megan. She says:

Figure 1-7:
Like Young
House Love,
most hobby
blogs turned
full-time job
derive their
revenue
from multi-
ple streams.

"A Girl Must Shop has helped me land consulting jobs. When a potential client sees my blog, [he's] confident that I can do the same for [him]. My blog also helped me launch my career into online marketing. Previously, I had been focused on traditional marketing. A Girl Must Shop was my proof that I could successfully manage a Web site and helped me land a 'job of my dreams' position as a Web content manager."

Developing a blog as a small business

Someone who develops a blog as a small business is usually motivated by the same thing as a hobby blogger who decides to go pro — a passion for a hobby or interest, and the desire to share knowledge and experiences with others. The main difference is that the blogger *starts* with the intent to build a blog to make money. That means having a plan from the very beginning.

The most common types of blogs as small businesses are magazines, review sites, and shopping blogs. Blog networks and communities, including hyperlocal sites, also fit into this category. Small business blogs typically make most of their money through advertising, sponsorships, and affiliate marketing. Not surprisingly, their business model often resembles that of a print magazine.

Here are some examples of blogs that are small businesses:

✔ **Blog Nosh Magazine:** The blog version of a literary magazine; see Figure 1-8 (www.blognosh.com)

✔ **Savvy Auntie:** An online community for aunts (www.savvyauntie.com)

 ✔ **ChambanaMoms.com:** A hyperlocal portal for moms in the community of Champaign-Urbana, Illinois; see Figure 1-9 (www.chambanamoms.com)

 ✔ **Palate Press:** An online wine magazine (http://palatepress.com)

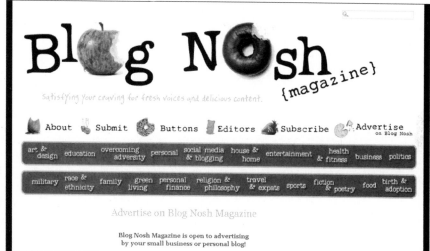

Figure 1-8: Online magazine Blog Nosh is the online equivalent of a literary digest.

Figure 1-9: Chambana-Moms.com is a hyperlocal community.

Understanding the common types of blog content

A blogger can write multiple types of posts, collectively referred to as *blog content*, although most limit themselves to one or two types. Content type isn't subject matter, topic, or tone; only your imagination and talent limit those. Here are some content types:

✔ **Essay:** Stories, sketches, and anecdotes about daily life. Many personal blogs use this type of content. For example, Mom-101, Woulda Coulda Shoulda, and Young House Love.

✔ **Review:** Product reviews. For example, Z Recommends, Cool Mom Picks, and Try Handmade.

✔ **Expert:** Blog posts that focus on one subject matter, written by one or more experts in the field. They typically have an educational, experiential focus. Blogs by professional services providers — such as public relations agencies, consultants, and attorneys, and corporate blogs — often take this form. For example, Marketing Roadmaps (my professional blog), It's Not a Lecture, and ReadWriteWeb.

✔ **Opinion/editorial:** A favored form in the political blogosphere. For example, Huffington Post and PunditMom.

✔ **Shopping:** Shopping blogs may have reviews, but the most salient characteristics tend to be explicit links to merchants and product pricing. For example, Cool Mom Picks, Want Not, and Green Mom Review.

✔ **News/events:** This type of post covers everything from news, reports, and analysis to entertainment news, rumors, and gossip. For example, MamaPop, TMZ, and PerezHilton.com.

Setting Your Professional Blogging Objectives

The first step in your professional blog plan is to set your objectives, just as you would with any business endeavor. In the simplest terms, determine

✔ **Who you're trying to reach:** To define your audience, build a *profile* of your readers — who they are and what they're interested in. Creating a tangible picture also makes it easier to write in a conversational tone for a person. You write for someone, not into the void.

✔ **What you have to offer, tell, or sell your readers:** You have stories, experiences, advice, and a product. Your readers and customers have interests, needs, and desires. Your blog is about where these things meet.

✓ **How you'll differentiate your blog from the competition:** You find a unique niche — a story only you can tell. This is what attracts readers to your blog instead of the competing activities they could be doing — reading other blogs, hanging out on Facebook, and so on.

✓ **Which monetization strategy fits you, your blog, and your audience the best, assuming making money is one of your goals:** You have choices. Lots of choices. I cover them in detail in Part II.

✓ **How you measure success.** Revenue? Readers? New business opportunities? You need to define what success means to you and develop a plan to evaluate your progress.

Be concise and as specific as possible, but don't treat the plan as inviolate. As you go through the process of developing your professional blog, you'll discover new things about blogging, your market, your audience, and possibly even yourself. Some of this discovery suggests a different course of action than you initially planned. Don't change your plan on a whim, but do change or add to it if it makes sense.

For inspiration, consider blogger and marketing professional Chris Hogan who writes men's fashion and style blog Off the Cuff (www.offthecuffdc. com). One of his goals when he started his blog was to see whether the blog could establish him as an expert in men's fashion, even though he has no formal training in fashion or design. He's succeeded almost beyond his wildest dreams. A leading authority in men's fashion recently retained him as a marketing consultant to help with the social media launch of an iPhone fashion application. Read the full story in the nearby sidebar, "Off the Cuff, a blog with style," in this chapter.

Narrowing your scope to find your niche

Marketing professionals use the proven tactics of differentiation and narrowing scope in their programs to improve their chances of success, and you can use the same strategies for your blog.

Don't try to be all things to all people. To separate your blog from the pack, find an unmet need in your market or focus on a smaller group than you originally intended. For example, shopping blog Cool Mom Picks (http://cool mompicks.com) reviews products for moms, as shown in Figure 1-10. Moms, particularly new moms, are a very attractive demographic group that buys lots of products — for their children, their families, and themselves.

Figure 1-10: Review blog Cool Mom Picks focuses on finding unique, cool products for moms and kids.

But Cool Mom Picks doesn't review everything. You can find reviews of diapers and the latest DVD from Disney on large parenting sites. Instead, the founders identified an unmet need for reviews of handcrafted and unique products from small online boutiques, independent designers, and entrepreneurs. These are the sort of products you'd find in a small, chic baby boutique in New York, London, or Paris.

Niche works. The site consistently ranks among the top parenting blogs.

Can you segment your market — either demographically or, as Cool Mom Picks did, by interest/content? If you have an interesting story for a market segment, you may want to start small and narrow. Stay focused, achieve your goals, and then develop your expansion plan. Read more about differentiation and finding your unique niche in Chapter 2.

Articulating your monetization strategy

Most professional bloggers earn their income from a variety of sources. Advertising, affiliate commissions, speaking and consulting fees, freelance writing, book deals, sponsorships, and in-kind compensation like free products and services are all part of the revenue mix.

When deciding what monetization options make sense for your blog, you have to consider your topic, your readers, and your own personal inclinations. For example, Chris Hogan's audience for Off the Cuff, covered in the nearby sidebar "Off the Cuff, a blog with style," in this chapter, spans more than 40 countries. He's considering adding advertising to his blog, but it has to be both international and fit with the Off the Cuff brand.

If you want to dig right into the details about your monetization options, skip ahead to Chapter 4.

Evaluating your plan

How do you know whether your plan makes sense? You should be able to make slight course corrections without changing your overall plan. If you can't — if the new thing that has caught your eye doesn't fit — don't force it.

The exception to this rule is a *game-changing event* that impacts your ability to reach your goals. A game-changing event is something that stops you in your tracks and prevents you from continuing on your path, such as finding out that a big publisher is investing thousands of dollars to create a site just like yours or that someone else owns the copyright for the name you've settled on. Luckily, those don't happen every day, not even in this fast-paced environment.

Blog aggregator kirtsy (`http://kirtsy.com`), which focuses on content for the women's market, faced a game-changing event early in its life. Originally, the site had a different name, and the site's founders had invested time, energy, and resources into their brand. Unfortunately, though, another online entity had trademarked the original name. Rather than engage in a costly and potentially losing legal battle, the kirtsy team chose to rebrand and enlisted the help of its community to suggest possible new names.

Being able to register a domain name for your blog, which I go into in Chapter 8, isn't an indication that you're free and clear of possible copyright issues. You need to make sure that someone else doesn't own the registered trademark for the name you want. I explain these issues in more detail in Chapter 3.

Off the Cuff, a blog with style

In 2005, Chris Hogan started menswear fashion and style blog Off the Cuff (www.offthe cuffdc.com) to express his passion for fashion. He'd always had an interest in men's fashion. His father was a sharp dresser in the East Coast Ivy League style, and as Chris got older, he realized he liked that style. Chris also worked at two Ralph Lauren stores during college, which gave him an appreciation for timeless style and attention to detail, and also helped him understand the power of brand management. He was equally interested in the history behind men's clothing, much of which is related to function. For example, the single, or double vent, at the rear of a man's jacket was to make it more comfortable when being worn on horseback.

Chris had a plan when he started Off the Cuff. He says:

> *"I like writing and enjoy being educational on the blog. Part of the plan was simply having an interest and talking to people about it. However, there was also a desire, almost an academic curiosity, to find out whether I — without any formal training, simply a genuine interest in menswear — could be viewed as an expert in men's fashion? And not just by the consumer, but by the experts in the field? How long would it take?"*

Chris realized his goal of being viewed as an expert by the experts was not so far-fetched when J. Peterman took his call. Well, not exactly. There was a messenger bag in the *J. Peterman* catalog that Chris wanted to review. He knew that the J. Peterman order line was actually staffed by people at the company, not a distant call center, so he called, delivered his spiel about the blog and asked whether there was a discount program for bloggers. He repeated the story a few times, clearly moving his way up a chain.

And then he was connected to John Peterman himself.

Chris had the presence of mind to deliver his pitch about the blog and the bag again. He heard typing on the other end of the line. Clearly, Peterman was checking out the blog. "It didn't hurt," Chris said, "when I told John that I was wearing J. Peterman pants at the time — which I really was." On the spot, Peterman made up his mind to send Chris a free bag for his review.

Chris has also gotten freelance writing assignments as a result of the blog. He wrote for Men's Flair (www.mensflair.com) for a couple years, which led to an assignment for an international men's fashion magazine, *The Rake* (www.therakeonline.com). Most recently, he was contracted by Nivea for Men to write a regular Fashion/Style column for Nivea's The Groom Room blog (www.nivea formenusa.com/local-content/ groomroom.html).

He wasn't running any advertising on the blog when I spoke with him in May 2010, but he was considering an opportunity with an online custom tailor that can ship worldwide. Off the Cuff has about 20,000 readers in more than 40 countries, so it's very important to him that any advertising on his blog be both international and fit with the overall Off the Cuff brand.

Chris has also gotten opportunities to work with marketers through Off the Cuff. He wrote a post about Nike's sponsorship of elite golf athletes and as a result, was recently invited to visit the *Oven,* the Fort Worth, Texas, facility where Nike Golf creates its PGA professional's golf equipment. He'll also attend a PGA event as a guest of Nike.

Like many bloggers, Chris focuses his attention on his content, not on promotion, but does participate on Facebook and Twitter.

The most rewarding thing about blogging for Chris is helping people:

"To paraphrase style icon Alan Flusser, in the privacy of the dressing room, every man wants to know how to dress well. Often, they're afraid to ask for help. Off the Cuff answers those questions about how to dress well."

His tip for new bloggers is to really love what you write about because that comes through on the blog and attracts readers. Also, if you think you may want to do something more with your blog down the road, start thinking like a professional upfront. He says:

"Treat your blog, and your writing, like part of your brand. That way, if the opportunity you dream about actually shows up someday, you'll be ready."

A common form of monetization for professional bloggers is consulting. Through connections, Chris met Alan Flusser, one of the most well-known menswear authorities worldwide and author of multiple books on men's fashion. Subsequently, when Flusser was looking for a social media marketing consultant—

someone who understood men's fashion and social media — to help him launch an iPhone application for men's fashion, Flusser remembered his meeting with Chris. He hired Chris to work on the project and the rest, as they say, is history. Chris says:

"Having the opportunity to work with Alan and his team is literally one of the most significant moments in my life. Alan has, quite literally, written the books on menswear and permanent style, so to actually sit in his office and work on a business plan is amazing. I am helping him learn more about the blogosphere and new ways to expand his brand and in return, I have the chance to learn from and work with the best in the business. In one way, I have achieved my initial goal of being considered an authority by the experts, but in a larger sense, everything is only now just beginning."

From dream blog to dream job; it doesn't get much better than that.

Off the Cuff
Classic. Modern. Style.

Tuesday, November 03, 2009

J. Peterman's Mailbag - The Best Bag Ever?

It's funny how sometimes things just come together. I am a bag guy; I have lots of different bags, from elegant leather briefs to beat-up nylon messengers.

One of my all-time favorites is the Counterfeit Mailbag, from the J. Peterman Company. In fact, it's one of the first bags I ever wrote about and was sent to me by John Peterman himself - it can't really get better than that.

The bag, based on the classic leather workhorse lugged across the country by a generation of letter carriers, is simple and classic. Unique enough to be modern and fit effortlessly into the current "heritage" trend it is also timeless enough to always look current.

I ♥ WHAT YOU'RE BLOGGING!
ONE OF SHINY MEDIA'S TOP 100 FASHION & LIFESTYLE BLOGS

About Me

OTC
Washington, D.C., United States
Off The Cuff is an award-winning site dedicated to the principle that classic style and modern life can live quite comfortably with each other. Founder and Editor-in-Chief Chris Hogan is a frequent contributor to leading

Setting realistic expectations

Setting realistic expectations is extremely important so you don't get frustrated and abandon your effort before your blog has had time to succeed. Here are some helpful tips to keep in mind:

- ✔ **Set milestones along your way to your long-term objective.** Achieve them and then move on to the next. For example, say your long-term objective is to make your living from your blog. A good first milestone is to build your audience to a level that attracts some advertisers. If you sell a product on your blog, forecast sales on the low side and adjust as you have real sales results from the blog. And so on.

- ✔ **Consider your own personality and style.** If you don't like criticizing things, starting a review blog probably isn't a good idea. Consider another type of blog to share your experiences and opinions with readers.

- ✔ **Don't expect to achieve your goals overnight.** Successful bloggers you've read about in the news include Heather Armstrong (www.dooce.com), who parlayed being fired from her job for blogging into a wildly successful and popular, personal blog, more than 1 million followers on Twitter, and a book deal. She had something to say that resonated with readers and worked hard to achieve her success.

  I hope you can be that successful. But keep in mind that overnight success is extremely rare. Sure, the success seems sudden to an observer, but almost always the person has worked long and hard in obscurity or delayed a dream like Paul Potts, the phone salesman and amateur opera singer who won the *Britain's Got Talent* competition in 2007.

In other words, getting to the top takes hard work, and you have to work just as hard to stay there. If you want to make your living from your blog, you have to treat it as your job.

Have realistic expectations for your blog, and start by being honest about the effort you're willing to put in. The reality is that readers don't come simply because you build it, so you have to be prepared to work hard — just like you would at any full-time job.

Sketching Your Preliminary Plan

After you define your objectives — you know what you want to achieve — decide how you're going to achieve them. That's the nitty-gritty of building a strategic plan for your professional blog.

In Chapter 2, I discuss defining the audience and a niche for your blog, and in later chapters, I discuss monetization strategies and blog development. However, before you dive into the detail, sketch a preliminary, strategic plan for your blog.

Here are the main questions that you need to answer:

- What do you really want to write about? What's your passion? How can you share that with readers in a meaningful way?

- Who will read it? What do they want that someone else isn't delivering?

- How will the blog fit into your existing Web site? How can you use them together to reach your objectives?

- How does a blog fit into your business strategy for your product/service? What are your overall goals?

- Is the blog the product? If so, how will you make money? Do you want to make money or simply cover your costs?

Take a few moments before you read on to jot down some ideas for your blog. You can then use the rest of this book to build upon your initial instincts to develop a blog and strategy that meets your objectives.

Chapter 2

Finding Your Niche in the Blogosphere

*H*ere's the unvarnished truth: Your new blog stands a far better chance of success if it's a unique offering that meets an unmet need of your audience. No matter how fascinating your idea, deathless your prose, or beautiful your design, you have an uphill battle to build your readership if you're just like all the other blogs. The problem is compounded if you're a late entrant to a crowded field.

If all you want to do is write for your friends and family, it may not matter that there are already tens or hundreds of people writing about the same thing. But if you want to create a professional blog that generates revenue, you need more than a few loyal readers to attract advertisers or generate an adequate sales volume.

To get, and keep, all your regular readers, you need to put a unique spin on your story. Tell them something they can't get anywhere else but on *your* blog. This unique content forms your editorial mission, and you build it in four steps (which I cover in detail in this chapter):

1. **Define your audience.**

   Who are you trying to reach? What would they be most interested in reading about? What information do they need?

2. **Analyze your competitors.**

   After you define who you want to reach, you can identify the competition for your reader's attention. What do your competitors offer? What's missing?

3. **Define your blog's niche.**

   This is the intersection between the audience's unmet needs and the information you can deliver based on your expertise, knowledge, and experience.

4. **Develop your editorial mission**

   You then take this clear picture of the target readers and their unmet needs to develop your editorial mission — a simple statement that tells readers what you and your blog are all about. I tell you how to do all of that in this chapter.

Building Your Blog-Analysis Toolbox

Solid business analysis is a combination of the questions you ask and the tools you use. In this chapter, I outline the questions you need to ask about your readers and your competitors so you can surface the unique opportunity for your blog. But before you can analyze, you need to do a little research, and for that, you need tools.

Many of these tools are useful for both discovery and determining influence, although I do recommend caution about taking any *one* of them as the last word. No single concrete definition of online influence exists; each tool measures it a bit differently, based on what the tool does. Plus, nearly every evaluative model I've seen has flaws, either in design or underlying bias. That's why I recommend using multiple sources of information and, then at the end, filtering all the data through the most accurate evaluative filter you have — your brain.

I focus on online tools you can use for free. Many market research firms and commercial software tools provide more granular data and analysis, but they tend to be expensive, making them more appropriate for larger businesses. Some give you a peek for free, so I give you a suggestion for how to use the free peeks in your own research. Also, keep in mind that new tools are developed all the time. For this reason, I tell you about the types of tools and give you some examples. Think as much about the kind of tool, and how you can use it, as you do the specific example, and be prepared to find new and improved ones every day.

✔ General search engines like Google and Yahoo! are your first step in any research, and you're probably already using them for this purpose.

✔ Use (with caution) blog search engines and ranking sites, such as Technorati and Alexa, that rank sites according to proprietary algorithms. These rankings have their limitations. For example, Alexa (`www.alexa.com`) bases much of its data on users that have installed its browser toolbar, which is not available for all browsers and platforms. The company says that it also uses other sources (unspecified), but the limitation of the toolbar does introduce some bias. Technorati (`http://technorati.com`) has had many problems with its algorithm over the years. Folks have also developed ranking algorithms for Twitter, such as TweetGrader.

None of these ranking engines is perfect, but if you use a few of them, patterns emerge that are useful for blog discovery and understanding influence.

✔ Check the sites of the commercial research tools to see whether they offer a free trial or some glimpse into their data for free. For example, Compete.com, which does comprehensive Web site tracking, lets you compare traffic on up to three URLs for free. In Figure 2-1, you can see a Compete.com comparison of the Web traffic on three domains. Only one, `http://simplyrecipes.com`, is a blog. The other two are commercial sites. This tool can be useful if you need to understand the relative influence of a site. The major drawback for blog research is that it's limited to full domain names; you can't compare sites at the subdirectory level.

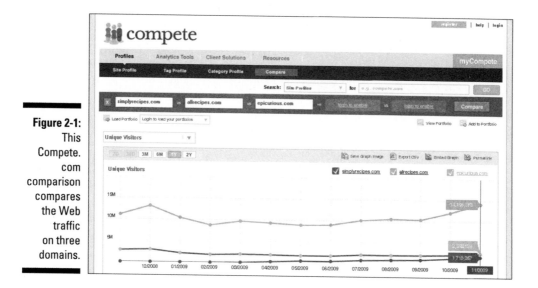

Figure 2-1:
This Compete.com comparison compares the Web traffic on three domains.

✔ Blog ad networks are an excellent resource for blog discovery. If they sell ads for individual blogs, as opposed to just the network in aggregate, the blog advertising rate card lists demographic data like the one at Federated Media for pop culture blog MamaPop, as shown in Figure 2-2. Even if the network sells only in aggregate, such as online community BlogHer, you generally find a list of the blogs in the network. Read more about ad networks and advertising in Chapter 6.

Figure 2-2: Rate cards for blog advertising often include demographic data.

Audience Demographics

98% Female

85% 18 - 39

51% HHI above 76k

44% Publish their own blog

Traffic

560,000
page views per month

✔ Content aggregators like Digg (http://digg.com) and kirtsy (http://kirtsy.com), which let registered users vote on the popularity of blog posts, are good for understanding what a community likes *right now*. Many community Web sites add this type of feature, so keep your eyes open for it.

✔ Check out social networks, such as Twitter, Facebook, LinkedIn, and so on.

Twitter's trending topics shows you what people are talking about in real time, and search tools like Twitter Search, TweetBeep, and TweetScan are great for looking at what the tweeting community has recently said about a company, brand, or blog. You can also look at the recent tweets of any Twitter user unless they've protected (hidden) their messages from the public. All you need is the Twitter username, and Twitter lets you search for that too.

Facebook and LinkedIn are useful when you need to *crowdsource* something. Crowdsourcing is exactly what it sounds like — asking the community for an answer or recommendations. You can crowdsource on Twitter as well, but the 140-character limit makes it difficult to ask long or complex questions. Facebook is also a good place to go to find out more about the conversation the blogger is having with his readers. Many bloggers have set up Facebook pages for their blogs; you can check out who likes the blog and what folks are talking about. Find out more about Facebook pages in Chapter 11.

Your most important tool is your own brain, and how you creatively analyze the data to understand your readers and competitors and your own unique place in the blogosphere.

Defining Your Audience

You may already have a rough idea of the audience for your blog. If you are developing a blog for an existing business, the blog readers likely correspond to some or all of your potential customers. If you've been blogging as a hobby, you probably already have some readers. Even if all you've done to date is read blogs, odds are pretty good that you've been reading some blogs that appeal to the same group you'll be writing for. Regardless, making a point to clearly define your audience and its needs helps you understand what the opportunity for your blog is.

As you progress through your research, you'll get a good idea of who is talking about your topic and what they are saying. You'll probably also get some indication of who your potential competitors are. Set up a folder of bookmarks of the sites you visit as you do your research (or keep some sort of list), and you can use that information later in the chapter when you identify and analyze the competition.

In the sections that follow, I tell you how to create profiles of the types of readers that you hope to attract and investigate what your anticipated blog readers' needs are. This rough idea is a good place to start defining your audience. However, this place is most definitely *not* where you should stop, so resist the temptation.

Profiling your ideal readers

I like to start by profiling the ideal readers of the blog. If this were a traditional marketing plan, you'd call it market segmentation, but all you're really doing is organizing your readers according to who they are and what they do. A blog is a conversation with your customers and readers, not with a market demographic. It's personal.

That said, the definition of your ideal reader creates a demographic selection that matches up to a category of readers. It sounds complex, but it's not. Just stay focused on who cares about your content. That's your reader, and that's who you are writing for.

Understanding the profile of your readers helps you determine how to develop a blog that will be valuable to a specific group of readers, but it also gives you another advantage: a definite leg up when evaluating advertising opportunities and making your case to potential advertisers. (See Chapter 6 for more details on how to attract advertisers.)

Outline the following information for each desired group of readers:

  ✔ **Relevant demographic data:** *Demographics* are variables that objectively describe people, such as age, gender, geography, income, and marital status.

  ✔ **Psychographic profile:** *Psychographics* describe personality attributes, such as attitudes, opinions, beliefs, and biases. For example, if your product is an environmentally *green* laundry soap, you'd include an environmentally conscious attitude in your ideal reader profile.

  ✔ **Customer behaviors:** Identify behaviors that are relevant to your topic or products, such as usage, purchase frequency, and loyalty.

You may start with more than one reader, or group, for your blog. That's okay. Define each one separately to get a clear picture of the total potential readership. When it comes time to define the editorial mission for your blog, you'll either find an area of common interest or eliminate some of the groups. What you don't want is to be too narrow at the start. You could end up boxing yourself into a corner.

A final word on the profile: It doesn't have to be perfect or cover every possible demographic or psychographic variable. All you need is a solid description that creates a picture in your mind of your reader — a real person just like you who will want to read your blog. Here are two examples of simple profiles:

Profile 1: Green mom

  ✔ Women aged 25–55 with at least one child under 18 years still living at home

  ✔ $75,000 per year annual household income or more

  ✔ Healthy lifestyle, interested in sustainable products

  ✔ Purchases something online at least once per month

Profile 2: Active adult

- ✔ Adults aged 21–35
- ✔ $50,000 per year personal income
- ✔ College degree
- ✔ Physically active, participates in sports at least weekly
- ✔ Interested in active travel

Understanding reader needs

After you know who your reader is, the next step is to find out what she wants so that you can construct an editorial mission for your blog that meets those needs. And particularly what she wants that she isn't getting from the blogs and Web sites she's reading already.

Most likely, you're already reading blogs that attract the audience you intend to write for. After all, your blog topic is something you're interested in — enough to build a business or a professional blog around it. The first thing you need to do is analyze the conversation on the blogs that you already read.

You need to look at both posts (the articles that the blogger writes) and comments (the blog readers' responses to those articles); you're interested in what the community has to say, not just the bloggers. Be sure to follow interesting links within posts and check out the *blogroll* (a set of links to blog posts and sites that the blogger recommends to readers) on the blogs to see who those writers are reading. This helps you understand the larger context that may impact your blogging plans. For example, the list of links on Nomadic Matt's travel blog, shown in Figure 2-3, is annotated and includes blogs and travel resources.

Your initial scan captures only the blogs you already know about and the general conversation. You need to go beyond what you already know (or assume) and find out where else your potential readers hang out online and dig deeper into what's being said about your specific topic.

To dig deeper than you're digging when you follow links in reader comments and blogrolls, turn to your preferred search engine, and search blogs for relevant keywords associated with the following:

- ✔ Your brand (if it's known already in the market)
- ✔ Known competitors
- ✔ Key themes and issues around your product/potential blog topic

For example, if you're a caterer specializing in vegetarian cuisine, you might be thinking about starting a blog about vegetarian holiday food. Do a Google blog search to understand your possible competition.

You should also make a practice of reading blogs every day. You can access them directly by bookmarking the URL or set up an application called a *feed reader*. A feed reader, such as Google Reader (`www.google.com/reader`), uses a technology called Really Simple Syndication (RSS). You subscribe to the blogs you want to read, and RSS delivers just the content of a blog post without the design elements. It looks a little like your e-mail application, as shown in Figure 2-4.

Figure 2-3:
The blogroll is a good place to start your research for similar blogs.

TRAVEL LINKS

Travel Blogs
Almost Fearless- Christine left Boston to become a free lance writer in Barcelona. She's a good motivator.
Amateur Traveler Podcast- A good podcast about various destinations in the world.
Amtrekker- Brett started out with a list of travel goals and wouldn't let himself go home until he finished them all.
Asian Ramblings- Steve is an ESL teacher and a photographer in China. His postings give a glimpse into Chinese life. His photos tell thousands of words.
Collazo Projects- Julie is a Matador Travel editor and runs an excellent travel blog about writing, meaningful travel, and shares her wonderful travel tips from her adventures living in multiple countries.
Cool Travel Guide- Musings of a

General Travel Information
Airline Numbers- All the airline telephone numbers you need.
Eurotrip- Good information and a forum about Europe by backpackers.
Lonely Planet- The guidebook king. They also have a good forum where you can ask about anything. There website is a good resource.
South Pacific Travel- South Pacific island destinations, airlines, news, events, maps, films, music, guidebooks, blog, and tips for trips by veteran travel writer David Stanley.
STA Travel- Worldwide student/young adult travel/tour company that provides good deals.
Couchsurfing- This website allows you to stay on people's couches or in spare rooms for free!! It's a great way to save money and meet people.
Backpacker Resources- Another good set of information for

Tour Companies
Black Sheep Inn Ecolodge- International Award Winning Eco-Lodge in Ecuador. Affordable guesthouse, bed & breakfast hotel in the heart of the rural Ecuadorian Andes. Enjoy horseback riding, mountain biking, & day hiking.
GAP Adventures- For those who want a tour that lets them do what they want, this is the company to go with. Their tours are geared toward independent travelers who just want the hassle of booking taken care of! (Cheap too!)
Intrepid Travel- Pretty much like Gap adventures but based out of Australia.
Contiki Tours- For those 18-35 who want to party and be herded like cattle.
HBF Travel Insurance - For Australians traveling within Australia or overseas. You can save 10% when

Figure 2-4:
A blog post in Google Reader.

Gmail Calendar Documents Reader Web more ▼ | ⚙ | Settings ▼ | Help | Sign out

Google reader [ ] All items ▼ Search

➕ Add a subscription

Home
All items (1000+)
Starred items ☆
⊟ Your stuff
  Shared items
  Notes
  Trends
  Browse for stuff
People you follow (32)
7 new followers View

Explore
Subscriptions
  Logic+Emotion (7)
  Maneuver Marketing Co...
  Marketing & Entre... (1)
  Marketing Conversation (21)
  Marketing Nirvana by ...
  Marketing Roadmaps
  Marketing to Women On... (6)
  Marketing Tom - Inter... (6)
  MarketingVOX - The Vo... (114
  Mary's Blog (7)
  media landscaping
  Morgan McLintic on PR (4)
  My Name is Kate (16)
Manage subscriptions »

Marketing Roadmaps »

Show: **Expanded** - List

Show: 0 new items - **all items** | Mark all as read | ▼ | Refresh | Feed settings... ▼

show details

Add star ☐Like Share Share with note ☐Email ☐Keep unread ☐Edit tags: Marketing Blogs

Thoughts on the FTC investigation of Ann Taylor LOFT blogger Apr 29, 2010 12:59 PM
event
by Susan Getgood

So many things queued up to write about, including last week's New Comm Forum, a slew of bad pitches that folks have forwarded over the past few months (Douches, Snakes and Brand Ambassadors) and a great visit to the Dana Farber Cancer Institute yesterday to learn more about the Jimmy Fund.

But the FTC went public this week with the results of its first investigation under the new endorsements and testimonials guidelines, and that news trumps the other (more evergreen) topics.

As reported in Ad Age, the FTC investigated an event held by Ann Taylor LOFT in January to launch its summer collection. The company invited bloggers to attend a special preview of the collection; those that posted about the event within 24 hours were entered into "mystery gift-card drawing" with a value between $50 and $500. (More about the event on Jezebel: February 3, April 28)

Reported Ad Age:

The event and the unusual request for posts to be submitted for a prize received media scrutiny and caught the eye of the FTC. "We were concerned that bloggers who attended a preview on January 26, 2010 failed to disclose that they received gifts for posting blog content about that event," Mary Engle, the FTC's associate director-advertising practices, wrote in a letter dated April 20 to Ann Taylor's legal representation.

According to the article, the FTC decided not to take further action because it was a single event, only a small number of bloggers participated (and some disclosed) and Ann Taylor subsequently adopted a written policy for blogger outreach.

Previous item | Next item

more than 20 items

Identifying the Competition

Understanding your competition is a necessary step before you can carve out a unique niche for your own blog. Knowing that people are interested in reading about a topic isn't enough to guarantee success if multiple competitors are already doing a good job covering it. Don't get me wrong; your writing may be so brilliant that your blog breaks through, but the odds aren't good. Your chances are far better if you can carve out a niche within your topic that isn't being addressed.

To do that, you need to know the competitive blogs and what they're doing. Also important, both at this planning stage and later when you're promoting your blog, is to understand which competitors have the most influence with the audience. By *influence*, I mean a combination of the blog's traffic and reader engagement. The tendency is to pay the most attention to blogs with lots of traffic and comments, and those are very important, but don't overlook blogs that may have fewer readers; their ideas get picked up by others and spread widely.

You also need to look at both direct and indirect competitions. Direct competitors are other bloggers who write about the same topic for the same audiences. Your indirect competition is everything else your readers might do instead of reading your blog, such as reading blogs on other topics and hanging out on Facebook.

Getting ready to gather data

If you've defined your audience as explained in the preceding section, you already have a list of some of your competitors. You can then take some of that initial research data and create a reference list of competitive blogs that includes your notes on the blog's topic, demographics, and influence. You will add data to that reference list as you continue to research your competitors.

You can organize that list any way that works for you. I like to use a spreadsheet, like the one shown in Table 2-1, but you could also use index cards or any other organizational tool. You don't need to put the blogs in rank order unless you really want to. This list simply forms the basis for your next task — evaluating the competitive blogs — and it doesn't matter which blog is number one and which is number ten.

Table 2-1		Blog Competitors		
Name	**Topic**	**Demographics**	**Influence**	**Blog Features**
Enter the name and URL of the blog.	Enter the blog's topic.	Note any reader demographic data you might have, including age, gender, geography, income, and marital status.	Include any information you have on the blog's traffic and reader engagement.	List design elements or popular features that might work well on your blog, too.

Keep the list as small as possible — include only the most influential blogs that are closest to your chosen topic. If your list starts to get really big, your research scope for *direct* competitors is probably overly broad. Some of them are probably indirect competitors. Start a second worksheet or set of index cards.

Finding your direct competitors

If you're planning to use your blog to promote a product, you already may have researched your direct competitors, and as I note in the earlier section, "Profiling your ideal readers," you will surface some data on your competitors when profiling your ideal reader. Add that data to your spreadsheet as long as it pertains to your blog's competition (not your product's competition).

To find your direct competitors, follow these general steps:

✔ Start with the blogs you've already read. Just as with the profile task in the "Profiling your ideal readers" section, reviewing the sites and bloggers with whom you are already familiar is the best place to start. Read posts and comments, follow links, and scan the blogroll for relevant sites.

✔ Next, turn to your preferred general search engine and do a search like the Google one shown in Figure 2-5 for *top 100 food blogs*. A search for the top blogs on your topic will surface articles and blog posts that rank blogs in that category. These are your direct competitors.

✔ Do a similar search on blog and Web search engines, such as Technorati and Alexa. As discussed in the earlier section, "Building Your Blog-Analysis Toolbox," none of them is perfect, but if you use a few of them, patterns emerge that help confirm which are the most popular and influential blogs about a topic. Figure 2-6 shows the results of the search on *top food blogs* in Technorati.

After you have a preliminary list of competitors, you can turn to other resources to fill in your information about the competition.

Figure 2-5:
A search for the *top blogs* in a segment surfaces lists, rankings, and resources for discovering influential blogs.

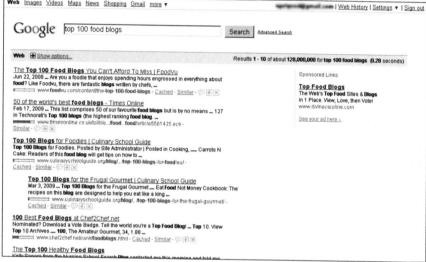

Figure 2-6:
Technorati is another tool for researching blogs.

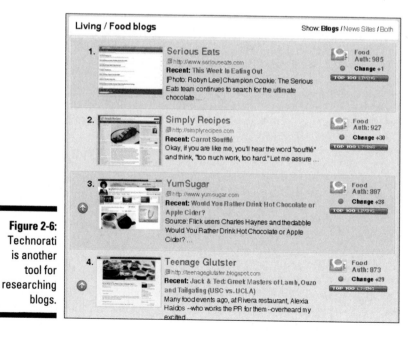

Uncovering your indirect competitors

Before you turn to analyzing your competitors (as described in the next section), take a quick look at your indirect competition. Indirect competition is everything that your ideal reader might do *instead* of reading your blog. For simplicity, limit your scan to online activities, but know that walking the dog and watching TV are also indirect competition for your blog.

For this book's purpose, the indirect competition that matters is

- ✔ Social networks, such as Facebook and Twitter.
- ✔ General-purpose Web sites and blogs that attract the same reader.
- ✔ Blogs in your general category. For example, if your topic is *vegetarian holiday food,* applicable general categories might be vegetarian, holiday, and food.

How do you find these indirect competitors? Read the blogs, check out the blogrolls, and follow links in posts. Be on the lookout for blog *badges,* those little graphics in the sidebars. If large numbers of blogs in your competitive list all link to a site, odds are it's a complementary site to them, and ultimately to you.

These indirect competitors are important for two reasons. First, you want to understand what appeals to your ideal reader about these sites and then incorporate those features on your blog where appropriate. Second, your indirect competitors are considered complementary sites and among the first places where you'll promote your finished blog.

Your analysis of indirect competitors doesn't need to be as in depth as your direct competition, but at a minimum, you should make note of their mission statements and readership demographics, and identify any design elements or popular features that could translate well to your blog.

Analyzing the Competition's Strengths and Weaknesses

After you identify the direct competition for your ideal reader's attention, you need to evaluate how well the competition meets the reader's needs. The gaps are the unmet needs that form the opportunity for your new blog. Hopefully, your idea is squarely in one of these gaps already; if not, you may need to tweak it.

To evaluate the competition's strengths and weaknesses, examine the data you've compiled, along with information on these five additional areas: theme and editorial mission; post content; comments and inbound links;

participation on other social networks; and promotions, products, discounts, and giveaways. I tell you how to do that in the sections that follow.

I take each area of investigation in turn and identify what you need to be looking for when you evaluate your competitors. The examples throughout this section are mostly from two successful travel blogs whose authors left the traditional work world to travel full time: AlmostFearless.com (http://almostfearless.com) and Nomadic Matt (www.nomadicmatt.com).

You can still use your spreadsheet or index cards to organize your research if that's what works for you, but at this point in the process, I usually start compiling the profiles of the top competitors in a word-processing document. This makes it easier if I ever need to compile a formal marketing plan.

The influence of the blog and blogger, as discussed earlier in the "Identifying the Competition" section, form part of an analysis of the competitor's strengths and weaknesses, but influence doesn't give you all the information you need to understand the unmet needs. For that, you need to evaluate your directly competitive blogs in the context of your market knowledge and its needs.

Much of this analysis is subjective, and that's okay. Readers decide what's hot and what's not, and you're part of your community, too. The main purpose with this exercise is to make sure that your blog idea is unique so that you don't spend months developing a brilliant site only to find half a dozen similar blogs and an uphill battle to build readership. Try to be truly objective in evaluating your own blog idea and its chances for success in the competitive environment.

If your blog promotes a product, you may be tempted to evaluate the competitive product. Stop. For this purpose, you need to evaluate the competitor's blog, not the product.

Theme and editorial mission

The theme and editorial mission are the heart of a blog and the most important part of your analysis. You can get a good idea of a blog's theme and editorial mission from its *masthead* (the graphic at the top of the page) and About page. A good masthead sets the tone and provides the framework for the content to follow. The About page should give you a sense of who the writer is and what he hopes to achieve with his blog.

Start with the mastheads of these example blogs, both of which are shown in Figure 2-7. Although these mastheads are visually very different, each uses the blog name and tagline to evoke an emotional response that effectively positions the blog:

- ✔ Nomadic Matt's Travel Site. Life Untethered.
- ✔ Almost Fearless. Work Wirelessly. Travel the World. Do Anything.

Before moving to the About page, which provides further clues, consider how the two taglines subtly differentiate these two blogs, even though they're rooted in a similar premise: full-time travel rather than a 40-hour workweek. Christine Gilbert, author of AlmostFearless.com, is more focused on work than Matt. She tells you how you can travel full time and still make a living, whereas Nomadic Matt shows you how to live and travel without all that "stuff."

Christine changed her tagline in Spring 2010. It used to be "Redesign your life. Travel the world." While I like the feeling of freedom that she's added with the concepts of working wirelessly and doing anything, the concept of redesigning your life was a very powerful one. However, her focus has shifted to working wirelessly — she's already redesigned her life — so it's a sensible switch to inform readers about what they will find on her blog.

The About pages on both blogs confirm the initial impression from the mastheads and help us get to know Christine and Matt better.

Christine Gilbert, who left the corporate world to travel full time and make her living as a freelance writer, writes:

> *"When I was first thinking about leaving corporate life, I spent too many hours researching, pouring over travelogues, trying to get some sense of what it was really like to give up everything for long term travel. I kept looking for someone like me — late 20s/early 30s, married (but no kids), workaholic, uber-ambitious and normally quite cautious (oh and if they have two big slobbery dogs, bonus). I never found exactly what I was looking for, but I promised myself I'd document the process for others, as best as I could."*

And Nomadic Matt says:

> *"This Web site is not only a chronicle of my travels but also a way for people to find inspiration, travel tips, destination advice, travel news, and beautiful photos. People always say to me how much they would love to do what I do, even if it is just for a little while. I'm here to tell you [you] can. I'm here to show you how. Travel doesn't have to be an expensive task nor does taking a Gap year require you to uproot your existence. If I, a lazy guy from Boston, can do this,* **you** *can do it too!"*

As you evaluate your competition, look for a gap that you can fill. Don't worry that your new blog has to be completely different from everything else, although it certainly can be. For example, if a competitive travel set were just these two blogs, one obvious gap would be full-time travel after retirement. (Of course, the travel blog segment is much larger than the two blogs in this example set, and blogs do in fact fill this particular gap.)

The important thing to remember is that subtle differences can be enough to differentiate blogs within a category. All you need is to give the reader sufficient incentive to read your blog, too!

Posts

To get a good sense of a blog, you need to read the blog over time, at least three months of posts, and preferably six. Past posts are perfectly fine. Here are some of the things to look for:

- Does the content deliver on the theme/editorial mission? In other words, does the content meet the readers' expectations?
- How often does the writer post? How long are the posts?
- How many authors does the blog have? If multiple authors, does the blog keep a consistent voice? If yes, how? If not, does the blog work?
- Does the blog have any special features, such as book reviews, tips, and so on? How about multimedia content, such as podcasts or video?
- Does the blog link frequently to other blogs?
- Is the blog well written? Yes, this is subjective, but important. You're evaluating a number of competitive blogs, and some will be better written than others.
- What's missing? What would you expect this blog to cover that it doesn't?

You won't have a "right" answer to these questions. Use these questions as a framework to guide your investigation. When you're done, you'll have a good idea of what topics and reader needs are well served by the competition and which ones aren't, thereby creating the opportunity for your blog.

Comments

Comments from a blog's readers are the direct measure of reader engagement. The more comments a blog has, as compared to other blogs in its category with a similar number of readers, the more engaged the readers are with the blog. Two key factors to examine are

✔ **Average comments per post over time:** You want to see a fairly regular pattern and volume of comments. Most blogs publish the number of comments right in the post byline so that you can quickly scan how many comments each post has (see Figure 2-8).

✔ **Comment content:** Comments that expand upon the point made in the post tend to indicate greater engagement in the content than brief notations like "Right on!"

Number of comments

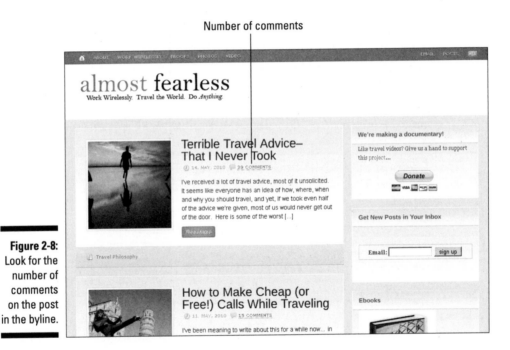

Figure 2-8: Look for the number of comments on the post in the byline.

When using comments as a measure of engagement, be sure that you compare apples to apples. Tools like Alexa, Technorati, and Compete.com's free comparison (which I discuss earlier in the "Building Your Blog-Analysis Toolbox" section) can help you figure out whether two blogs have a similar number of readers. Some blogs also publish their Really Simply Syndication (RSS) subscriber numbers.

Some blogs use tools like Chat Catcher (http://chatcatcher.com) to automatically append comments from Twitter to the post. If this is common practice among the blogs in your competitive set, it's valuable additive information about overall community engagement. However, these comments don't necessarily reflect regular readers of a blog, so don't give them undue importance unless they're substantive. This indicates that the person actually read the post and didn't simply *re-tweet* (repeat someone else's comment). Comments left on a blog and that add to the conversation are worth more. You can easily tell the difference between comments left on the blog and ones appended through Chat Catcher. (See Chapter 11 for details.)

Inbound links

Inbound links are the direct measure of the community's engagement with a blog. An inbound link is a link from another blog or Web site to your blog. It's simply the equivalent of one blogger saying to his readers, "Hey, you should read what this other blogger is writing." A high number of inbound links as compared to other blogs in a category indicates that many other bloggers are talking about and referencing the post.

The point? If someone writes a blog about the same idea and their blog is wildly popular, with tons of positive comments and inbound links, you probably need to retool your idea. If their blog isn't popular and you truly think you can do better, it may be worth the effort.

Inbound links are value-neutral; they can be positive or negative. To get an accurate assessment of the blog's position within the community, you have to read some of the posts. It's the only way you will know if someone agrees or disagrees with the blogger. Most of the time, an inbound link will be positive, but don't make that assumption.

Yahoo! Site Explorer is a good, free tool to discover the number of inbound links to a blog. To review a list of sites that link to a URL, follow these steps:

1. **Navigate to Yahoo! Site Explorer at** `http://siteexplorer.search.yahoo.com`.

2. **Type a URL in the text box at the top of the page and then click the Explore URL button.**

   The results appear on the page.

3. **Click the Inlinks button to review the sites that link to this URL, as shown in Figure 2-9.**

Participation on social networks

Social networks are increasingly important for both sharing content and building relationships with customers and readers. If social networks like Twitter, Facebook, and LinkedIn are important in your community (and they probably are), you need to know how active the competition is within these networks. Also look for private or branded communities that form around specific interests. Some are formal branded sites, others less so, but they're all gathering places for their communities.

If the competition is participating in a network, you need to be, too. If it has missed an important network, it's an opportunity for you.

Start by looking for the sidebar buttons and badges that bloggers use to promote their participation, as shown in Figure 2-10. If you can't find any and you know a particular network is important to your readers, do a search within the network for the competition by name and brand.

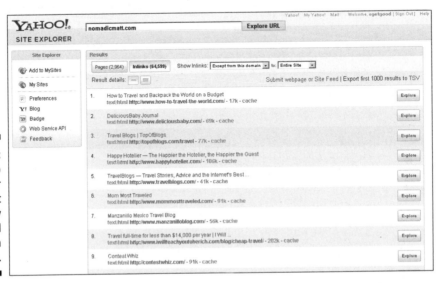

Figure 2-9: Use Yahoo Site Explorer to find out how many inbound links a blog has.

Figure 2-10: Buttons and badges for social networks tell you the community sites in which a blogger is active.

Links to source networks

Do a survey of your readers

You may also consider doing a survey of your readers. Free survey tools, such as SurveyMonkey (www.surveymonkey.com) and Zoomerang (http://zoomerang.com), are an excellent way to gauge market sentiment at a very low cost. The principal limitation is that you can send invitations to participate only to known contacts, or you can publicize the survey URL broadly on blogs and social networks, such as Facebook and Twitter.

Surveys work best when they go from general to specific questions. Your general questions might be about the industry or general market conditions, moving into selection criteria for products or blogs, following that with specific content-related questions, and wrapping up with brand and demographic questions.

You can also use survey tools to fill in data blanks about your readers. This can be particularly useful when it comes to psychographic questions about attitudes, opinions, and lifestyles.

Promotions, products, discounts, and giveaways

Promotions, products, discounts, deals, contests, and giveaways all give the reader a reason to keep coming back, especially if new ones are added regularly. For example, Christine Gilbert of Almost Fearless sometimes offers her e-books free to her subscribers for a limited time and then charges a nominal fee.

Evaluating the competition's promotions and contests is bound to be subjective — either you like them or you don't. That's okay. Make note of the ones that seem particularly successful or total flops, and think about what you might do differently.

Understanding the competition's products and promotions delivers two benefits:

- ✔ You know what you're up against, which is especially important for close competitors.
- ✔ You can benefit from competitors' mistakes and successes; avoid the first and improve on the second.

If you do contests and giveaways on your blog, you need to set up the contest or giveaway properly, and if you get free products from companies for your contests, you need to disclose that fact in your post. For more on these topics, Chapter 3 covers disclosure, and Chapter 11 offers some guidelines for contests.

To understand the impact of a competitor on your plans, you need to evaluate both how close its content is to your idea and its influence with the audience. The fact that a blogger writes a similar topic for her mother and her five best friends is one thing. The fact that the blog is a top blog in your segment with thousands of readers is another.

Discovering Your Niche with a SWOT Analysis

A SWOT (Strengths, Weaknesses, Opportunities, and Threats) analysis is a commonly used marketing tool to understand market potential for a product or service. First, look at the competition and identify its strengths and weaknesses. (I show you how to do that analysis in the section "Identifying the Competition," earlier in the chapter.) Then evaluate the opportunities and threats those strengths and weaknesses pose for your product — in this case, your new blog. Later in this section, I use a fictitious example to explain how to use a SWOT analysis to find the unmet market needs and define the unique niche for your blog.

Some people like to use a grid format, with a box for each element, as shown in Figure 2-11. Others prefer a list. Use whichever method works best for you. List the competitor's strengths and weaknesses, and then assess how those either threaten your idea or create an opportunity for it.

Competitor Name

Strengths	Weaknesses
Opportunities	Threats

Figure 2-11: Identify your competition's strengths and weaknesses.

Follow this process for each competitor (that's why you want a fairly small list of direct competitors) and then create an aggregate picture of overall competition strengths and weaknesses. That's what you use to refine your own idea and find your opportunity.

For example, earlier in this chapter, I mention a caterer thinking about doing a blog about vegetarian holiday food. Assume you did a complete competitive analysis and discovered many blogs that specialize in vegetarian recipes and regularly include holiday and party recipes. This (fictional) scan of the competition also showed that general food/recipe blogs feature vegetarian holiday recipes from time to time. That's *strong* competition and a *threat* to the success of the caterer's idea, which indicates that this (fictional) caterer needs to refine the idea and do something beyond just recipes to promote his business.

Time to turn to what's missing and come up with an idea that capitalizes on a market need that isn't being well served by the competition. Their weakness, your opportunity. Your niche in the blogosphere.

If you're developing a brand-new blog and using this analysis to refine what it should be, your blog doesn't have strengths and weaknesses yet. However, if you have an existing blog and are using this book to redevelop it, you may want to do a SWOT analysis on your own blog. In that case, look at your strengths and weaknesses, and then consider where these expose you to the competition and where you have the advantage. You want to sustain your advantage and eliminate the exposure.

Creating Your Editorial Mission

If you've followed along so far, remember that preliminary blog plan I asked you to jot down at the end of Chapter 1? Based on what you've discovered about your competition, add some information to it:

What I Discovered	*What I Will Do*
I will differentiate my blog from competitive blogs by focusing on:	
This will attract readers because they want:	
I am uniquely qualified to deliver this content because:	

These answers form the core of your editorial mission. You want to pretty the prose for your About page and come up with a killer name and tagline that encapsulates your blog (which I cover in Chapters 8 and 9), but you're well on your way to a professional blog.

Chapter 3

Protecting Your Blog with Appropriate Business Policies and Practices

*A*lthough you don't have to set up a formal business entity for your professional blog, there are distinct advantages to doing so, such as credibility for your endeavor and liability protection.

This chapter starts with a general overview of the business end of setting up your professional blog, including business formation and how a lawyer and an accountant can help you get started on the right foot.

I then move on to U.S. laws and regulations that impact your blogging business and suggest best practices to help you comply with the laws.

Setting Up the Business End of Things

Does your blog need a business — as in a legal business entity, a corporation, or a limited liability company (LLC)? The answer is probably yes. If you're on your own, without partners or employees, you could use your Social Security Number for tax identification purposes. The minute you add any complexity — such as partners, revenue streams, or third-party contracts — set up a business entity and formal agreements that spell out everyone's rights and responsibilities. Even if you don't have partners, liability issues make forming a business a good idea.

In the sections that follow, I tell you why you need to set up a business for your blog, help you determine which type of business to establish, discuss the importance of lawyers and accountants, tell you about Employer Identification Numbers (EINs), and give you some tips on how to handle adding a blog to an existing business.

Knowing why to establish a business entity

Kim Kramer, a small-business attorney based in Boston, says that the benefits of establishing a legal business for your blog far outweigh the costs:

> *"The primary benefit is liability protection. If you operate your business under your name, you personally will be sued for any unpaid bills or to satisfy other debts or liabilities of the business. This opens the door to creditor liens on your residence, bank accounts, and other personal assets. If you operate as an entity, whether a corporation or a limited liability company, the entity will be responsible for the debts and liabilities of the business, and your personal exposure will be limited, except to certain circumstances such as where you have personally guaranteed payment."*

Other benefits of operating your blog as a legal business include

- You can more easily evaluate the financial performance of the business against your objectives.

- A business structure often has more credibility than individual ownership, even when the employees are me, myself, and I.

- As I mention earlier, if you have partners, you have a defined, formal structure for setting up terms of ownership.

- Your legitimate business expenses can be paid directly by the business rather than from your personal income. This may also offer you tax advantages, which you need to discuss with your accountant.

Deciding what type of business to set up

After you decide to set up a formal business for your blog, you need to decide whether to create a corporation or a limited liability company (LLC), the two entities most commonly used in the U.S. The following list points out the similarities and differences between these two types:

- **Similarities:** Both the corporation and the LLC offer liability protection and are formed by publicly filing a certificate and paying a fee to a state agency. In many cases, you also need to get a federal tax ID number, or

Employer Identification Number. (I tell you more on that in the upcoming "Getting an Employer Identification Number" section.)

✔ **Differences:** The principal difference between the corporation and the LLC is the organizational structure. The way you run the business and how you account for profits are different for the two entities as well.

- *In a corporation,* the rights and responsibilities of the principals are described in the corporation's bylaws, and fairly rigid rules dictate what needs to be included in these bylaws. For example, a corporation must have an annual meeting of shareholders and file an annual report.

- *In an LLC,* the rights and responsibilities of the principals are set out in an operating agreement document that has to cover all contingencies, including dissolution. Says Kim Kramer:

  "The operating agreement and the opportunity it affords for creativity is what fundamentally distinguishes the LLC from a corporation. Because the owners are not required to follow strict corporate structure with shares representing ownership, a board of directors, officers, [and so on], there is an incredible amount of flexibility in setting up the operational and governance structure of an LLC. This flexibility can be freeing or daunting, depending on your perspective. It can also be expensive, as the drafting of the free-form operating agreement is generally done by the business' attorney billing by the hour."

If you want to create a tax-exempt nonprofit organization, you must form a corporation and comply with specific rules, such as IRS rules governing nonprofits. Don't try to do this yourself; talk to a lawyer.

Otherwise, the choice is really up to you and how you want to run your business. Many resources are online, at the library, and at your local bookstore that go into all the differences between the two forms, including *Limited Liability Companies For Dummies,* by Jennifer Reuting and *Incorporating Your Business For Dummies,* by The Company Corporation. If you have a lawyer, he can advise you on the most appropriate choice.

Hiring legal and financial advisors

Although you can legally form your company, and the paperwork for a simple entity isn't that difficult, I don't recommend it, and I don't do it. Books and Web sites are useful resources, but they aren't experienced, expert counselors who know you and your situation. Good legal and financial advisors help you make the best choice for your circumstances and make sure that you don't miss important steps in the process. They're also resources that you can call later with operational, legal, and tax questions.

Your lawyer can help you with the formation of your business and can advise you about things like operational policies, liabilities, contracts and business agreements, trademarks, and copyright protection. You also may want to get a business liability insurance policy. The specific type of coverage depends on your business and its potential liabilities, and your lawyer can help you weigh these factors.

You also never know when you might need a lawyer to represent your firm in a dispute or contract negotiation; it can be very useful to already have an attorney who knows your business.

Whether you decide to do-it-yourself or retain a lawyer, here are two Web sites that offer free legal information, legal forms, and a directory of lawyers:

- ✔ **Nolo:** www.nolo.com
- ✔ **FindLaw:** www.findlaw.com

Legal fees vary depending on the services your lawyer provides you, but expect to pay in the range of $500–$2,000 for a small-business attorney to draft incorporation papers or an operating agreement.

Your accountant helps you with the practical financial matters of operating your business. The most important thing is preparing your taxes; however, he can also help you set up your books or select a bookkeeping service.

Many states have accounting trade associations with online directories of members. To find an accountant in your state, try searching in your preferred search engine on the name of your state and the term *accounting association*. Your local chamber of commerce directory is also a great place for finding accountants in your area.

Note that an accountant doesn't have to be a Certified Public Accountant (CPA); however, CPAs must pass a professional certification exam.

Getting an Employer Identification Number

An *Employer Identification Number (EIN)*, or *Federal Taxpayer Identification Number,* is the business equivalent of your Social Security Number. You need an EIN if you form a new corporation or a multi-member LLC. If you form a single-member LLC as a pass-through or disregarded entity, you use your Social Security Number as the LLC's EIN. Your lawyer or accountant can help you with this process.

What to look for in a lawyer

Kim Kramer suggests these tips on what bloggers need to look for when hiring a lawyer:

✔ *"Look for someone who works with clients like you and businesses like yours. There is no need to be a small fish in a big pond. You want someone who is familiar with the issues that commonly come up for business owners operating in your space.*

✔ *If you are forming a new business, make sure the lawyer customarily handles entity formation. Her familiarity with the process should lead to efficiency, and [because]*

lawyers usually bill by the hour, you may be able to save some money.

✔ *For discrete issues, ask the attorney if he or she can offer a flat fee for this service. Many attorneys will be willing to do so if the scope of the work is readily determinable at the outset.*

✔ *Finally, you should hire a lawyer you like talking to and who is willing to spend some time, off the clock, to get to know you and your business. As your business and legal needs grow, you may find yourself spending a lot of time together."*

Just like you provide your Social Security Number to an employer, you give your EIN to anyone who pays funds to your business, such as advertisers. Usually the company also asks you to fill out federal tax Form W-9 and sends you Form 1099 in January to summarize all payments made to your company during the previous year.

You can apply for your EIN online, and the IRS Web site offers resources to help you through the process. Start here: www.irs.gov/businesses/small/index.html.

Your state also has requirements for filing taxes, including sales tax, unemployment insurance, and workers' compensation. The IRS small-business Web site is a good place to start your research: www.irs.gov/businesses/small/article/0,,id=99021,00.html. This is also something that your accountant can help you with.

Considerations for an existing business when adding a blog

If you already have an established business and your professional blog is simply an offshoot of that business, you probably don't have to do as much on the legal front.

However, if you change the nature of your business in a material way, consult your legal and financial advisers to protect your business. For example, if you bring in coauthors to create a group blog, decide whether they're employees, independent contractors, or partners and then take the appropriate legal steps to ensure that everyone understands their rights, responsibilities, and compensation. You may also want to review your business insurance coverage, such as Errors and Omissions (E&O) and liability insurance, and if you're adding employees for the first time, check into the workers' compensation rules in your state.

 Often bloggers operate multiple businesses, representing different blogs and partner relationships. This way each entity can be kept fairly simple, and issues in one don't impact the others. If you suspect that this type of setup might benefit you and your business, discuss it with your lawyer.

Understanding U.S. Laws That Impact Your Blog

Whether your professional blog is a new business or an addition to an established one, you need to understand and comply with a number of U.S. laws and regulations — some of which apply to all businesses, others to those operating online. These include

- Trademark and copyright protection
- Online privacy laws, including the Children's Online Privacy Protection Act and data security regulations, both state and federal
- The CAN-SPAM Act
- The FTC guidelines for endorsements and testimonials
- Libel

The remainder of this chapter covers these laws in more detail.

Applying Trademark, Copyright, and Licensing Protections to Your Blogging Efforts

Nearly every blogger uses or refers to material produced or owned by others. For example:

- Excerpts to clarify a point
- Art or photos to paint a picture

✔ Quotations to tell a story

✔ Links to provide additional information

Respecting the intellectual property rights of others is an important part of successful, ethical blogging. And likewise, you want others to respect your work, and both use and acknowledge it appropriately.

In the following section, I explain trademarks and copyright, and discuss how you can protect your content and respect others' rights.

Examining the differences between trademark and copyright protections

There are many kinds of protected content, including patents and trade secrets. However, the two categories that are most common in blogging are trademark and copyright:

✔ **Trademark:** A symbol, phrase, word, or design that distinguishes the goods or services of a business. An unregistered trademark is asserted by the trademark holder with the symbol ™. You can also register a trademark with the United States Patent and Trademark Office (www. uspto.gov). Registered trademarks are identified with the symbol ®. Figure 3-1 shows some very well-known trademarks.

✔ **Copyright:** Federal copyright law protects original works — literature, music, choreography, visual art, and architecture — from being stolen. In general, a protected work may not be displayed, published, performed, or used derivatively without the permission of the copyright owner.

Figure 3-1:
The logos for Starbucks, Apple, and Amazon are very well-known trademarks.

Your original blog content is copyrighted. Whether you label your blog with a copyright symbol or statement (which I cover later in this chapter), you own the copyright to the words and images you create.

Your blog name, masthead, logo, and tagline are all elements that you can trademark. Assert the trademark with the ™ symbol.

Understanding the exceptions to trademark and copyright protections

Using someone's trademark or copyrighted material on your blog (and someone using your trademark or copyrighted material on his blog) is restricted under state and federal law and subject to certain exceptions, dubbed *fair use*.

Trademark fair use

Fair use as it applies to trademarks is a little different from fair use for copyrighted material. You also need to know that copyrighted material might also be subject to certain licensing terms. I discuss copyrights and licensing later in this section.

For trademarks, the three most common exceptions under federal law are

- ✔ **Classic fair use** is when the trademark is generally descriptive of the goods or services and you use it to describe your product. For example, stating that you provide *topnotch writing services* doesn't violate the rights of the owner of the Topnotch Writing Services trademark.

- ✔ **Nominative fair use** is when you use someone else's trademark to describe their product, such as in a sales flyer or a comparison of your products to theirs.

- ✔ **Noncommercial use** of the trademark in comment or criticism in which the usage isn't likely to cause confusion among consumers is also considered fair use. For example, an article reviewing the various features of a product branded with a trademark.

These are the most common exemptions under federal law. If you have a specific question about the law in your state, contact a local attorney for guidance.

Copyright fair use

The fair use exemption under U.S. copyright law (www.copyright.gov/title17) lets you quote material from copyrighted works on your blog. This act allows reproduction *with attribution* (identifying the owner of the copyright) for criticism, comment, news reporting, teaching, scholarship, and research. Factors used to determine whether the reproduction of the copyrighted work is fair use include

- **The purpose:** Commercial or nonprofit, educational use. For example, excerpts of a written work used in a review or critical commentary.
- **The nature of the work:** For example, a parody.
- **The scope of the portion used compared to the work as a whole:** For example, a summary accompanied by brief quotations from the article.
- **The reproduction's effect on the market value of the work:** For example, a review of a book or film.

You can also use copyrighted material under a license from the copyright owner. For example, Figure 3-2 shows the agreement for stock photo site iStockphoto, which allows you to license artwork royalty free for a nominal fee. Online magazines and content portals often license blog posts for reproduction on their sites, a practice dubbed *syndication.* I discuss syndication at length in Chapter 7.

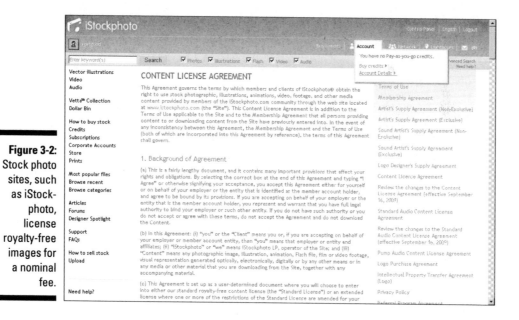

Figure 3-2: Stock photo sites, such as iStockphoto, license royalty-free images for a nominal fee.

A license you often see on blogs and social networking sites is a Creative Commons license (see Figure 3-3). Creative Commons lets content owners specify how they want to share their copyrighted content with others. At the Creative Commons Web site, content owners choose the license conditions that they want to apply to their blog and then use a widget to create the license code. (You can find out more about the Creative Commons license at `http://creativecommons.org`.)

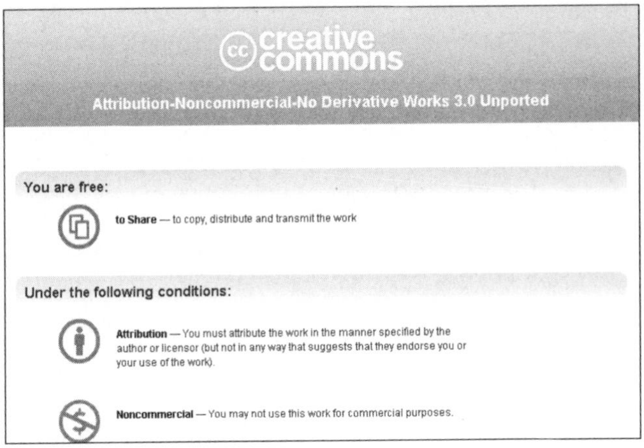

Figure 3-3:
A Creative
Commons
license lets
content
owners
share
copyrighted
content
under pre-
defined
terms.

The six main Creative Commons licenses are

- ✔ **Attribution:** Lets others distribute and build upon your work, even commercially, as long as they credit you for the original creation.

- ✔ **Attribution Share Alike:** Lets others remix, tweak, and build upon your work even for commercial reasons, as long as they credit you and license their new creations under the identical terms.

- ✔ **Attribution No Derivatives:** Allows for redistribution, commercial and noncommercial, as long as the work is passed along unchanged and in whole, with credit to you.

- ✔ **Attribution Non-Commercial:** Lets others remix, tweak, and build upon your work non-commercially. Their new noncommercial works must acknowledge you, but they don't have to license on the same terms.

- ✔ **Attribution Non-Commercial Share Alike:** Lets others remix, tweak, and build upon your work non-commercially, as long as they credit you and license their new creations under the identical terms.

- ✔ **Attribution Non-Commercial No Derivatives:** Is the most restrictive Creative Commons license. This allows others to share your works with others, but they can't change them or use them commercially.

Protecting your work

Trademarks are valuable assets, especially for companies that have invested to build brand equity and goodwill among customers for their trademarks. Likewise, the imagery and content you create for your blog represent a significant investment in time and effort. You need to protect your investments.

 Although a trademark doesn't need to be registered to have protection, if you develop a unique brand name, phrase, or logo, consider registering your trademark so that you can use the ® symbol. This gives you more protection than simply asserting your trademark with a ™ symbol.

Register a trademark with the United States Patent and Trademark Office (www.uspto.gov). Be prepared; it's a long process that requires lots of documentation about your use of the trademark. Start by putting the ™ symbol next to any trademarks you want to protect. Also, a good idea is to keep dated printouts that prove when you first started using your trademark.

A copyright exists, even if the material isn't labeled with a copyright symbol © and the phrase All Rights Reserved. However, proactively asserting your rights to your content with a copyright statement using the symbol is a good idea. Label your blog and other online content, such as photos on Flickr and other photo-sharing sites, with your copyright notice.

You don't need to label every post on your blog. Simply put a copyright statement, such as "Copyright 2010 *Your Name*. All Rights Reserved" in the *footer* (a blog element that appears on every page) of your site or at the bottom of a sidebar column.

If you want to offer a Creative Commons license, discussed earlier in this chapter, display your Creative Commons license in the same place. To create a Creative Commons license, go to the License Your Work page on the Creative Commons site (www.creativecommons.org/choose), and follow the simple directions on the site to generate the license.

In addition to displaying trademark, copyright, and Creative Commons licenses, you may want to proactively protect your content from theft. There are two kinds of theft you need to be on the alert for — plagiarism and spam-scraper sites:

- ✔ **Plagiarism** is when someone uses your content or images as though they're his own. The thief may change some details, or if it's a recipe on a food blog, a few ingredients or the image, but the work is substantially your work.

That's what happened to blogger Megan Jordan, who writes the popular blog Velveteen Mind (www.velveteenmind.com/velveteenmind) and created the Blog Nosh Magazine blog (www.blognosh.com). In April 2009, she discovered that someone had copied two of her posts pretty much word for word. In her investigation, she found out that the same person had plagiarized from other blogs in the past. That made her think this instance wasn't an honest mistake, but rather a consistent pattern of abuse. She reported the incident to the blog host, Blogger. Shortly thereafter, the plagiarizing blog disappeared.

✔ **Spamscraper sites** — usually on the free platforms Blogger and WordPress — *scrape,* or copy, content from the Really Simple Syndication (RSS) feeds of popular blogs without permission. They use the feeds to create a new blog whose sole goal is to drive clicks to Google ads for search engine marketing revenue.

Here are some ways to protect your content:

✔ **Publish a partial, rather than full, RSS feed.** This defeats the spamscrapers but can also be annoying to your legitimate readers who want to read your blog in their RSS reader instead of having to click through to your site.

✔ **Use the Copyscape tool.** Copyscape (www.copyscape.com) checks for plagiarized content. This tool isn't free, although you can check your URL and see the first ten results. To see the full results, you subscribe and pay five cents per search.

✔ **Link to your own blog somewhere in your post and set up a Google Alert for links to you.** A lazy spamscraper may not check for inbound links within your post, so you get an alert that someone has linked to you. Go to www.google.com/alerts to request an alert.

✔ **Add watermarks to your photos.** A watermark is a small image that overlays your photo, as shown in Figure 3-4. There are many ways to add a watermark, including photo-editing software, utilities, and plug-ins for your blogging platform. A quick search for *watermark photos* on your preferred search engine delivers many options.

Respecting other people's rights

Respecting the intellectual property rights of others is an important part of successful, ethical blogging. And likewise, you want others to respect your work, and both use and acknowledge it appropriately.

When you use someone else's trademarks or copyrighted material on your blog without explicit permission, you rely on the principle of fair use. (If you aren't sure what fair use means, review the "Understanding the exceptions to trademark and copyright protections" section, earlier in this chapter.)

Figure 3-4:
A water-mark identifies the owner of a copy-righted image.

When using someone else's copyrighted material, always give the proper attribution (identify the copyright owner), and if the source is online, link back to it. Simply put, say who said what first and provide a way for your readers to find the original if they want.

Copyright fair use allows you to use a portion of a written text for criticism or commentary; it does *not* allow you to reproduce the entire item without per-mission. If you want to use the entire piece, you must get permission from the author.

Using a *portion* of a photo or illustration is hard. The safest course is to assume that you have to obtain permission or license the item to use it on your blog. Don't use images you find online without the proper permission.

Generally, photos that you license from royalty-free stock photo sites don't require a photo credit, but always read the license to find out what your responsibilities are. If you've paid for use of an original piece of artwork or photography, the terms and your permitted uses are spelled out in the contract.

On the other hand, if you use a photo under a Creative Commons license, *attribution* — in this case, the photo credit — is required.

If you want to do something that doesn't appear to be covered under the fair use exceptions, you can ask permission to use the trademark from the owner. Be clear about what you want to do and be prepared for rejection. Companies invest quite a lot in their trademarks and usually don't allow third parties to modify them. However, if you don't ask, the answer is definitely no.

Protecting Privacy

The United States online privacy law is concerned with the protection of personally identifiable information under two general circumstances: the information of children under the age of 13 (the Children's Online Privacy Protection Act) and information collected and stored by financial institutions (Gramm-Leach-Bliley Act and other federal and state data privacy regulations). Additional laws apply to specific types of information. For example, the Health Insurance Portability and Accountability Act (HIPAA) protects the privacy of patient healthcare information.

In this section, I review the various U.S. privacy laws so you can determine whether they apply to your blog, and I suggest some best practices for your privacy policy.

Complying with the Children's Online Privacy Protection Act

The *Children's Online Privacy Protection Act (COPPA)* requires Web site operators that collect personal information (name, address, phone number, e-mail address, and so on) from children younger than 13 to publish a privacy policy that spells out exactly what information they collect and how they use it, including the circumstances under which that information might be shared with third parties. The site must also obtain verifiable consent from a parent. You can find more information at www.ftc.gov/bcp/edu/pubs/business/idtheft/bus45.shtm.

If you collect personal information from children on your blog, you must comply with COPPA.

Protecting your customers' financial data

The *Gramm-Leach-Bliley Act (GLBA)* and the state data privacy regulations are concerned with the protection of financial information — name, Social Security Number, and financial accounts. The goal is to protect consumers from identify theft and credit card fraud. GLBA, which applies to financial institutions, spells out requirements for collection and disclosure of personal financial data as well as the obligations of the institutions to safeguard the information. GLBA also includes specific written notice requirements to consumers.

State data privacy regulations may have additional requirements. The FTC has many good resources to help with data security requirements at www.ftc.gov/infosecurity.

If you sell products on your blog and collect your customers' personally iden-tifiable financial information, such as name and credit card number, you may be subject to data privacy laws. If a third party, such as a payment processor, handles the transaction for you and you don't have possession of the cus-tomers' financial information, the laws likely don't apply to you, but you need to find out how the payment processor secures customer information.

Blogging with other regulations in mind

You also need to be aware that some regulated industries have restrictions on the kind of content you can publish and what you can collect on your blog. For example, the *Health Insurance Portability and Accountability Act (HIPAA)* protects the privacy of patients online and off. The short version of HIPAA: Healthcare professionals may only share patient healthcare informa-tion with people who need it to properly treat the patient. The patient can share whatever he likes.

If you blog professionally as an extension of your participation in a regulated industry, be sure to look into this and work with your attorney to craft a pri-vacy policy for your site that protects your visitors and your business.

Preparing a privacy policy

If your blog is for an adult audience and you aren't in a regulated industry, current privacy law probably doesn't apply to your blog. That said, most sites collect some information even if it's just an e-mail address to subscribe to a newsletter. And even if you don't directly collect any information, a pri-vacy policy is a best practice that gives your readers important information about your business practices.

A *privacy policy* tells your visitors what level of privacy they can expect on your site. This policy needs to include who owns the site and your data collection practices, including data collected explicitly (such as an e-mail address to subscribe to a newsletter) and data collected in the background (for example, cookies).

 Be clear and factual about the information you collect and how you intend to use it. You don't have to use official-sounding legal language (except in the circumstances when such language is required by law), but stay away from hyperbole and marketing speak. Tell your visitors

- ✔ What data you collect
- ✔ Why you collect that data
- ✔ How the data will be used

✔ Who you share the data with, and what they use it for

✔ How your visitors can remove themselves from your database

Put your privacy policy on a separate page on your blog and link to it from your footer. That's where most commercial Web sites put it, so your readers will know to look for it there.

Preston Koerner, the founder of environmental design blog Jetson Green (http://jetsongreen.com) is a practicing attorney. He runs the blog as an LLC and not surprisingly has an extensive Terms and Conditions page, a comment policy (more about comment policies in Chapter 10), and a privacy policy, all of which can be read or accessed here: www.jetsongreen.com/legal.html. Another good example of a privacy policy is women's blogging community BlogHer at www.blogher.com/privacy-policy.

The Federal Trade Commission (FTC) has a number of resources to help you, including these tips for a privacy policy, www.ftc.gov/bcp/edu/pubs/articles/art09.shtm.

You can also include a list of trademarks you want to explicitly assert and disclose your general business practices; however, these items need to follow the privacy disclosures.

After you publish your policy, you're legally obligated to follow it. If you don't, the FTC considers that a "deceptive trade practice." You can, however, change your policy at any time, so be sure to review it whenever your business practices change.

The following isn't regulated, but another best practice for privacy is to blur out personal information, such as license plate numbers, home addresses, and children's faces from photos that you post online, unless you have explicit permission.

Keeping your e-mail marketing campaigns legal

If you use e-mail to market your business, you must comply with the CAN-SPAM Act. This law, which has tough penalties for violations, applies to "any electronic mail message, the primary purpose of which is the commercial advertisement or promotion of a commercial product or service," including content on a Web site or a blog.

This includes your promotional newsletter, bulk e-mail marketing campaigns, and even individual messages to customers whose primary intent is *commercial* (to sell something) rather than *transactional* (related to the ongoing business relationship or a current transaction).

Under the CAN-SPAM Act, when you send a commercial e-mail, you must

- Identify yourself as the sender and provide accurate information in the message header.
- Use an accurate subject line and clearly identify the message as a commercial message.
- Include a valid physical address.
- Provide a clear and conspicuous explanation of how to opt-out of further e-mail communication.
- Honor opt-out requests within ten business days.
- Make sure that any vendors helping you with e-mail marketing comply with the law.

A key element in the law is the distinction between commercial and transactional e-mail. Examples of transactional e-mails include

- Order confirmations or download information for an electronic product
- Warranty or recall information
- Notice of change in terms or other information related to an ongoing commercial relationship

These transactional messages can't include false routing information, but otherwise are exempt from most provisions of the CAN-SPAM Act, which makes sense. You really don't want people to opt-out of receiving important safety information or subscriber notices.

TIP

Even though your transactional e-mail is exempt from many CAN-SPAM provisions, include your valid physical address and contact information in these messages.

The FTC is responsible for the enforcement of the law and provides extensive resources on its Web site to help businesses understand and comply with the law. Start here: www.ftc.gov/bcp/edu/pubs/business/ecommerce/bus61.shtm.

The simplest way to make sure that your e-mail marketing programs comply with the CAN-SPAM Act is to use a reputable e-mail marketing software package, such as iContact, Constant Contact, or MailChimp. Not only do these programs make managing your e-mail lists easier, but they also have built-in safeguards to ensure that e-mails sent comply with the law.

Be wary of vendors offering e-mail lists for sale. You may find them tempting, but the best e-mail list for your blog consists of people who proactively subscribe to your updates.

Reviewing the FTC Guidelines for Endorsements and Testimonials

In December 2009, the FTC revised its guidelines for endorsements and testimonials (`http://ftc.gov/os/2009/10/091005revisedendorsement guides.pdf`) to include social media like blogs and review sites. Under the revised guidelines, bloggers and word-of-mouth marketers have specific disclosure obligations when they

- ✔ Are compensated directly for their post or comment
- ✔ Write about products they received for free from manufacturers
- ✔ Have a material relationship with a company

Bloggers also may be held liable for false statements about products in their posts.

The original purpose of the FTC guidelines was to help advertisers understand how the agency intended to enforce truth in advertising laws when advertising messages contain endorsements and testimonials. Things like weight loss results, "I lost 50 pounds with the Flabinator," and efficacy claims, "This product was so good it cured my *(insert name of malady here)* in only five days." The guidelines also covered celebrity endorsements and anyone with a material relationship with the company.

What the customer understands is the underlying principle. When a speaker or writer is compensated, either directly or with free products or services, her words are considered commercial speech. If the consumer clearly understands that the message is a paid advertisement or the speaker is an interested party, disclosure isn't required. If the relationship with the company isn't clear on its face, she must disclose it.

Looking at why the guidelines were extended to bloggers

Over the past few years, the opinions shared on blogs and social media have become increasingly influential. Because of this, companies have increased their marketing efforts to people actively engaged in these channels, offering them free products for review, all-expenses-paid trips to company headquarters for blogger meetings, and paid post programs. (I tell you more about pay-per-post blogging in Chapter 7.) All are designed to positively influence the opinion of the bloggers in the hope that those opinions will, in turn, drive consumer behavior.

Nothing's wrong with this commercial activity; it helps get valuable information about products and services to the consumer and helps the bloggers as well. The problem is that it wasn't always clear in the resulting posts that the products or services were provided to the blogger for free. Consumers, however, might evaluate the post and the blogger's opinion differently if they had this important information — if they understood that the blogger had a relationship with the company.

A relationship with a company doesn't mean the blogger isn't ethical or was somehow bought by the free product or compensation. People simply don't expect that the average Joe gets stuff for free. People also expect that when someone is paid to endorse a product, it's obvious or declared.

Under the FTC standard for deception, a blog post is considered *deceptive* if it misleads reasonable consumers about something important to their purchase decision. The potential for consumer confusion is what led the FTC to extend the guidelines for endorsements and testimonials to blogs and social media. The guidelines include five examples that apply specifically to social media; I discuss them generally in a bit and you can read the full text of the revised guidelines at `http://ftc.gov/os/2009/10/091005revisedend orsementguides.pdf`.

The FTC intends to focus its enforcement efforts on the companies and advertisers that use social media and blogs to promote their products rather than the individual bloggers who are writing about the products. This is consistent with historical practice — advertisers have always been responsible for deceptive advertising. However, blogger, advertiser, or both, if you have relationships that fall under the guidelines, you must comply with the guidelines. In the next section, I tell you how.

Complying with the FTC disclosure requirements

Disclosure is a requirement in the U.S. under the circumstances outlined by the FTC. More important, disclosure is a best practice that lets you share the affiliations that may influence your opinions with your readers; it's the embodiment of transparency. When you disclose your business practices and relationships, you're *transparent*.

You disclose in two places. The FTC requirement is to disclose your relationship or compensation in the post that mentions or reviews a specific product.

In your privacy and disclosure page, you outline your general policies and practices about products, reviews, and marketing relationships.

In the next section I tell you how to properly add a disclosure statement to a blog post and then give you some guidelines for creating your disclosure policy. After that, I give you some tips on how to handle the disclosure issue when you're the one giving away the free goods and/or services.

Disclosing a relationship with a company in a blog post

If you're compensated by a company or its agent, either directly or with a free product, and subsequently write a blog post about the product, trip, service, or company, you must disclose the relationship in your post.

The disclosure must be clear and conspicuous. You can include it in the text of the post or in a notice at the top or bottom of the post, as shown in Figure 3-5.

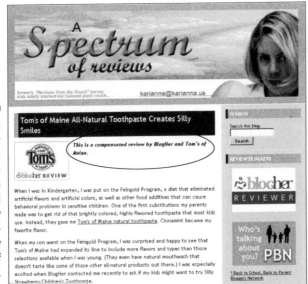

Figure 3-5: The blogger places the disclosure about the sponsored post clearly and conspicuously at the top of the post.

In addition to disclosing a relationship, also be careful about claims you make about products because you can be held liable for any misrepresentations. In commercial speech, general claims must be substantiated. Using the FTC's skincare lotion example (see Example 5 in Section 255.1 of the guidelines, posted online at http://ftc.gov/os/2009/10/091005revisedendor sementguides.pdf), there's a big difference between saying, "This cream cures eczema" (wrong) and "This cream really helped my eczema" (specific, your experience). As the FTC explains:

> *"The advertiser is subject to liability for misleading or unsubstantiated representations made through the blogger's endorsement. The blogger also is subject to liability for misleading or unsubstantiated representations made in the course of her endorsement. The blogger is also liable if she fails to disclose clearly and conspicuously that she is being paid for her services."*

If you use *affiliate marketing links* (hyperlinks that contain a special code identifying your blog) in your posts (more about those in Chapter 6), you must disclose that you're an affiliate of the seller, and that if the reader follows the link and makes a purchase, you receive an affiliate commission. You can do this within the text of your post by explicitly stating that the link is to an affiliate by saying something like, "You can purchase this product at my affiliate store *X* at this affiliate link."

That can get a little awkward, especially if you use many affiliate links on your blog. I like blogger Mir Kamin's solution at shopping blog Want Not: She uses hover text over the affiliate link, as shown in Figure 3-6, and describes her policies in a comprehensive disclosure policy.

Figure 3-6: Shopping blog Want Not uses hover text to disclose affiliate links to readers.

Affiliate marketing. The main source of revenue here at Want Not is commissions I make off of sales generated through affiliate linking. (Cliff Notes version: I have an existing relationship with a store whereby using a special link gives me a percentage commission of any sales made through that link.) Per the new FTC rules, although I previously disclosed those affiliate relationships on my About page, any link through which I stand to make money will now be clearly marked as an affiliate link via hover text.

Example:

This is a non-affiliate link to Amazon.
This is an affiliate link to Amazon.
(Holding your mouse over each link will show you the difference.)

> This is an affiliate link; shopping through it makes me a little money and makes you even prettier than you already are.

From December 1st, 2009, and forward, all affiliate links which appear on this site will have the hover text disclosing them as such. If a link doesn't have that text, well, it's not an affiliate link. It's just a link. I am not an affiliate with every merchant I feature here.

Creating a disclosure policy

A clear disclosure policy that explains the general practices on your blog is a best practice that helps your readers and the marketers that might want to work with you understand what you, and your blog, are all about.

As with your privacy policy, after you publish your disclosure policy, you're legally obligated to follow it. If you don't, the FTC considers that a "deceptive trade practice." You can, however, change your policy at any time, so be sure to review it whenever your business practices change.

Your disclosure policy needs to include

✔ **Any information about you that helps your readers more easily understand your point of view:** For example, biographical information, affiliations, and information about any existing business relationships, such as brand ambassador, consulting, or affiliate marketing agreements. See an example in Figure 3-7.

✔ **Your review policy:** State whether you do reviews and under what circumstances. Outline the type of products you are (or aren't) interested in. Say what you do with products after the review.

✔ **Advertising:** Tell readers (and potential advertisers) what kinds of advertising you accept on your blog and where they can get rate information. Let readers know whether you do paid posts.

Full Disclosure

Per the new FTC regulations about bloggers and disclosure, this is a crib sheet on exactly how I handle anything involving compensation here at Want Not.

Want Not began as a hobby, and has since grown into a commercial enterprise. Simply put: This is my job, now. I get paid for doing my job, just like you get paid for doing yours. The following should clarify any questions about that.*

Free stuff. Sometimes I accept free items from marketers or companies, and then almost all of the time I use those free items as contest prizes here on Want Not. On the rare occasions when I keep one of those items for my own personal use, I will disclose that I received the item for free if it is discussed here on the site. If I tell you I love my 3-handled family credenza beyond measure and I never mention that it was a freebie? That's because it wasn't.

Sometimes I accept even "bigger" free items in return for discussing them here on the site, such as my participation as a Frigidaire Test Drive Mom. Those campaigns are also fully disclosed so that there's no confusion as to whether or not such a thing is sponsored.

Product reviews. I do not do paid product reviews, with the notable exception of occasional contracts with BlogHer to participate in targeted campaigns where I am reimbursed for my time. Those reviews will be clearly labeled as such. Any *other* product review I do will either disclose that I received the item in question for free

---

Figure 3-7:
The disclosure policy of shopping blog Want Not.

Be careful when you use generic disclosure policy templates. Writing your policy is always best, but if you use a template, consider it a starting point and not the finished product. Review the template carefully and modify it to fit the policies you practice on your site. And keep in mind that your disclosure policy does not replace the need for disclosure in any posts that fit the FTC parameters.

If you accept free products for review and keep them, don't forget your tax liability. Talk to your accountant. The IRS may not care about a few CDs and books, but free trips, appliances, and cars? You bet the IRS cares.

Understanding your company's obligations under FTC endorsement guidelines

If you give a free product to other bloggers for review or provide other compensation — payment, free trip, affiliate commissions, and so on — you need to understand your company's obligations under the guidelines. Companies using social media marketing tactics have an equal, if not greater, obligation than bloggers do under the revised FTC guidelines.

Companies using word-of-mouth marketing and their agencies are required to

✔ Disclose their relationships when posting, commenting, tweeting, or reviewing products.

✔ Provide guidance to people participating in their campaigns about their obligation to disclose.

✔ Monitor to ensure both compliance with the disclosure requirements and information accuracy.

✔ Take steps to correct inaccurate or misleading information.

Your programs probably aren't on the same scale as a large consumer goods company, but still

✔ **Include information about the disclosure requirements in your materials, with a specific example for your program.** For example, if you invited the blogger to a special event during which she gets a free makeover and a gift bag of free products, you might include something like this in your invitation:

> *We look forward to seeing you at* (event) *on* (date). *Please remember that if you choose to write about the free makeover or our products, you must disclose that you were invited to the event and received the makeover and products for free. This is both best practice and a requirement under the FTC guidelines on endorsements and testimonials.*

✔ **Monitor the blogs to make sure that the bloggers included the proper disclosure and didn't misrepresent your product.**

✔ **Do your best to correct any errors.** You can't make someone fix an inaccurate statement on his blog, but documented proof that you attempted to get the error fixed is essential to protect yourself. You also need to provide the correct information on your blog.

✔ **Always identify your blog and your interests when commenting on your products.**

Avoiding Libel

Libel is the intentional publication of false or defamatory statements or representations of a living person, usually with intent to damage the person's reputation. To be a libelous statement, it has to be distributed to someone other than the target. In other words, statements in an e-mail or letter to someone, and only that person, aren't libel, but the same content on a public blog might be.

If you're libeled, seek the advice of your attorney and weigh the long-term impact of the statements on your business. A lawsuit can be costly and may not be your most effective form of redress.

The best strategy to avoid being accused of libel is to avoid making this type of statement about others online, including on your blog, in blog comments, and on social networks like Twitter and Facebook. When criticizing or disagreeing with others, attack the idea, not the person. There is a vast difference between "Jane's idea is stupid" and "Jane is stupid."

Take the time to reread your blog posts and comments before clicking the Send button. This is a good strategy for any electronic communication, including e-mail. After you send a message, you have no control over who it might be forwarded to; incautious, hasty words can damage your reputation even if they don't cause legal problems.

Part II
Making Money with Your Blog

The 5th Wave   By Rich Tennant

"Just how accurately should my blog reflect my place of business?"

In this part . . .

Chapter 4 provides an overview of the options available to you to make money with your blog. The subsequent chapters in this part delve into each area — sales, consulting, advertising, and sponsored conversations (or paid posts) — in detail.

I include real-world examples throughout so you can hear from people just like you who have developed successful blogs.

Chapter 4

Monetizing Your Blog Strategy

*W*hether you want to make a living from your blog or merely enough money to pay for the family vacation, you need a plan for monetizing your blog. Your plan doesn't have to be 40 pages with charts, graphs, and footnotes. An outline of your goals and how you intend to achieve them is enough to get started, although a financial plan is a good idea.

The most important part of your monetization plan is selecting ways to monetize that fit your skills, blog, and audience. There is no one-size-fits-all solution.

In this chapter, I give a brief overview of the various ways you can make money from your blog. The rest of the chapters in this part go into the details.

Having Realistic Expectations

You need to be realistic about the effort you're willing to put into your blogging endeavor. Most blogs don't make a lot of money. In a the survey that I conducted for this book, only 56 percent of the bloggers reported making money from their blog, and most of them attributed less than 10 percent of their income to their blog (see Figure 4-1).

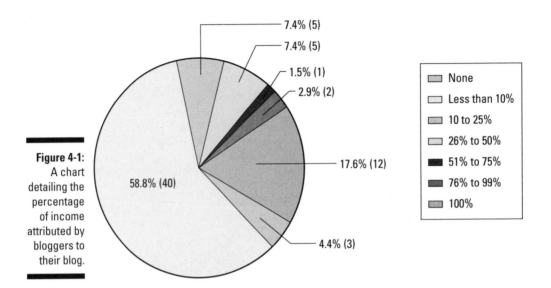

Bloggers That Make Money from Blogging, Percent Attributed to Blog

7.4% (5)
7.4% (5)
1.5% (1)
2.9% (2)
17.6% (12)
58.8% (40)
4.4% (3)

Legend:
- None
- Less than 10%
- 10 to 25%
- 26% to 50%
- 51% to 75%
- 76% to 99%
- 100%

Figure 4-1:
A chart detailing the percentage of income attributed by bloggers to their blog.

Source: Professional Blogging For Dummies survey, Susan Getgood, 2010

The good news, if you want to earn your living from blogging, is that almost 18 percent of those making money from their blog are doing just that. The key to success is matching your effort and plan to your desired results. If you want to earn a living from your blog, plan on treating it as your job. If your goals are smaller, your effort can be too.

To see the complete results from the survey I conducted for this book, check out my blog Marketing Roadmaps at `http://getgood.com/roadmaps`.

Understanding Your Monetization Options

Advertising is the first thing that comes to mind when people think of making money from a blog; it's also the most common strategy. More than 70 percent of the bloggers who made any money on their blog reported advertising as a revenue source (see Figure 4-2). However, you have other options, and the most successful bloggers use more than one strategy. Other lucrative options include income from freelance writing, syndicating your posts to larger sites, commissions and referrals, book sales, and speaking fees. I cover your options in more detail later in this chapter.

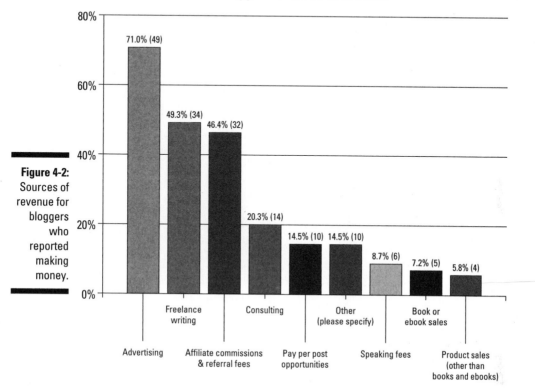

All Bloggers: Sources of Revenue

Figure 4-2:
Sources of revenue for bloggers who reported making money.

Source: Professional Blogging For Dummies survey, Susan Getgood

Matching Monetization to Your Business Goals

There are no shortcuts or easy answers. You make your monetization choices based on your business objectives, the range of opportunities available to you (often influenced by your blog topic), and the level of effort you want to invest.

Starting point: Your blog objectives

Your blog plan or objectives — the ones you can outline in Chapter 1 — are your starting point. Of the opportunities available to you, which ones fit with your blog objectives and which ones don't? For example, if your blog is a consumer watchdog site, you may want to avoid keyword-based advertising. Otherwise, you might find an ad on your blog for a company you've been critical of simply because of a keyword match that you didn't add to your filters (more about this in Chapter 6).

If you're a consultant, you may want to avoid advertising altogether to keep your prospecting options open. You may have a hard time pitching a company on your services if an ad for its competitor runs on your blog. This is how I handle my professional Marketing Roadmaps blog.

If your blog is a shopping or review blog, on the other hand, your readers want information about products. They're highly likely to be buyers; therefore, advertising and affiliate marketing are good choices.

Identifying the opportunities

After you've considered what generally makes sense given your overall blog plan, research the specific opportunities for making money that fit your blog *and* your plan. Generally speaking, they fall into three broad categories:

- ✔ Advertising
- ✔ Product sales
- ✔ Consulting and writing

These categories aren't absolute, and sometimes they blur into each other, but they provide a basis for laying out a monetization plan.

Monetization means you get paid. After you've established a successful blog, you may be approached with all sorts of offers, such as including your content on blog networks and link exchanges. If the offer does not include compensation, it's a promotional opportunity, *not* monetization. Evaluate these offers based on the promotional value to you. Does the offer make sense for your blog and your readers? Are you getting sufficient exposure for your blog? Read more about this topic in Chapter 12.

Advertising

Advertising includes

- ✔ **Online advertising, both direct and through ad networks:** With advertising, you're paid on a promise. The person clicking through on an ad on your blog *might* purchase something. This is a numbers game based on your blog traffic.

✔ **Affiliate marketing:** With affiliate marketing, you're paid on a *result,* not a promise. The person clicked an affiliate ad on your blog or a link in your post and then actually purchased something. In effect, affiliate marketing is commission on a sale.

✔ **Advertorial, also known as pay-per-post:** In pay-per-post, the advertiser hires you to write a post on your blog about its product. It looks like editorial content, but it is really advertising — hence the blended name, *advertorial.*

✔ **Direct blog sponsorship:** The company pays a fee to the blog to be listed as a sponsor, similar to underwriting on public television. A blog may have multiple sponsors or a single sponsor.

Product sales

To make money from product sales, you have to sell a product directly from your blog: It can be your own product, someone else's product, or even a store with many products. Your product can be offline or online — perhaps on a network like eBay (www.ebay.com) or Etsy, a community of online sellers of handmade crafts and artisan items (www.etsy.com).

The difference between product sales and an affiliate relationship is that if you're selling a physical product, you carry the inventory and the corresponding risk. The upside, of course, is that you get to keep all the revenue.

Even if you use your blog to promote your product, you don't necessarily have to sell it yourself. For example, if your blog promotes your book, you may prefer to drive buyers to Amazon (www.amazon.com) rather than have the headache of dealing with direct sales.

Consulting and writing

Your blog can lead to opportunities for freelance writing, consulting, or speaking even if you have never considered this kind of work before. Spokesperson work, which is when you are hired to represent a brand, is also included in this category. Acting as a spokesperson is different than when a company sponsors your blog because you personally perform tasks (such as promotional appearances) for the advertiser. You may also get the opportunity to have a previously published blog post featured on a Web portal for a fee. This is called *syndication.*

Keep in mind that if the other site is making money from you or your content, so should you!

Deciding how hard you're willing to work

Be realistic about the time you have to devote to your blog. Each of these ways to make money requires a different amount of direct effort on your part, and you need to set your priorities against the expected return:

- ✔ Consulting, speaking, and freelance writing are labor intensive. You have to obtain the work and then you have to actually do it. Likewise, negotiating with a potential sponsor can take a very long time.

- ✔ Selling a product, even one you produce, is more about the promotion plan than your labor. You probably need to invest in some advertising. If you're opening your own online store or carrying physical inventory, you also have a higher degree of risk and financial investment.

- ✔ Advertising and affiliate marketing seem simple and require less apparent effort. You sign up with a network, put the ads on your blog, and collect the payments. Easy, huh? Except . . . not so much. They're only less effort if you don't count building your audience or monitoring special offers from your affiliates so you can inform your readers. Plus, many advertising networks and affiliate programs have thresholds that they expect you to meet, such as minimum page views per month, before they even consider your application. You may end up selling ads directly, at least in the beginning, and that's time-consuming work.

Combining different strategies

The best way to successfully monetize your blog is to combine multiple strategies. When I interviewed a number of successful bloggers, everyone who attributed 100 percent of their revenue to their blog cited multiple sources of revenue.

Jaden Hair, the author of the Steamy Kitchen blog (see the nearby sidebar "The plan, boss, the plan"), says that combining strategies is the only sensible strategy. For many bloggers, the fourth calendar quarter is terrific for advertising revenue due to holiday buying, but the rest of the year, you have to supplement your income with other sources of revenue. In Jaden's case, book sales, speaking fees, freelance writing, and sponsorship round out her monetization plan.

Matt Kepnes, of Nomadic Matt's Travel Site at www.nomadicmatt.com (which I feature in Chapter 2), reported a similar revenue mix of advertising, affiliate commissions, product sales, and e-book sales. According to my survey, advertising, freelance writing, and affiliate commissions are the most common sources of revenue for bloggers who make their livings from their blogs, as shown in Figure 4-3.

What does this mean for your blog? Follow the leaders. Don't rely on a single strategy to make money. Diversify.

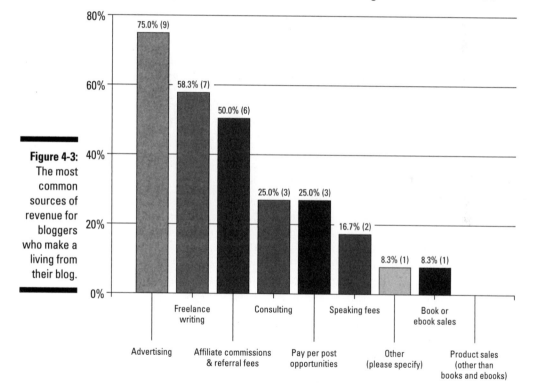

Bloggers Who Earn 100% of Revenue from Blog: Sources of Revenue

Figure 4-3: The most common sources of revenue for bloggers who make a living from their blog.

Source: Professional Blogging For Dummies survey, Susan Getgood, 2010

Promoting your blog: The key to success

Ultimately, how well you promote your blog to build an audience is the key to successful monetization. Why? Because nearly every way of making money on a blog requires readers.

Advertising networks and sponsors want to know that lots of people will see their ads on your blog. You can't collect affiliate commissions unless people buy products from your links. Ditto for product sales: no readers, no buyers, no sales. Even consulting and freelance jobs require that you reach the right readers — the ones who can hire you. When making money through work for hire, it's more about influence and talent than volume, but you still need readers.

Don't get so caught up in the mechanics of monetization that you forget that the total formula for success requires good content and effective promotion as well as a monetization strategy. Commit this formula to memory:

Success = Solid strategy + Good content + Effective promotion

---

The plan, boss, the plan

Very few bloggers start out on day one with a business plan. In the survey that I conducted for this book, only 33 percent of the bloggers surveyed had any sort of a plan when they started (see the following figure). Sixty-three percent say that they subsequently added a plan though.

The most successful bloggers come up with a plan pretty quickly if they don't have one to start with. One example is Jaden Hair, author of the food blog Steamy Kitchen, www. steamykitchen.com, as shown in the following figure.

Jaden started her blog as an offshoot of classes she was teaching at a local cooking school near her home in Florida. She was simply looking for a way to share her recipes with her students and realized very quickly — about three months into it — that her niche of authentic Asian cuisine for the home cook was unique and had the potential to be a profitable business. So she

took steps to make it happen. She wrote a business plan, incorporated, and created a virtual board of advisors of experienced food bloggers that she respected.

She also made a point of diversifying her revenue streams. She started by targeting multiple media outlets — print, television, radio, and public speaking — and literally created opportunities for herself. She tells the story:

"Instead of waiting around for someone to notice me, I contacted the tiniest local community newspaper. You know, the free one they throw in your driveway. I offered to write for it once a month with a recipe and a photo, for free. They said yes. I built a following, and eventually the Tampa Tribune offered me a weekly column. I did the same thing with television. I called the tiniest local ABC affiliate and offered to appear. Gradually, bigger and bigger stations contacted me, and now I am on a syndicated show, Daytime, twice a month. A lot of people *are so afraid of rejection, they don't call. I just picked up the phone. Any no's that I got only meant that the right opportunity was one step closer."*

Jaden is now a nationally recognized food writer and speaker. The Steamy Kitchen blog gets more than 600,000 page views per month, and in October 2009, she published *The Steamy Kitchen Cookbook* with Tuttle Publishing.

When writing your business plan, Jaden advises bloggers to create something that

inspires them. In her case, that meant ditching the written plan in favor of something that suited her personality better — a visual representation:

"I made a collage with images and words cut out of magazines to represent what I was trying to achieve, and called it my Vision Board. I framed it, hung it on my office wall, and it became the most inspiring piece of artwork."

Recognizing How Monetization Can Impact Your Blog Design

Think about monetization in a general way even before you begin designing your new blog. This doesn't mean that everything has to be locked down before you start. In fact, you can't lock down everything beforehand, because some of your opportunities, like advertising on the more exclusive ad networks, don't exist for you until you have an established blog audience.

Knowing what you might want to do, however, helps you make smarter choices about your design. The following sections detail some things to consider.

Deciding what display advertising sizes you plan to offer

Luckily, online advertising has standard formats, so you don't have to worry about oddball ad sizes; however, you may not want to offer every possible ad size on your blog. Think about how and where you want the ads and then develop your design to suit. The Interactive Advertising Bureau publishes the design specs at

```
www.iab.net/iab_products_and_industry_
          services/508676/508767/Ad_Unit
```

You're probably already reading blogs that attract the advertisers you want to have someday. Find out what ad sizes they offer. If they work with an ad network, such as Federated Media or Blogads, you can find this information on their Web sites:

```
www.federatedmedia.net/marketers/adspecs
```

```
http://web.blogads.com/Documents/Examples_of_3.0_ad_types/
```

If not, the blog may have its own list of advertising rates and sizes, called a *rate card,* or you can just eyeball it. Support the same ad sizes on your blog. Doing so doesn't guarantee anything, but if you can use ad inventory that the advertiser has developed already, it makes it just a little bit easier for them to choose you.

Just because the blog you're emulating is part of an ad network doesn't mean that you have to be part of that network to approach the *advertiser* about your blog. Being part of the network helps, but it's not a requirement.

Selling products on the blog

To sell products on your blog, you need an electronic payments solution (see Chapter 7), and if you're going to offer more than one or two products, you may want a *storefront* — an e-commerce section on your blog that can be organized into categories — and a virtual shopping cart.

Before you choose your blogging platform, make sure that you like the way it supports e-commerce. Is there an easy-to-use off-the-shelf e-commerce option that offers the experience you want in your store? Does the e-commerce solution integrate nicely with the blogging platform and the payments solution, or does it look like a clunky afterthought? Don't get stuck with something you don't like, or worse, paying for custom software development when you don't have to. I cover this topic in Chapter 5 and provide some examples of currently available solutions.

Looking for a corporate sponsor

If your blog topic is a good fit — and I mean a really, really good fit — for a corporate sponsor, spend some serious time on the sponsor's Web sites. You want your blog to complement the main site of your proposed sponsor, in content, looks, and especially color palette so the company's logo looks good. Your blog doesn't have to match the company's site, but you want your potential sponsor to feel comfortable with your site, and making your blog feel familiar is a good place to start.

Creating a Financial Plan

You don't need a financial plan to make money blogging. However, the discipline of a financial plan can help you surface issues before they become problems and make smarter decisions about opportunities. Chances are, you'll reach your goals faster.

For your first plan, all you really need is a monthly revenue forecast, expense budget, and cash flow projection. I detail these reports in the upcoming sections. As your business grows, you can add more formal financial reports, such as a profit and loss statement, as well as a balance sheet. You need them if you apply for loans, seek investors, or sell your blog.

If you're using an accounting package, such as QuickBooks, for your business, it can generate all three reports for you. You can also use a spreadsheet program, such as Microsoft Excel.

If you are using QuickBooks, *QuickBooks All-in-One For Dummies* by Stephen L. Nelson is a good additional resource, as is the QuickBooks Web site:

```
http://quickbooks.intuit.com.
```

If Microsoft Excel is more your speed, Microsoft offers a library of templates for the documents I recommend in the following sections (and more) at

```
http://office.microsoft.com/en-us/templates/
        FX100595491033.aspx
```

You don't need a plan to start your blog. But, using simple financial planning tools is a good way to get in the habit of thinking about your blog as a business.

The monthly revenue forecast

The *monthly revenue forecast* lists your expected sources and estimated revenue from each source, as shown in Table 4-1. Use this table as a guide to measure your performance and fine-tune your strategy. Every month, compare your actual results to the forecast, for each revenue source, and then adjust your strategy accordingly.

Table 4-1	Monthly Revenue Forecast	
Revenue Source	*Forecast Amount*	*Actual Amount*
Advertising		
Google AdSense		
Other ad network		
Direct sales		
Affiliate Income		
Affiliate, by network and/or store		
Sponsorship Fees		
By company name		
Consulting/Writing Fees		
Project 1		
Project 2		
Syndication fees		

When you first get started, you don't know how much money you'll make, but it's still worth building a first forecast to use as a baseline. You just have to use conservative estimates until you have actual data from your own blog. For advertising and affiliate revenue, other bloggers may be willing to give you guidance based on their experiences, especially if you aren't competitive directly.

Professional bloggers like Darren Rowse who make their living helping other bloggers succeed are also a good source of information to calculate your estimates. For example, his post on the Amazon Associates program gives some pointers for estimating affiliate potential based on the types of products you might feature:

```
www.problogger.net/archives/2007/06/29/amazon-affiliate-
                          program
```

If you're selling a product or a book, you can find industry sales figures and projections online from the government, trade associations, industry analysts, market research companies, and business groups such as your local chamber of commerce. Web sites like About.com are also good sources for up-to-date references.

For example, a Google search on *monthly sales figures* surfaces the U.S. government's monthly and annual retail trade report at `www.census.gov/retail`. You can also search your favorite search engine for *market research about [insert name of product or industry here]* and get a pretty decent list for investigation.

If you've been selling the product in a bricks and mortar store, use your sales figures from the store to create an estimate based on the number of visitors required to make a sale. If it takes 100 visitors in your store to make one sale, assume the same for your blog.

Don't forget to account for seasonality. Advertising and affiliate revenues are generally higher in the fourth calendar quarter due to holiday sales.

On some level, *what* you forecast for the first few months doesn't matter, as long as you don't overspend on blog development and promotion. Get in the habit of looking at the forecast every month and make adjustments if things aren't producing as expected. After you have actual data, of course, use it to calculate your forecast.

Expense budget

Your monthly *expense budget* lists what you plan to spend to operate and promote your business. This budget includes things like blog development, hosting costs, software fees, computer hardware purchases, travel and office expenses, legal fees, and marketing costs.

Cash flow projection

The monthly *cash flow projection* tells you how much cash you have on hand to fund your business. This projection lists your sources of revenue and subtracts your expenses — how much is coming in less how much is going out.

Even if you don't want to do the forecasting at first, do the monthly cash flow projection from the very beginning. Think of it this way: The revenue forecast and expense budget describe what you hope for; the cash flow projection documents what is; and you need that information to run your business on a day-to-day basis.

Deciding Whether to Stay or Sell

Here's a fourth way to make money from your blog: Sell it. Keep in mind that buyers look for revenue, or at least the potential for revenue, so you still have to figure out how to make money. And then use that story to convince a buyer.

If acquisition is a good long-term strategy for your blog, think about who you might like to be acquired by and then build your blog and monetization strategy to fit. I don't mean copy the design or content. Glean information from the company's business model and use a similar strategy on your site. The potential acquirer can more easily see how you might fit into its model if you already look a bit like it.

You also want to do a lot of homework on *valuation* — what your blog and its readers are worth — before you approach or respond to potential buyers.

Value is not an absolute thing. What someone is willing to pay for your blog often depends on why they are acquiring it. Your blog may be a competitor, and buying it gets you out of the way. Or the company wants a blog that covers your topic, and it is cheaper, and faster, to acquire your blog and its readers than to create a new one. Whatever the reason, the buyer will base its offer at least in part on the revenue potential of your blog and readers post-acquisition.

To estimate future revenue, start with current revenues and factor in growth. You can use your current growth rate or industry growth, but be prepared to justify your choice. Be sure to exclude earnings that rely on you personally, although post-acquisition you'll probably have to stay on for a transition period to ensure that the results meet expectations. And don't be surprised if your final payout is tied to these results.

In addition to future results, your asking price can include intangibles such as the goodwill you have earned with customers and readers. You can also use a multiplier to account for potential over time. Don't try to do this part yourself. Get advice from people in your networks who have merger and acquisition (M&A) experience. When it's time to negotiate the details, hire a lawyer with M&A expertise.

Finally, have your price in mind when talking with potential buyers, but don't tip your hand. It can be better to wait for the offer than state a price, especially if you aren't in a hurry to sell and they really want to buy.

Getting Paid

Paying with a company check is most common for consulting and other work for hire, advertising, affiliate marketing networks, and direct sponsorships. Advertising and affiliate networks may also offer direct deposit. You can also accept payment through PayPal or Google Checkout, but you will have to pay a fee, as I explain in a minute.

Firms that operate their own affiliate programs (for example, Amazon) may offer store credit as a payment option. However, use caution when selecting this method of payment. You don't want to end up with more store credit than you could reasonably use.

If you sell products directly from your blog, you have to set up electronic payment processing. For most bloggers, online payment processors, such as PayPal (www.paypal.com) and Google Checkout (http://checkout.google.com), are the simplest solutions. With these processors, you don't have a monthly fee; instead, you pay a fee to the payment processor for every transaction.

As of April 28, 2010, the fee for transactions on both PayPal and Google Checkout starts at 2.9 percent of the amount of the transaction plus $0.30 per transaction. As monthly volumes increase (starting at more than $3,000 per month), the percentage basis decreases; however, you still pay the per-transaction fee, and your account must be approved before the lower fees take effect.

If you already have a merchant account to process credit cards offline or your transaction values or volumes are high enough, you might prefer to work with your bank and a service called an *Internet gateway,* such as Authorize.Net (www.authorize.net) or Payflow Gateway (www.paypal.com/us/cgi-bin/webscr?cmd=_payflow-gateway-overview-outside) to accept credit card payments directly. The gateway is simply the virtual version of a credit card reader; it securely transmits the buyer's credit card information to the bank and authorizes the transaction.

In this case, you pay fees to

- ✔ The credit card issuer for each transaction based upon the amount of the transaction. Check with your bank to see what rates they are offering, but plan on at least 2 to 2.9 percent.

- ✔ Your bank for the dedicated merchant account. Around $10 per month plus $0.25 per transaction.

- ✔ The gateway service. You pay a setup fee, a monthly fee of at least $18 to $20, and per transaction fees. For example, the simplest gateway solution from PayPal costs $20 per month and charges $0.10 per transaction after the first 500 transactions.

For most bloggers, a merchant account would be overkill. I'd only recommend it in the following situations:

- ✔ You already process credit cards offline in your business by using a merchant account, in which case your incremental cost is the gateway service.

- ✔ You want the perceived value of buyers purchasing directly from you — for example, if you sell a high-ticket luxury item or offer many different items. In these instances, having your own online store is part of your marketing strategy. You may want to consider linking your blog to an e-commerce Web site rather than selling the product on the blog. I discuss this topic in more detail in Chapter 5.

Finally, keep in mind, that if you do not already have a merchant account to process credit cards, you will have to qualify through your bank's credit program; this process can take four to six weeks.

Chapter 5

Selling Products or Services on Your Blog

. . . .

. . . .

You can use your blog to sell just about anything you could sell on a traditional Web site. The difference is that on your blog, you lead with your passion for your topic. Your posts share your expertise and opinions; any products you sell are a small part of the overall experience. At a typical e-commerce site, on the other hand, the products are the focus, and the experiences of customers, such as reviews and ratings, are secondary. Important, but secondary.

Keep in mind, however, that using your blog to sell products or services is more than simply tacking on a store. In this chapter, I cover the most common ways to sell products on your blog, the key considerations for each, how to integrate sales authentically, and how your thought leadership and expertise contribute to success.

Selling Products and Services

You've decided to sell products on your blog as part of your monetization strategy. Your next step is to answer these questions:

> ✔ What are you selling? Are you selling your own product or service or someone else's? How many different products do you plan to sell?

> ✔ Are you selling physical products that require inventory and shipping, electronic products like e-books or software, or professional services?

✔ Where are you selling? Will you sell on your own store, through a service like PayPal or eBay, or through an affiliate store like Amazon's aStore?

Selling one or two products or an e-book

If you plan to sell only a few products, and especially if you sell a download-able product like an e-book, adding product sales to your blog is pretty straightforward. Simply set up your product page(s) and then use a payment processor, such as Google Checkout (`http://checkout.google.com/sell`) or PayPal (`www.paypal.com`).

Signing up for a payment processor

Setting up Google Checkout or PayPal is very simple. Both Google Checkout and PayPal offer solutions for single products purchased one at a time by using a Buy Now button, like this one:

Google Checkout
Fast checkout through Google

When customers click this button, they see a Google Checkout form, as shown in Figure 5-1. Or if you're selling multiple products, you can provide a virtual shopping cart, as shown in Figure 5-2.

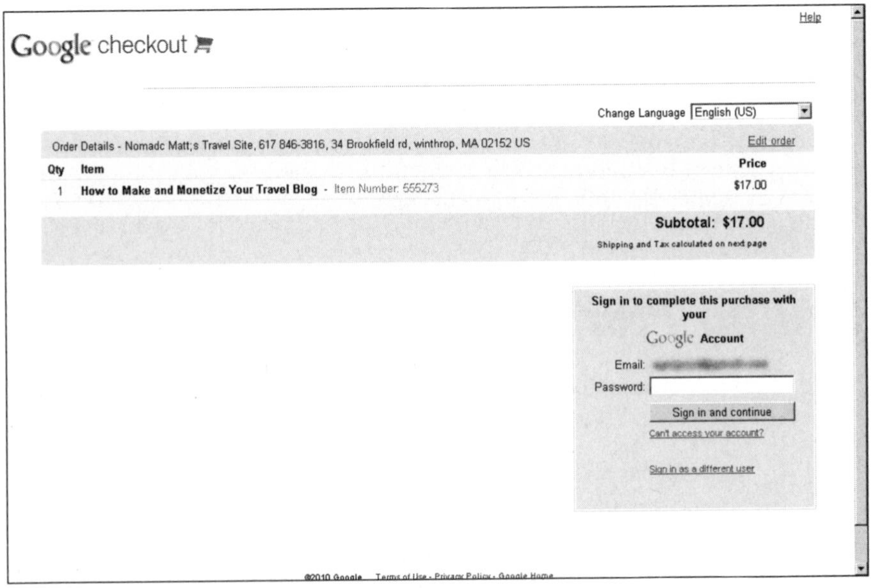

Google checkout

Help

Change Language English (US)

Order Details - Nomadc Matt;s Travel Site, 617 846-3816, 34 Brookfield rd, winthrop, MA 02152 US

Edit order

Qty	Item	Price
1	How to Make and Monetize Your Travel Blog - Item Number: 555273	$17.00

Subtotal: $17.00
Shipping and Tax calculated on next page

Sign in to complete this purchase with your
Google Account
Email:
Password:
Sign in and continue
Can't access your account?

Sign in as a different user

©2010 Google · Terms of Use · Privacy Policy · Google Home

Figure 5-1:
A Google Checkout order form.

The following steps show you how to sign up for Google Checkout and set up a Buy Now button or virtual shopping cart, but the process is similar to signing up for PayPal:

1. **Go to the Google Checkout page at** `http://checkout.google.com/ sell`**.**

2. **Indicate whether your business has a Google Account for services like AdWords or Gmail. If you don't have a Google Account, select No and then follow the instructions to set up an account.**

   If you sign up for a new account, Google sends the account verification instructions to the e-mail address you provided.

3. **Next, you must decide whether you want to have a single account for all Google services. If you already have a Gmail login that you want to use, click OK and log in by using your personal user credentials. If you want to set up a separate account for your business, select No and follow the prompts to set up a new account.**

   After you sign in, the Tell Us About Your Business page appears, as shown in Figure 5-3.

4. **In the Private Contact area, enter your personal contact information.**

   Google uses this information to keep in touch with you about your account.

Google checkout 🛒 More leads. Lower costs.

Set up Account ▸ **Enter Business Information**

Tell us about your business.

1. Private contact information [?]

How can Google get in touch with you?
Google will use this information to contact you if needed. This information will not be displayed to your customers.

Contact person:

Contact person's email:

Location: United States

Don't see your country? Learn More

Address:

City/Town   State   Zip [?]

Phone number:

2. Public contact information

How can your customers get in touch with you?
This information will be made available to your customers when they make a purchase.

Business name:

Customer support email:

Common Questions

- What is Google Checkout?
- How does Google Checkout help me increase sales and lower costs?
- How much does it cost to process transactions through Google Checkout?

Figure 5-3:
Enter information about your business to sign up for Google Checkout.

5. **In the Public Contact area, enter contact information for your customers to use.**

    Customers can use this information to contact you after they make a purchase.

6. **In the Financial Information area, enter your monthly sales volume as well as a Federal Tax ID/Employer Identification Number (EIN) or Social Security number and credit card.**

    Google uses this information to verify your credit history.

7. **Accept the Terms of Service and then click Complete Sign Up.**

8. **After you've signed up, navigate to the Settings tab on Google Checkout. Choose whether you want to add a Buy Now button for a single product or a simple shopping cart, and follow the instructions on the site.**

    There's a nice chart on Google Checkout that compares the various checkout options offered by Google at `http://checkout.google.com/seller/integrate.html`.

    When you're finished, Google displays HTML code that you copy and paste on your blog.

When your buyers click a Buy Now button or add products to a cart and then check out, they are directed to the payment processor. After the transaction is complete, you fulfill the order.

Fulfilling the order

For physical products, you have to ship the product and send a notification to the customer. For e-books, you can either use the payment processor's application programming interface (API) to deliver a download key or fulfill by e-mail:

✔ E-mail is easier at smaller volumes, because you don't have to worry about securing the content. Simply e-mail the e-book to the buyer.

✔ If the book is too big to be sent by e-mail or you are worried that buyers will redistribute your content, secure your book in some fashion. For example, require a key or secure the download site from unauthorized access. Many commercial products can help; start with your preferred search engine and search on *securing e-book sales* for the latest copyright protection and digital rights management products like:

- *SoftLocker:* www.softlocker.net

- *LockLizard:* www.locklizard.com

- *Secure e-Book:* www.secure-ebook.com

Securing your electronic products from theft is your responsibility. If you freely distribute software and ask users to pay what they want as a donation, go full steam ahead with something simple like PayPal or Google Checkout. If you need to be paid first, consider working with a payment processor that specializes in software fulfillment, such as RegNow (formerly Digital River, www.regnow.com) to help you sell, register, and deliver your products securely. In addition to a secure payment solution optimized for software sales, these firms offer digital rights management to protect your intellectual property.

Offering professional services through your blog is even easier. Set up a page on your blog that describes your services and link to it prominently on your site. See the Marketing Roadmaps blog, which has a Consulting/Speaking tab, shown in Figure 5-4, that links to my speaking/consulting services.

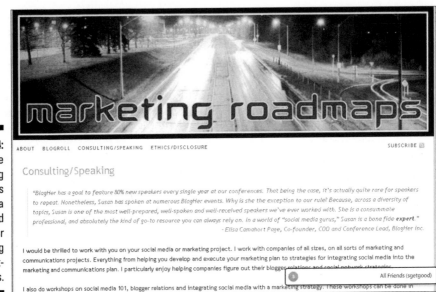

Figure 5-4: The Marketing Roadmaps blog has a dedicated page for speaking and consulting services.

Selling many products: eBay, Etsy, Amazon, and e-commerce

The simplest alternative to selling products on your blog is to list your products on eBay. Setting up an eBay store is fairly straightforward, and eBay handles the transaction and includes your products in its search engine. But keep in mind that there are disadvantages to this setup: Your buyers have to leave your site to make their purchases, and you're limited to the eBay tools and customization options.

You can find some alternatives to eBay:

✔ **Etsy and Artfire:** If you make handmade goods or sell vintage products, you can open an Etsy store (www.etsy.com; see Figure 5-5). A similar site for artists is Artfire, www.artfire.com.

✔ **Amazon Advantage:** If you're selling media products (books, DVDs, CDs, and so on), you have North American distribution rights, and the products have scannable UPC, EAN, or ISBN numbers, the Amazon Advantage self-service consignment program is an option (www.amazon.com/gp/seller-account/mm-product-page.html?topic=200329780).

Through the program, you make your products available for sale to Amazon, and it purchases amounts of each item that meet current customer demand plus potential sales for a few weeks. You ship to Amazon, and Amazon takes care of everything, presenting your products in its store like any other Amazon offering.

You set the suggested retail price and get 45 percent of sales. Amazon keeps 55 percent, but any discounts it chooses to offer are taken out of its share, not off the top. Your other costs are a $29.95 membership fee and the cost of shipping product to Amazon's warehouse.

✔ **E-commerce solution:** The most common alternative to eBay for selling many products is to create your own customized storefront, an e-commerce section on your site with a virtual shopping cart and "aisles" or categories that make it easier for buyers to browse. You can still use Google Checkout or PayPal as your payment processor; both services offer hundreds of third-party shopping carts, some of which may also integrate seamlessly with your blogging platform. For example, WP e-Commerce is a free shopping cart offered for the popular blogging platform WordPress (www.getshopped.org).

The more integrated the store is with your blog, the more it's going to cost you to develop it, including fees for e-commerce solution providers and Web developers. But, you have far more control over your brand with your own store.

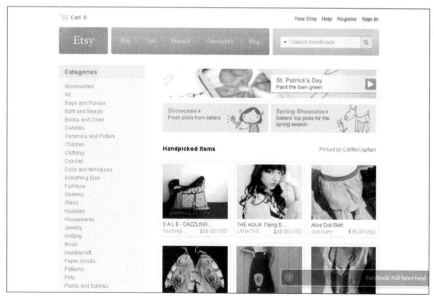

Figure 5-5:
Etsy offers an alternative sales channel for handmade and vintage goods.

A popular e-commerce solution is Shopify `www.shopify.com`, as shown in Figures 5-6 and 5-7. Other e-commerce providers that you can use to create your store include

- *Amazon WebStore:* `http://webstore.amazon.com`

- *eBay ProStores:* `www.prostores.com`

Comprehensive e-commerce solutions like the ones listed here also offer integration with Internet payment gateways such as Authorize.net, PayPal Website Payments Pro, and QuickBooks Merchant Services.

Figure 5-6: The main page for a Shopify store.

If you choose eBay or a Web site like Etsy, you use its payment-processing solution. If you set up your own e-commerce site, you also need to have a payment processor (see Chapter 4). And no matter which of these options you pick, you have to fulfill the orders!

Also, if possible, provide an offline way for buyers to obtain your products, either via the telephone or a bricks and mortar store where the products are sold. Some folks still don't like to buy online.

I've briefly touched on the mechanics of adding product sales to your blog. If you are expecting a significant percentage of your revenue to come from direct product sales, you also should check out *Starting an Online Business All-in-One For Dummies* by Shannon Belew and Joel Elad and *Web Stores Do-It-Yourself For Dummies* by Joel Elad.

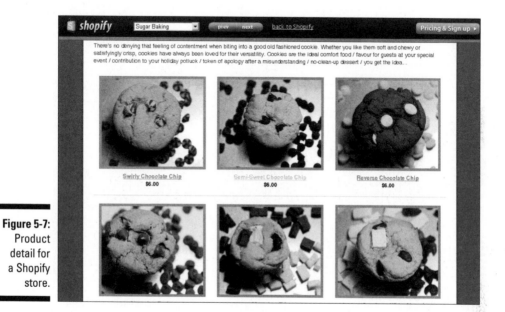

Figure 5-7:
Product detail for a Shopify store.

Adding an affiliate store

An alternative to selling products directly on your blog is to add an affiliate store, such as an Amazon aStore, to your blog. This is a good choice if you want to offer recommended products to your readers, but don't want to carry inventory or deal with shipping.

The home-design blog Young House Love offers an Amazon aStore (see Figure 5-8) in addition to its design consulting and direct art-prints sales. (You can read more about Young House Love in Chapters 1 and 6.)

After you're an Amazon affiliate, setting up an aStore is pretty simple, and if you have more than one blog, you can even have multiple stores under the same affiliate account. Chapter 6 covers affiliate marketing in depth, but if you'd like a head start, go to `https://affiliate-program.amazon.com` to see all the options in the Amazon Associates program.

Ecoblog Sustainablog (`www.sustainablog.org`) takes a different approach. Sustainablog works with affiliate aggregator ShopWiki to build its Sustainablog Green Choices store of environmentally-friendly products (see Figure 5-9).

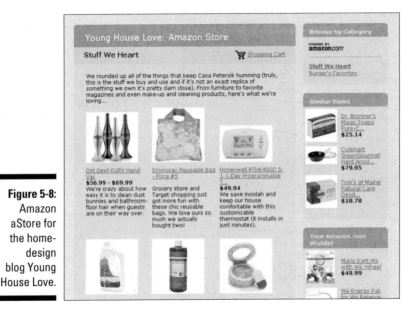

Figure 5-8:
Amazon aStore for the home-design blog Young House Love.

The ShopWiki platform acts like a product search engine for Sustainablog and finds products from its various affiliates that meet the Sustainablog criteria. ShopWiki handles the affiliate relationships; all Sustainablog does is manage a site that works with ShopWiki and then delivers the interested buyers. (Read more about Sustainablog in the sidebar "You have to have something they can buy," later in this chapter.)

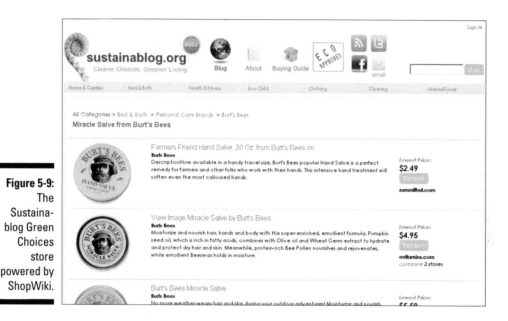

Figure 5-9:
The
Sustaina-
blog Green
Choices
store
powered by
ShopWiki.

Other products that help you create an e-store for your affiliate relationships include:

- ✔ **Datafeedr:** A WordPress plug-in to create an affiliate store that works with the major affiliate networks. Pricing starts at $27 per month for a single store. (www.datafeedr.com)

- ✔ **PopShops.com:** An affiliate aggregator that works on any Web platform. The site offers a free 30-day trial, and subscription plans start at $14.99 per month. (http://popshops.com)

- ✔ **StoreStacker:** Web site development software for affiliate store sites. The purchase price ranges from $97–222, depending on number of affiliate networks included. (http://2.storestacker.com)

You can't integrate an affiliate store to sell your own products unless they're carried by an online store, which may be the case depending on what you manufacture or produce. For example, I offer this book on my Web site through my Amazon affiliate store rather than deal with the hassle of managing inventory and shipping.

Integrating Sales Authentically

Regardless of how you choose to include product sales on your blog, you must do so authentically. Products are *part,* not all, of the visitor experience. If your readers feel that your blog is merely an excuse for pushing products at them, they'll leave. Even if your blog is a shopping blog, and is in fact all about products, your posts need to entertain and inform, not just sell.

If you aren't sure whether your content is too salesy, follow the old rule: When in doubt, take it out.

The following advice from shopping blogger Mir Kamin regards affiliate links, but it's equally applicable to any product sales:

> *"No one is going to use those [affiliate marketing] links unless you're able to establish yourself as a trusted, helpful authority. That means you don't just link to stuff to get sales. It means that you build a track record of linking to things that your audience will find interesting and useful. It also means that sometimes you link to stuff where you don't stand to gain financially; I link to plenty of stores that either don't have affiliate programs or for whatever reason haven't accepted me into their programs. The minute your linkage is all about the dollars, traffic will plummet because people will immediately be able to tell you're more interested in making a buck than in helping them."*

Measuring Sales Results

The nice thing about selling a product directly on your blog is that you have 100 percent visibility into your results. You know how many products you've sold. Depending on your e-commerce tools, you may also have sophisticated reports to understand your most popular products, buyer demographics, and other trends. Reporting is part of what you're paying for with the more robust commercial tools.

But even if you simply sell a downloadable e-book or a single product straight from your site, you still have your Web analytics, which can help you understand product interest and demand.

To take full advantage of your Web analytics like Google Analytics for forecasting and promotional decisions, don't sell your product direct from your blog home page. In your analytics, Web hits — to and from the home page — show up at the root-level, and you can't tell what drove the action. Chapter 13 goes into detail about analytics, including how to add the free Google Analytics to your blog. Instead of selling the product right from your home page, put a link on the home page to an "inside" page that explains the product offering in detail and links to your payment-processing solution. As shown in Figure 5-10, you can then study the reports for that "inside" page to understand traffic sources and productive keywords. Chapter 13 has more detail on how to interpret Web analytics.

Figure 5-10:
A Google Analytics report for a blog page.

You can also overlay your sales figures against the Web traffic for a raw conversion number of how many visits result in sales, which can be useful in forecasting.

Becoming a Thought Leader

The other product you sell on your blog is yourself. Not literally, of course, but part of the blogging dynamic is how well you establish your expertise in your domain. Your product recommendations are valuable only if you're a trusted, expert source.

This is particularly true if your product is your intellectual property, such as a book or consulting services. Establishing your thought leadership is critical.

Understanding thought leadership

Unfortunately, *thought leadership* has become something of a buzzword, but underlying the buzziness is an authentic and important strategy for establishing your personal reputation and expertise.

Essentially, you identify a few important issues in your field and then use your blog to establish yourself as both an expert and a visionary. Strive to be ahead of the curve on the thinking about your chosen topics. The leadership component is critical. It's not enough to be knowledgeable; you have to use your knowledge, expertise, and opinions to create new, original ideas.

This doesn't mean that you can't write about other topics. You should have varied interests. But when you can, as often as you can, relate your topic to your core issues.

 Avoid being too narrow or too broad: Too narrow is limiting, and too broad is just hard to do. The tendency is to believe that the jack-of-all-trades is a master of none, and to be a thought leader, you need to be a master. Be selective.

For example, I write a marketing blog. Marketing is a big topic. I focus on integrating social media tools with the marketing plan. That's still a pretty big topic. So I try to narrow it down to

- ✔ **The intersection of marketing and customer service:** Who owns the customer relationship? How can organizations manage the fact that many groups within the company interact with the customer and need access to customer insights, including what customers are saying about the company on blogs, Web sites, and social networks?

- ✔ **Blogger relations:** This includes best practices to reach customers through social media, but also how people use things like blogs, Twitter, and Facebook to engage with the community.

- ✔ **Ethics and social responsibility:** This includes everything from what it means to be a responsible blogger and citizen, to detailed analysis of regulations like the FTC Guidelines for Endorsements and Testimonials and privacy legislation.

Do I write about other things on the blog? Sure, but the purpose of Marketing Roadmaps is to showcase my expertise as a marketing professional to organizations that might hire me as a consultant or a speaker. I stick to the things I know best *and* am passionate about. Opinion and passion were also the driving forces behind the Bad Pitch Blog, featured in the nearby sidebar interview with founder Kevin Dugan.

Kevin Dugan: Outing bad pitches since 2006

Kevin Dugan started the Bad Pitch Blog (http://badpitch.blogspot.com) in 2006 with an idea, an opinion, and a passion.

It had always bothered him that a few poor practitioners of public relations tarnished the image of the entire profession. He asked fellow PR pro Richard Laermer, whom he had met through his personal blog Strategic Public Relations, to join him on the blog, and the rest, as the saying goes, is history.

As the name suggests, the blog uses the device of outing bad public relations pitches to focus attention on best practices. Initially, the goal was to shame the offenders into doing a better job but "we quickly realized that, while that probably will never happen, we CAN have an impact with younger practitioners and students." He says that hearing from people in the industry that his work has helped them is the most rewarding thing about blogging.

Like many whose blogs are focused on their professions or career objectives, Kevin makes a little money from advertising, but most of his blogging-related revenue comes from consulting and speaking fees. And blogging has led to other opportunities for him, most recently helping him land his current job.

Kevin's advice for new bloggers is to have passion and patience. He says:

"Passion better be the foundation of your blog if you want it to ultimately succeed. Patience helps. But have some goals one way or the other and plan accordingly. I am not the poster child for patience or planning. But I would argue I am for passion. How else can you explain the fact that I am still blogging after eight years and not earning a significant amount of income off my blog?"

The weirdest search term ever used to find his blog? Oscar Meyer Weiner:

"I wrote a post about the Weinermobile. I still get people telling me why they should win a ride in the fuel-injected frank."

Parentopia: Helping parents create a happy parenthood

Because the Parentopia blog was a business endeavor designed to build community with the readers of their book, *Mommy Guilt*, authors Devra Renner and Aviva Pflock had a plan from the get-go. Devra says:

"Our blog is an extension of our professional identity, so we felt a formal plan to incorporate our point of view as experts was important to implement in the design of our site. We also wanted to use the blog as a way to connect with potential clients for speaking engagements and consulting opportunities."

Devra and Aviva don't do advertising or affiliate marketing on their site, and the few product reviews they do are very carefully vetted to ensure that they fit well with both their readers and professional identity.

Devra says the most rewarding thing about blogging is:

"the serendipitous connections Aviva and I make online, and in real life, with our readers. Nothing makes me happier than finding out a post I penned gave a reader support, insight, encouragement, or just a much needed laugh. Our Web site was designed to help make parenthood more enjoyable. Just as parents strive to give their children a happy childhood, Parentopia is the place where moms and dads can create their own happy parenthood."

And the weirdest search term ever used to find their blog? Devra reports:

"Diapered husbands. Every single month since we began our blog, at least once, someone is searching for diapered husbands. For the record, we've never blogged about diapered husbands, and we don't diaper our husbands or recommend doing so to others."

Parentopia – The official blog for Aviva Pflock and Devra Renner
co-authors of the award winning book – Mommy Guilt

Promoting your book

Many authors start blogs as a promotional tool for a new or in-progress book. When doing this, it's important that the book's promotion isn't the *only* reason for the blog. You always want to add value for your readers beyond your promotional purpose. Also wise is to develop your blog around the same theme as your book, but not specifically the book.

Travel writer Edward Hasbrouck, who writes The Practical Nomad at www.
hasbrouck.org/blog (see Figure 5-11), developed his first Web site in the
'90s to promote his travel books, and the blog grew out of that. He now uses
his blog to publish shorter, more-timely articles that don't fit into his books.

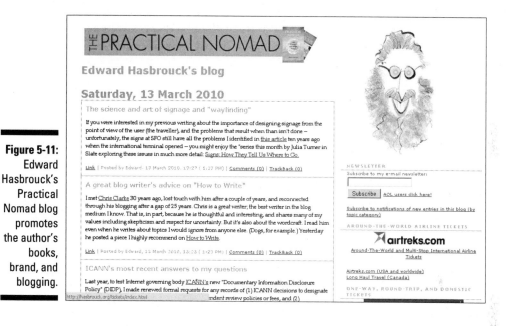

Figure 5-11:
Edward
Hasbrouck's
Practical
Nomad blog
promotes
the author's
books,
brand, and
blogging.

In the process, he promotes his brand and books as well as develops his reputation as a travel expert. But the blog isn't about the books: It's about travel.
The most rewarding thing about blogging for him is

> *"Hearing from people who say that reading my blog empowered them to
> travel, and that travel was a life-changing personal growth and educational
> experience."*

Devra Renner and her coauthor Aviva Pflock started their parenting blog
Parentopia (www.parentopia.net/blog/) to connect with readers of their
book *Mommy Guilt* and to build a community and professional identity online.
Read more about the Parentopia blog in the nearby sidebar interview with
Devra.

If you plan to use your blog to promote your book, here are some tips from
Yvonne DiVita, president of self-publishing house Windsor Media Enterprises:

- ✔ **Shoot a book trailer.** Think of a movie trailer, but use the cover as your visual, read a bit of the intro, and tell the reader why you wrote it. Keep your trailer to three minutes or less. Add music. Don't hire a voiceover person, unless your voice is too hard to understand.

- ✔ **Don't expect your blog to sell your book.** Connect with influential bloggers who've read the book and like it. Promote them and their work, and then thank them for reading your book. They'll keep the conversation going and promote you better than you ever can.

- ✔ **Be realistic about blog book tours.** A *blog book tour* is when you set up interviews, usually over the phone, with bloggers about your work. Some are good; others aren't worth the time. Blog book tours need to be done carefully and thoughtfully — with the expectation that you're serving the bloggers and the readers, not vice versa. Be open and authentic and share some insights, if you get interviewed.

You have to have something they can buy

Jeff McIntire-Strasburg, the founder of the ecoblog Sustainablog, says, *"If you are going to make money with your blog, you have to have something your readers can buy."*

And he would know.

Since he started Sustainablog, shown in the following figure, in 2003, he's tried a variety of business models, and he's settled on an affiliate shop through ShopWiki as the best way to meet both his goals of blogging a greener world *and* his readers' needs.

Jeff started Sustainablog as a hobby with dreams of someday turning it professional. In 2005, the rise of environmentalism opened up new opportunities for green bloggers, so he left his full-time job as an English professor for a job with a St. Louis-based dot.com, and in 2006, he cofounded the environmental blogging network Green Options.

The Green Options idea was to develop a blog network of environmentally focused blogs that would meet people where they were in terms of their readiness and interest in green solutions with a variety of niches — sustainability, green parenting, energy, crafting, and so on. The business model was advertising.

When Green Options was acquired in 2008, and the management team centralized on the West Coast, Jeff didn't go. In part for family reasons, but also because he had come to the conclusion that the advertising model wasn't the right one for an environmental blog. There just wasn't enough control over the advertising in most ad networks.

He took back his blog and embarked on a new plan. With a new partner, he acquired the exclusive rights to offer green products on shopping aggregator ShopWiki and created the Green Choices store of environmentally-friendly products. ShopWiki uses criteria and categories set by Sustainablog to search affiliate networks for appropriate green products for the store.

The blog is separate from the store and focuses on issues, not products. There's a link to the store on the blog, and vice versa, but you won't find affiliate links about products in blog posts.

(continued)

(continued)

It's the halo effect of Jeff's more than seven years blogging about the environment that makes him, and Sustainablog, a trusted source for product recommendations.

With the change to a product versus advertising model, Jeff says search engine optimization (SEO) has become a larger part of the promotional mix, and his blog is turning up on page one searches for all sorts of products. However, he stresses that what makes everything work is the combination of a blog focused on important environmental issues and a store that appeals to the same audience. He doesn't promote products on the blog.

The measure of success? Prior to launching the store, Sustainablog was getting around 40,000 page views per month. Since the Green Choices store launched, it's been getting about 145,000 page views per month, and the revenue is building.

The most rewarding thing about blogging for Jeff is the relationships he has forged in the community:

"It's been a lot of fun to see the green blogosphere grow from basically nothing to what it is today. And to realize that it is human voices doing it for the love of it. To make change in the world."

Here are Jeff's tips for bloggers who are just starting out:

✔ **Write good, original content every day.** Readers want to see regularly updated content, especially at first. After you get established, maybe there's some wiggle room but to get search engines to pay attention, you have to write every day.

✔ **Write because you're passionate about your topic.** Even before he really paid attention to his page rank, Sustainablog had a Google page rank of 7 because he was writing about things his audience cared about.

✔ **Pay attention to SEO.** Writing is what builds your relationships. SEO is the nuts and bolts that can get you to your business goals.

Chapter 6

Making Money from Advertising

*A*dvertising: It's one of the first things that comes to mind when you think about making money on a blog. In this chapter, I clear up some of the mysteries about the three main types of blog advertising — sponsorship, display advertising, and affiliate networks — so you can decide which, if any, is for you.

Gaining Perspective on Blogging for Money

Seventy-one percent of the bloggers in my professional blogging survey confirmed that advertising is by far the top source of blogger income (see Figure 6-1). Nearly 60 percent of the survey group reported earning less than 10 percent of their income from their blogs. Only 17.6 percent of the bloggers in the survey said they earned 100 percent of their income from their blog (see Figure 6-2).

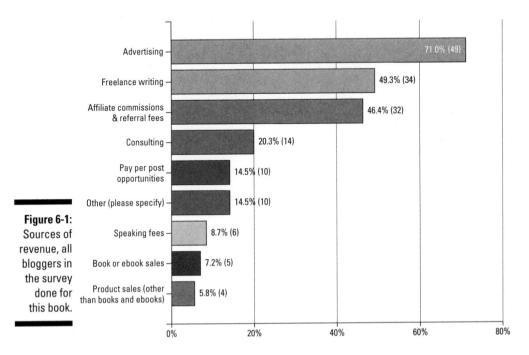

Sources of Blogging Revenue, All Bloggers

Figure 6-1:
Sources of
revenue, all
bloggers in
the survey
done for
this book.

Source: Professional Blogging For Dummies survey, Susan Getgood, 2010

Blogging is hard work. Blogger Sherry Petersik, co-author with husband John, of top home-renovation blog Young House Love (which I profile in the sidebar "Hobby to career: Young House Love" later in this chapter), says it best:

> *"If you can't do something for zero compensation for at least a year, blogging is not for you. We blogged for 300 days with no comments. We made maybe 30 cents a day. It's a natural selection process. If you don't love blogging, you won't make money because you'll give it up before you make any."*

What Percentage of Your Income Do You Attribute to Blogging? (All)

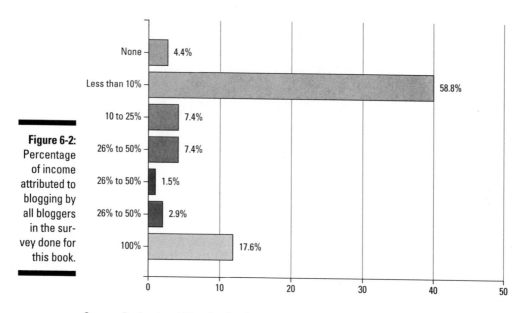

Figure 6-2:
Percentage of income attributed to blogging by all bloggers in the survey done for this book.

Source: Professional Blogging For Dummies survey, Susan Getgood, 2010

Getting a Sponsor

Most bloggers dream of getting a big corporate sponsor like General Motors (GM). That's exactly what happened to the Manic Mommies, podcasters Erin Kane and Kristin Brandt when GM sponsored their first escape weekend to Newport, Rhode Island, in 2007. GM brand Saturn subsequently became the name sponsor of the Manic Mommies podcast, which was "Driven by Saturn" throughout 2009 (see Figure 6-3).

Although some element of luck is always involved in deals like this, you make your own luck. GM didn't sponsor Manic Mommies because it had nothing better to do with its marketing budget. Erin and Kristin built a brand that delivered the audience GM wanted to reach and an experience — the escape weekend — that GM wanted to be associated with.

Figure 6-3:
The Manic
Mommies
work with
sponsor
GM.

Direct sponsorship, like any business relationship, has its advantages and disadvantages. If you think a corporate direct sponsor makes sense for your blog, here are some of the things you need to consider:

- **Who the sponsor is and how hands-on it's going to be:** The Manic Mommies were fortunate with their sponsor; GM understood that the value came from association with the Manic Mommies and took a very hands-off approach. Many companies aren't so willing to let you run your own show. Concern about how hands-on a sponsor might want to be is one of the reasons blogger Christine Koh hasn't pursued a big sponsor. Read more about Christine in the "Blogger spotlight: Christine Koh, Boston Mamas" sidebar, later in this chapter.

- **What you're offering for sponsorship:** Are you offering your entire blog, a section of your blog, or an event? The more of your property you offer to a sponsor, the more reliant you are on that sponsor for your revenue stream.

  Are you offering an exclusive sponsorship, and if so, are you valuing it properly? Price the sponsorship too high, and you'll have no takers; price it too low, and you've reduced your revenue potential.

- **How well the sponsor is aligned with your brand and your goals:** Don't be blinded by dollar signs. Do your homework, and be sure that the sponsor's brand and your blog are good bedfellows.

✔ **What the sponsor expects from you:** In any good relationship, set the right expectations upfront. Make sure that everyone knows and agrees on the terms and conditions. The last thing you want the day before you launch your new blog is to find out that the sponsor expected its logo to be bigger than yours in the masthead.

✔ **Your potential interest in being acquired by a sponsor:** If you're interested in being acquired by a sponsor, you may want to tailor your blog more closely to the company than you might otherwise. Just don't be too obvious and tip your hand. That gives too much power to the sponsor and could end up reducing both the sponsorship fee and your ultimate asking price.

✔ **What you should charge:** Your fee depends on the sponsor and what it is sponsoring, but the short answer is: what the market will bear. Here are some ideas for setting your price:

- Compare your readership or traffic numbers with a blog that advertises on one of the popular ad networks and use its ad rates as a basis. Both Federated Media and Blogads publish their ad rates.

- Consider the amount of work you will have to do and calculate the monthly sponsorship fee based on your hours times a reasonable hourly rate. What's reasonable? In my opinion, $50–$75 per hour is a reasonable range if you are approaching the sponsor. You can probably use a higher rate if the sponsor approaches you.

- Calculate your costs plus a markup. Take what it costs you per month to run the site — development, writers, promotional costs, and so on — and mark it up. Standard markups in PR and ad agencies are between 15 and 20 percent.

You should also plan on giving a price break for a longer sponsorship commitment.

Crafting a pitch

For the most part, when it comes to sponsorship, you approach brands with a value proposition: a *pitch,* in other words. The type of sponsorship that works best for both sides is a sponsorship of a specific feature, a section on your blog, or an event. Solid parameters make it easier for you to tailor advertising or content, as desired, to the sponsor without impacting your whole site or brand. You can also more easily measure results.

You need to build a solid business case for the sponsorship. Be prepared to answer these questions:

✔ Why is your blog (or event) a good fit for the company?

✔ Who is your audience? Why does that audience matter to the sponsor?

✔ What do you want? Don't go in with a vague *let's work together* pitch. Have something specific in mind and be willing to negotiate.

✔ How will you measure success? You want to build this into the program in advance. Views of pages that display the sponsor's information are a good start, but you should also consider things that get the readers to take an action such as a coupon or discount code for the sponsor's product or a direct response ad that delivers visitors to the sponsor's Web site.

Be creative

The more creative and unique your pitch, the more likely it is to succeed. For example, the *SocialLuxe Lounge,* a party thrown the night before the BlogHer women's blogging conference in 2009, attracted marquee sponsors like Swiffer, Kodak, Lands' End, LEGO, and M&M because it offered a unique opportunity to showcase brands. Allison Czarnecki (www.petitelefant. com), one of the organizers, describes SocialLuxe as a way to treat bloggers to a night of pampering before the BlogHer conference, somewhat like the suites and such that surround the major award shows.

Anyone could RSVP for the party, which offered beauty and spa treatments as well as the opportunity to socialize with friends. The whole thing was capped off by an awards ceremony, but there were a limited number of spaces — around 500, roughly one-third the attendance at the BlogHer conference.

Allison says they approached companies with whom they already had great relationships:

> *"If you're a big user of a specific food, cleaning product, or makeup, it makes sense to approach a company whose product you adore. It has to be an organic relationship or it will feel stilted. If we'd done the party with sponsors who didn't reflect our everyday lives, it would have come across as artificial and disingenuous to the attendees, and likely wouldn't have been the big success that it was."*

Ciaran Blumenfeld (www.momfluential.net) was also one of the organizers of the 2009 party and says that a key to a successful sponsorship program is crafting messages that work for the sponsors and the event (or blog):

Blogger spotlight: Christine Koh, Boston Mamas

When freelance writer and designer Christine Koh started Boston Mamas (www.boston mamas.com), the city didn't have a good all-in-one resource portal for parents. She says:

"I saw a hole and wanted to fill it. I also was in the process of planning my exit from my decade-long career in academia. I channeled all the frustration I experienced during my postdoctoral fellowship into positive energy with the creation of Boston Mamas."

Although Christine makes money from advertising on her blog, and related consulting and speaking engagements, she doesn't rely on it for her livelihood. She admits to thinking:

"It would be fantastic for a big sponsor to come through so I could devote more time

to Boston Mamas and build out the site further, [but] I know it's tough to come by that kind of money in these times. I also know that with major sponsorship can come major headaches, in the way of clerical and legal matters, tussles over editorial, [and so on]. So at the moment, I'm continuing with what I'm doing, with the general goals of creating meaningful and interesting content, fostering a sense of community, and connecting with others in the space."

Her advice for someone starting a new blog:

"Do not try to shoehorn yourself into a peg that doesn't fit; be organic and true and write about what speaks to you, not about what you feel you should write."

"Many of us (women bloggers) use Swiffer products to clean our homes on a daily basis, but how is this relevant to a party about pampering and primping? I came up with the concept of "Clean Up Beautifully," and a fun activity — dressing up and taking photos as your favorite retro housewife. It was something almost everyone present could relate to, and enjoy."

She agrees that you need to start with brands and products with whom you have a relationship, and advises that a media kit and slide presentation are key tools to summarize what the brand gets from sponsoring your blog or event.

The *media kit* is a sales tool borrowed from traditional publishing. It acts as your online brochure and includes information about rates, the audience, expected attendance or readership, previous results if you have them, bios of organizers/authors, and anything else that you think will convince the sponsors. A slide presentation makes the case for a specific sponsor, connecting the dots from the media kit to the marketing benefits for that sponsor.

If you want sponsors, whether for a section of your blog or a special event, Allison advises the best way to make that happen is to approach the brands you like with an idea and be persistent:

> *"If there's a company or product I like, I go to the Web site, find an e-mail address, and start writing. You can't sit back and wait for people to contact you if you want to get things done. You have to go out there and make it happen. Create an experience and think of sponsors who'll fit the bill, and then start knocking on doors. Even as a known blogger, I still get more no thank you's than I get yeses, but I still keep asking. If you have something you're passionate about, with clear goals, and a specific return on investment for the sponsor, it's totally possible to make it happen."*

For more tips on pitching your ideas to companies, read Chapter 12.

Selling Ads

You can sell your ads directly to advertisers, or you can work with one or more advertising networks. If your contractual agreements allow, you can combine approaches.

When you first get started, you won't have the track record necessary to apply to a premium ad network. There's absolutely no harm in putting up an Advertise Here button on your site in case sponsors find you first. If you're lucky, what happened to Sherry and John Petersik of Young House Love will happen to you:

> *"We didn't chase after advertisers. We focused on the blog — building our readership and delivering good content. All we did was put up a little button, Advertise with Us. Brands found us, and our readers became our first sponsors."*

But don't count on it. Definitely plan to start with advertising options that have low barriers to entry, such as the Google AdSense pay-per-click advertising program and the Amazon Associates affiliate marketing program, both of which are covered later in this chapter.

If you choose to pursue direct sales of advertising on your blog rather than an ad network, be prepared to invest time building a media kit, putting together your online brochure of rate and readership information, and working with your advertisers on their programs — reporting results, helping with ad creation, and advising on optimum placement. Under certain circumstances all this work can be well worth it, but don't forget the value of your time when you compare the expenses of selling your ads directly versus using a network that retains a share of the proceeds.

If you decide to sell your own ad inventory, look into an ad management system, such as DoubleClick for Publishers (DFP) Small Business (formerly Google Ad Manager) at `www.google.com/dfp/login/info/welcome.html`. An ad manager makes rotating ads in and out of your site easier than having to go into your code every time you need to make a change.

For most bloggers, a network makes more sense: It handles the selling duties, and you can focus on building your blog. The question is, which network, and how can you make the network work for you?

Participating in an Ad Network

When you run ads on your blog, you're the *publisher.* The company running the ad is the *advertiser,* and the *ad network* is the intermediary, facilitating the relationship on both sides. The ad network keeps a commission on sales.

Online advertising is basically sold in two ways:

- **Pay-per-click (PPC):** You're paid based on the number of times prospects click the ad to connect to the advertiser's Web site.

- **Impressions:** Ad rates are based on an anticipated audience. Multiple compensation models exist, but the most common are flat rate and cost-per-thousand impressions (CPM). Both are based on providing an *opportunity* for ad views; the monthly page views of your blog are important for setting your rates.

    - With *flat rate,* the advertiser pays for the ad to appear for a defined period of time and pays a fixed amount based on anticipated ad views.

    - With *CPM,* the ad is displayed a fixed number of times, called *impressions.* Ad rates are set per thousand views.

I take a closer look at both in the upcoming sections.

Pay-per-click

The most well-known example of a pay-per-click (PPC) advertising network is Google, which divides its network into two programs: Google AdSense for publishers and Google AdWords for advertisers. Web site and blog publishers — that's you — join Google AdSense to have ads appear on their sites. Advertisers sign up for Google AdWords and bid on what they're willing to pay-per-click to have their ads appear on search engine results and Web sites in the ad network. Advertisers can also choose pay-per-impression (or views) or pay-per-conversion, such as request for information or sale, but pay-per-click is the most common. You may end up participating in both programs — AdSense to offer ads on your blog and AdWords to advertise your blog on the Google network.

Google matches the keywords that the advertiser purchases with the content and keywords on your site. The ad is displayed. Someone clicks. You get paid.

I used to have a devil of a time keeping AdSense and AdWords straight until I came up with this: Advertisers use key*words* (Ad*Words*) to set up their ad buys, and publishers get a few *cents* (Ad*Sense*) whenever an ad is clicked on their site.

Joining Google AdSense

You can easily become a Google AdSense publisher, which makes it a good choice for bloggers just getting started with an advertising program. To be eligible for AdSense, you must be over 18 years old, and your site must comply with Google's policies, as detailed here:

`www.google.com/adsense/support/bin/answer.py?answer=48182`

Like with other Google services, you also need a Google Gmail account.

For a complete tour of the network and to access the online application, start at `www.google.com/adsense`. You can also check out *Google AdSense For Dummies,* by Jerri Ledford.

The application, shown in Figure 6-4, is very simple to fill out. It asks for your Web site URL and contact information, and requires you to explicitly agree to the AdSense program policies. Google will take about two to three days to review it and will inform you of your acceptance by e-mail. Most applications are accepted.

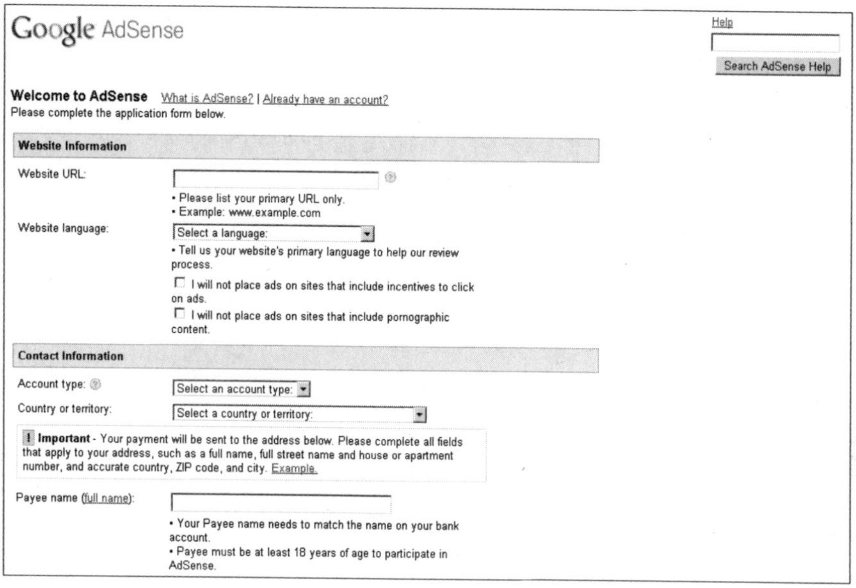

Figure 6-4:
The Google
AdSense
application.

Setting up your ads

After your application is accepted, use the AdSense Wizard to set up your ads.

Log in to your AdSense account, navigate to the AdSense Setup Tab, select AdSense for Content, and follow these steps:

1. **Specify the ad type by choosing whether you want to build an ad unit or a link unit. Then click Continue to move to the next step.**

   As shown in Figure 6-5, an *ad unit* can be a text or graphic ad. You select which type you want to build by using the drop-down list. A *link unit* is a list of topics that links to a page of related ads. Google allows you to place up to three ad units and three link units on your page.

2. **On the next page, choose the ad size from the Format drop-down list and then choose the color palette you want from the Palettes drop-down list (see Figure 6-6). Click Continue twice to advance to the Save and Get Ad Code page.**

3. **Name your ad unit and then click Submit and Get Code.**

4. **Copy the AdSense code, shown in the AdSense Unit code window in Figure 6-7, and then paste it to your blog where you want the Google ad unit to appear. Be sure to save the changes to your blog.**

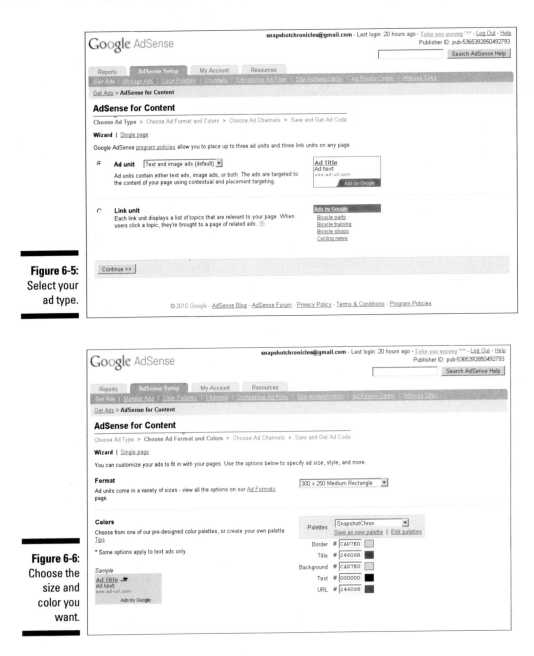

Figure 6-5:
Select your
ad type.

Figure 6-6:
Choose the
size and
color you
want.

Figure 6-7:
The code
for your
AdSense
ad that you
copy to
your blog.

Note: Your publisher ID is included in the code. Google assigns this unique code when it accepts your application, and it is used to keep track of the activity associated with your publisher account across all your ads.

That's all there is to it.

Don't click ads on your own site or post content encouraging fake ad clicks. These are violations of the terms of service, and your account may be disabled.

If you prefer, you can set all the ad settings in a single scrollable page. Instead of clicking Wizard on the first AdSense setup screen (refer to Figure 6-5), click Single Page.

Maximizing your AdSense results

Setting up AdSense is easy, but maximizing your revenue takes a little more work. The more an advertiser is willing to pay-per-click, the higher your earnings will be. Assume that advertisers of higher-value products are willing to pay more — it's only common sense. If you write about dime-store products and topics, expect dime-store revenues. If you write about more expensive things, odds are, your earnings will be better.

You can test this against your own results by looking at your AdSense reports and analytics. What posts and topics delivered the most revenue? To run your AdSense reports, navigate to the Reports tab in AdSense and select Advanced Reports. You can run a report of page impressions, clicks, and estimated earnings for any period of time. Then use your analytics (covered in depth in Chapter 13) to analyze which posts and topics were the most popular on your high-revenue days. Usually the popular post will be the one you published that day, but sometimes older posts get a new lease on life.

If you're using Google Analytics, you can click right over from a link at the top left of the AdSense screen.

The more relevant the advertisers are to your content, the better your results. Jodi Grundig, author of the Mom's Favorite Stuff blog (www.moms favoritestuff.com), says that Google ads tend to do well on her review blog because the ads are relevant to the product posts; however, Google ads don't do as well on her personal blog, where the topics are less connected. That stands to reason. People who read reviews are probably shopping and more likely to click ads.

Make sure that Google actually has ads for the keywords you use. I read this tip on ProBlogger, and it was an ah-ha moment. All you have to do is search on Google for your commonly used keywords. If no ads appear on the search engine results, Google doesn't have any ad inventory for you. Pick some new keywords.

These are just a few tips to get you started. If you want to be a power AdSense publisher, you need to do a lot of experimenting and analysis of your results. I also recommend that you invest in *Google AdSense For Dummies,* by Jerri Ledford.

Other pay-per-click networks

Google isn't the only advertising network that pays per click; it's just the most well known. Two others with interesting models are

- ✔ **Chitika:** Chitika (www.chitika.com) targets advertisements to visitors who have come to your site via a search engine based on the search term they used (see Figure 6-8). This can create a funny situation: If the search term isn't all that relevant to your content, the ad may be more relevant than the post! Visitors who arrive directly or from other referring sites don't see the ads.

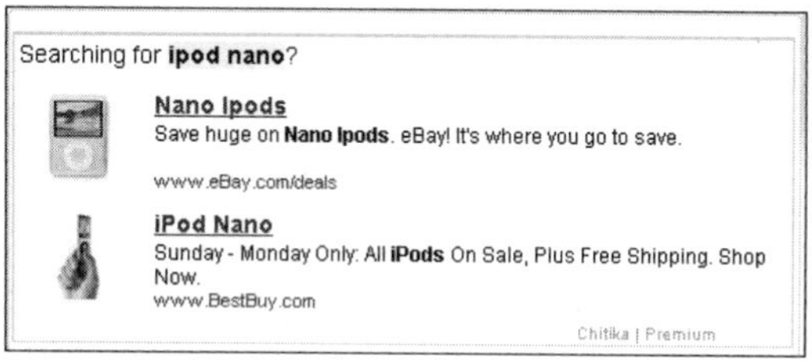
Searching for ipod nano?
Nano Ipods
Save huge on Nano Ipods. eBay! It's where you go to save.
www.eBay.com/deals
iPod Nano
Sunday - Monday Only: All iPods On Sale, Plus Free Shipping. Shop Now.
www.BestBuy.com
Chitika | Premium

Figure 6-8: Chitika shows ads based on the search terms used to find your blog.

- **YouData:** YouData (`www.youdata.com`) pays both the publisher/blogger and the consumer/site visitor. After you sign up for the service, you are provided with HTML code to install on your blog sidebar that displays an ad widget, as shown in Figure 6-9. As with most networks, the widget includes code that identifies your blog to the network for tracking and payment purposes.

You should have been paid to read this.
Create your MeFile™ and stop letting other people sell your attention.
Sign Up
More Info
Login

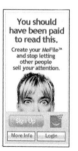

Figure 6-9: A widget.

Individuals sign up and create a personal profile, called a MeFile, by answering a fairly comprehensive questionnaire about their interests. When they come to your site, they log in through the widget and are presented with ad opportunities targeted to their interests. If they decide to view the ads, they get paid for the click. They can also share the revenue with you or send it to a charity (see Figure 6-10).

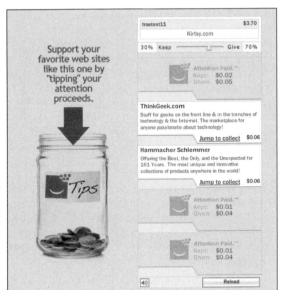

Figure 6-10:
Users can
share their
YouData
revenue
with you.

Impression or ad view-based models

Premium ad networks set rates based on *impressions,* or ad views. The
network sells the ads on your behalf and takes a commission on earnings,
anywhere from 30–50 percent depending on the network. Your monthly page
views are important for getting into the network and setting your rates.

Each network is a little different, but the most common compensation
models are

- **Flat rate:** The advertiser pays a fixed rate to run an ad on your blog, usually for a defined period of time.

- **Cost-per-thousand impressions (CPM):** An ad is displayed a fixed
number of times or views, called impressions. Ad rates are set per thousand views.

Premium advertising networks are highly selective, and at the time of this
writing, many of them aren't accepting new publishers. That said, if your blog
is a runaway hit, you may be able to get in. However, before you apply, you
need to understand a network's requirements to make the best possible pitch
for why it should add your blog. It can also be helpful if you know another
blogger in the network who can introduce you to the decision makers.

Very broadly, premium networks break down into two types:

- ✔ **Aggregators:** Aggregators look, and operate, very much like traditional publishing networks. In a nutshell, they aggregate, or collect, a variety of blog properties. Ads can be purchased on individual blogs or groupings. The following are some examples:

  - *Federated Media:* www.federatedmedia.net
  - *Blogads:* www.blogads.com
  - *Glam Media:* www.glammedia.com

- ✔ **Community-based media companies:** Community-based companies produce original content and sell ads on the community Web site as well as on the blogs that are part of the network. Typically, advertisers purchase ads on the entire network, called "run of network," or blog groupings, not on individual blogs. The following are some examples:

  - *BlogHer:* www.blogher.com
  - *Foodbuzz:* www.foodbuzz.com

To apply to an ad network, click the Publishers, Authors, or Bloggers link, usually found in the top-level navigation. Alternatively, look for a Contact Us link. Typically, you see a contact form or an e-mail address for contacting the network, not an application like on Google AdSense.

When you contact or e-mail a network, explain why your blog matters to that network. The network may not be *publicly* accepting new applications, but if you've got something great, and make a good case, it will consider you. It's simply good business.

Make sure that you include the following information:

- ✔ Your URL
- ✔ Your page views and other statistics about your blog — readership, influence, mainstream media coverage, and so on
- ✔ A strong description of your blog and your audience
- ✔ Your name and e-mail address

The upcoming sections look at some aggregators and community-based media companies in further detail.

Federated Media

Federated Media (FM) represents many of the most popular blogs, such as

- **The Pioneer Woman:** www.thepioneerwoman.com
- **Apartment Therapy:** www.apartmenttherapy.com
- **dooce.com:** www.dooce.com
- **Mashable:** www.mashable.com

FM is very selective, and page views are paramount. There are no guarantees, but your blog probably stands a better chance of being selected by FM if it doesn't already have deep coverage in your area, and you have lots and lots of page views.

A *rate card* is published for each blog that lists the type and sizes of ads offered. (See Figure 6-11 for the FM rate card for dooce.com.) Ad types include text and graphical ads sold at a flat rate, and graphical ads sold on a CPM basis. Advertisers can purchase ads on individual blogs or on a federation, such as a group of blogs devoted to topics like automotive or parenting.

Figure 6-11:
An FM
rate card.

FM also does sponsored-conversations programs for its advertisers, in which bloggers in the network contribute themed posts. Instead of the sponsored posts appearing on individual blogs, FM sets up a microsite for the content, such as the one for the Hoover Clean Freak Confessions campaign, as shown in Figure 6-12.

Figure 6-12: Hoover's Clean Freak Confessions is a sponsored conversations program.

Blogads

Blogads also has a pretty venerable stable of publishers, including

- **Daily Kos:** www.dailykos.com
- **Talking Points Memo:** www.talkingpointsmemo.com
- **I Can Has Cheezburger?:** www.icanhascheezburger.com

Ads are priced at a flat rate for a time period (a week, month, and so on), as shown in Figure 6-13, and can be purchased for individual blogs or *hives* (groups of related blogs) such as liberal blogs, conservative blogs, and baby and parenting blogs.

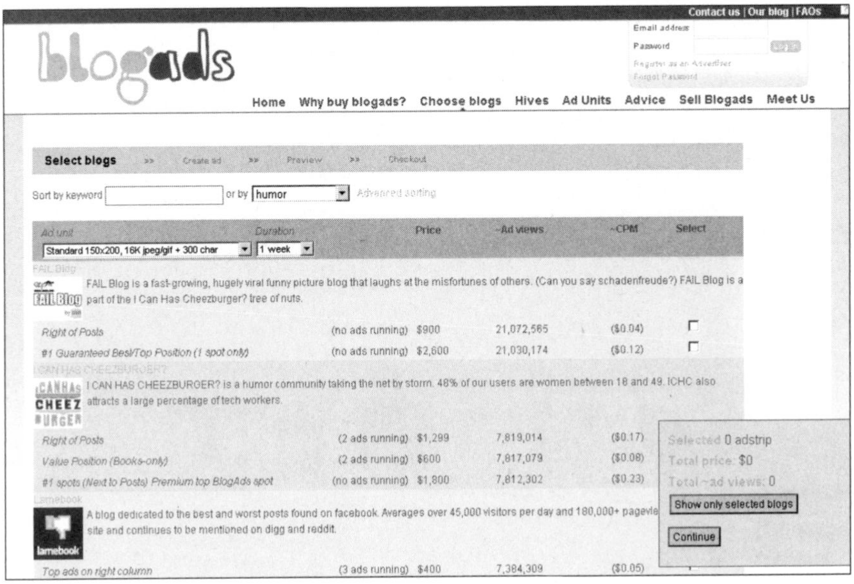

Figure 6-13:
Blogads
sells ads for
a flat rate,
individually
or as part
of hives.

Blogads has a unique format: a combination of image and text links, which is meant to look more *bloggy*. Figure 6-14 shows three ad variations:

- A standard ad with an image and multiple links to the advertiser's content
- A mini-format with an image and a single link
- A text, or classified, ad

Like other premium networks, Blogads isn't actively recruiting new publishers; however, the network considers blogs that are popular or important, have been consistently updated for at least six months, and have an average of 1,000 page views per day. Blogads also wants a sharp focus on a topic and the best ad placement.

BlogHer

Online media company BlogHer runs a community-based ad network, sharply focused on the demographic of women bloggers. Elisa Camahort Page, COO and co-founder, says the biggest point of difference between BlogHer and other networks is that BlogHer focuses on quality of content over traffic:

> "We look for bloggers who produce strong editorial content that's consistent with our mission of 'Life well said.' We also believe very strongly in the separation of advertising and editorial, and have strict guidelines for product reviews and other compensated content."

Figure 6-14:
Blogads's
unique
format is
meant to
look more
bloggy.

BlogHer sells advertising across the network by category — parenting, food, do-it-yourself, entertainment, and so on — and shares the revenue with bloggers based on actual impressions tracked through the ad code on each blog. The general requirements BlogHer looks for and the blog categories are shown in Figure 6-15. The network supports the Internet Advertising Bureau package for standard display advertising formats.

Figure 6-15:
BlogHer
sells
advertising
across its
network by
category
and pays
participating
blogs
based on
impressions.

Hobby to career: Young House Love

When Sherry and John Petersik started Young House Love (www.younghouselove.com) in 2007, as a way to keep friends and family informed about their house renovations, it was simply a hobby blog about their renovations. They didn't have a business plan at first because they had no idea it could become their career. They simply had a passion for renovating their house and wanted to share it with others.

They both worked on the blog part time for a year before it started earning enough for Sherry to do it full time, and in 2010, they turned the corner where they could both blog as a full-time job. Today, Young House Love gets about 1.5 million page views per month, and between 60,000–70,000 page views per day on weekdays.

Sherry thinks one of the reasons they were successful so quickly is because it's written by both of them together:

> *"People who read our blog tell us they like it because we don't take ourselves too seriously and we're approachable. And they like getting the perspective from the husband and the wife. We like to think that people can relate to our situation because we were them once — just two people who were looking to fix up our house without spending an arm and a leg. We strived to create a site that we would have found helpful back then."*

She adds that they also focus on making the site really easy to navigate, like a manual, so readers can find what they need.

From the very beginning, Sherry and John focused on creating good content and building their readership, thinking that would provide the business case for approaching potential sponsors. They had a little Advertise with Us button, but before they got around to reaching out, potential sponsors were contacting them.

They sell ads and sponsorships directly and through ad networks, offer a decorating advice service (which sells out every Monday within 15 minutes), and sell their own prints as well as products through an Amazon Associates affiliate store. Initially about 90 percent of their revenue came from consulting services and their stores. Now sponsorship supports the blog. Sherry jokes, "One hundred prints is not the same as one million views."

Young House Love opened many doors for them, including a regular column "Ask Sherry and John" in the *Better Homes & Gardens* title *Do-It-Yourself.* They've also been approached by TV networks, producers, and book publishers but aren't interested in TV because filming would take six or seven weeks away from the blog.

Sherry says:

> *"The blog is our passion. It's our first love. "It's too easy to say yes to everything, and then you lose yourself and the thing that you love. We're open to things that won't take too much time away from the blog, but we're homebodies. We love our house."*

Sherry says that the most rewarding thing about blogging is writing what she wants:

> *"I was an ad copywriter and spent my workdays writing based on other people's parameters. I love the freedom of expression and spontaneity with the blog. I can have an idea in the evening, and the post can be out there the next day."*

She advises new bloggers to manage their expectations and be prepared to work hard:

"Don't quit your day job. Success doesn't happen overnight. We blogged for over a year, just for friends and family, before we started earning any significant money. We may have gotten some lucky breaks, but we still worked our butts off. It's like any other business. If you want to succeed, you've got to put in the time and the effort."

Like Blogads, BlogHer looks for the preferential position. BlogHer ads must be in the top ad spot on your page. The only things that can be promoted above the BlogHer ads are your own products and services, and the BlogHer ads must be above the fold on the page. *Above the fold* is a newspaper term that means on the top half of the page. In the online context, this means on the first screen of content.

A key feature of the BlogHer ad network, as with many community ad networks, is that the ad widget shares blog headlines across the network, as shown in Figure 6-16.

BlogHer also lets bloggers in the ad network participate in sponsored conversations. Read more about BlogHer's program in Chapter 7.

Figure 6-16:
The BlogHer ad widget shares blog headlines across the network.

Choosing the Right Advertising Network

There are many, many advertising networks across demographics, geographies, and anything else humans might be interested in. Federated Media, Blogads, and BlogHer (which I discuss in the preceding section) are just representative examples of what you find when you start digging into your blogging niche.

When making your choices, you have to understand what the network you want to join requires *from you,* and you need to ask the right questions about what it's offering *to you:*

- ✔ What are the network's criteria? What sort of blogs is it looking for? Consider doing a survey of your blog audience to show that you reach a desirable demographic.

- ✔ Does the network want exclusivity or a specific position, such as above the fold? Can you run your own house ads or sell ads yourself?

- ✔ Do you have right of refusal on an advertiser?

- ✔ What sort of tools does the network provide to understand your sales, and how transparent is the network about how it calculates commissions? What do you get paid on? When do you get paid?

- ✔ How many blogs are in the network, and how does the network cross-promote them?

✔ What percentage of your available ad space can you expect will be sold? If that space isn't sold, what remnant programs does the network work with? *Remnant advertising* refers to ad inventory that the advertising network was unable to sell. Rather than run house or public-service ads, often the space is made available to remnant programs, like Double Click, that sell the space at bargain prices. The remnant ads fill in the gaps in your ad schedule. As a publisher, you do *not* want a lot of your inventory sold at remnant prices, but you do want to know that your ad network will maximize your revenue. A remnant ad is better than no ad!

✔ What percentage of the ad sales on the network is *run of network,* in which you share the revenue across the network versus ads specifically on your blog?

✔ Does the network allow pop-up ads and rich media like Flash and video, and do you get a premium on those?

✔ Can you meet the sales team in person?

Julie Marsh, Director of Advertising Sales at Cool Mom Picks (`www.cool mompicks.com`), says it has chosen a hybrid approach. Cool Mom Picks sells most of its site banner ads through Federated Media (FM) to take advantage of the network's ability to attract large advertisers. However, Cool Mom Picks retains some spots to sell directly to advertisers that don't have the budget for an extensive campaign with FM but are still willing to pay a premium to be on Cool Mom Picks. Cool Mom Picks also sells newsletter and gift-guide ad placements directly because it's very important that these advertisements fit thematically with the editorial product.

Julie says:

> "*Networks are the way to go for bloggers, even niche bloggers, for banner ad placement. However, niche bloggers have a great angle for pitching larger campaigns to brands that would be a good, specific fit with their site and their audience. But I'd issue the usual cautions about ensuring that scope is clearly documented, that compensation is in line with scope, and that the topic really is a good fit for them.*"

Understanding Affiliate Marketing

Joining affiliate marketing programs is a great place to start an advertising program for a new blogger — a *no-brainer,* as my childhood friends would have said. In the survey I conducted for this book, more than 46 percent of the bloggers who make money from their blogs reported revenue from affiliate commissions (refer to Figure 6-1). And although affiliate marketing seems very complicated, it's really very simple.

You put ads and links for stores on your blog. Ads go in your sidebars and other ad slots (see Figure 6-17), and product links go in your posts (see Figure 6-18). When your visitors follow your links (with your embedded affiliate code) to the store and purchase a product, you get a commission on the sale, which is anywhere from 3–12 percent, depending on the program.

Figure 6-17:
Affiliate ads.

Figure 6-18:
An affiliate link within a post.

Seating, storage, magic

by HiR on MAY 5, 2010 in HOT HOT HOT!

I've been looking for a few storage ottoman's for the kids' space, even though intellectually I *know* they will only end up crammed full of "treasures" and make me insane, a hopeful and emotional side of me believes that it will help magically hide the mess and make things more organized.

I know, it's cute when I'm like this.

Anyway, at just $16, I can certainly afford these nesting storage ottomans from Kohls, because at that price, I can afford to have my hopes and dreams dashed.

(Shipping is just $.99/item right now. Anyone can use coupon code THANKS1498 for an additional 15% off, too.)

COMMENTS (0)

Save $5 on
your $50 order.

Shop Target.com ›

Clearance ▶
Indulge in a little
bargain hunting!

SHOP
KOHLS.com

overstock.com
$20 Off
$500
Media & Electronics
Excluded

Puritan's Pride.
BUY 2
GET 3 FREE
Shop Vitamins

This is an affiliate link; shopping through it makes me a little money and makes you even prettier than you already are.

WANT NOT ARCHIVES

Select Month ▾

Select Category ▾

With a few exceptions, such as Amazon and some high-end retailers like B&H Foto and Electronics Corp., most stores run their affiliate marketing programs through networks, or gateways, such as

- ✔ **LinkShare:** www.linkshare.com
- ✔ **Commission Junction:** www.cj.com
- ✔ **ShareASale:** www.shareasale.com
- ✔ **Google Affiliate Network:** www.google.com/ads/affiliatenetwork

This means that applying to a store's program is a two-step process when you're getting started:

- ✔ Join the network if you don't already belong.
- ✔ Apply to the specific store program.

Getting into the networks is pretty easy. Getting into the store programs, however, can be more difficult. Some programs are very lenient and take all comers. Most, however, look for the right fit. They want to know you have the buyers and the page views to move products.

Building Your Affiliate Marketing Program

Start by applying to Amazon's Associates program. Amazon runs its own affiliate program and accepts just about everyone. The application is very simple; start at affiliate-program.amazon.com. If you have any existing Amazon account, log in. If not, create a new customer account. After you're logged in, follow the prompts to enter your account information and Web site profile.

After you're accepted into the program, you have lots of options for highlighting Amazon products on your blog, including

- ✔ Build an Amazon aStore of products you love and then link to it from your blog (see Figure 6-19, in which I link from the Snapshot Chronicles blog).
- ✔ Create blog widgets for product categories, aStore items, and all sorts of other things, depending on what fits your blog format (see Figure 6-20).
- ✔ When you write about products available at Amazon, remember to link to them by using an Amazon affiliate link that contains your unique affiliate code.

Figure 6-19:
The Amazon
aStore
for the
Snapshot
Chronicles
blog.

Figure 6-20:
Amazon
makes it
easy to cre-
ate widgets
to promote
its items.

After you highlight your Amazon products on your blog, you should apply to
the major affiliate networks; it costs nothing but a little of your time to apply.
All the application forms are pretty similar; visit each network and follow the
instructions it provides:

✔ **LinkShare:** www.linkshare.com

✔ **Commission Junction:** www.cj.com

✔ **ShareASale:** www.shareasale.com

✔ **Google Affiliate Network:** www.google.com/ads/affiliatenetwork

Most networks will accept your application. This is *not* true of the stores within the network.

After you're accepted into a network, you can access its *dashboard* (which is the control panel or interface). They're all a little different, but generally, they give you an overview of your earnings in the network, a list of available advertisers (stores), and detailed reporting on your earnings within the network.

Start by scanning the list of advertisers in the network in the categories most relevant to your blog topic. Figures 6-21 and 6-22 show the list of advertisers for the Flowers category on LinkShare and Google Affiliate Network, respectively.

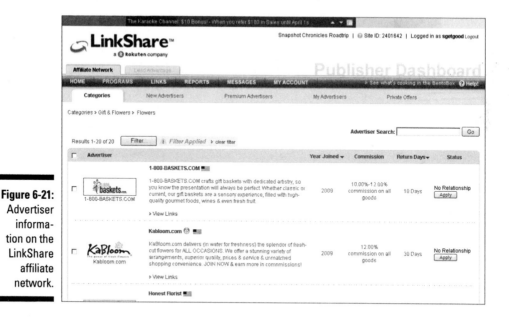

Figure 6-21:
Advertiser information on the LinkShare affiliate network.

Each store listing has the details about its commission structure and any requirements it has for selection. Pay attention to this. If a store says it wants a certain number of page views per month and you don't meet the criterion, you aren't going to be accepted. Figure 6-23 shows some of the detail for an advertiser on the Google network.

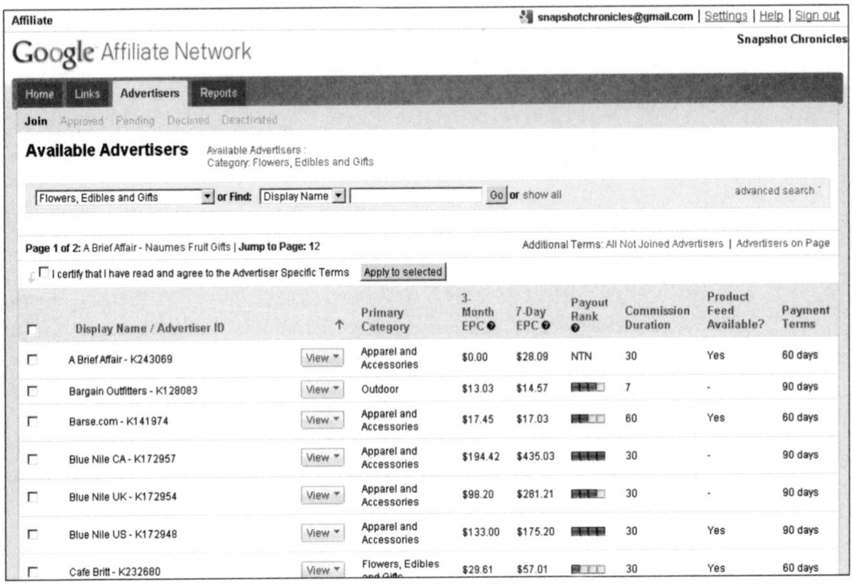

Figure 6-22:
A list of
advertisers
on Google
Affiliate
Network.

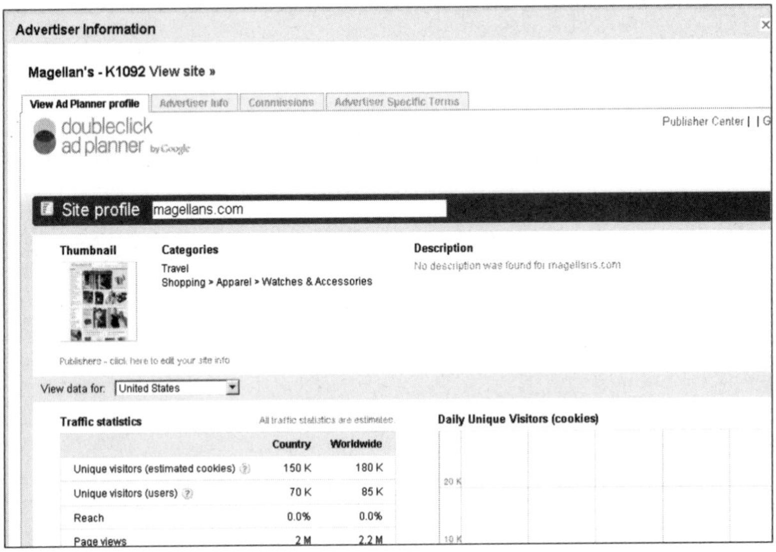

Figure 6-23:
Advertiser
informa-
tion on the
affiliate
networks
includes
commission
rates and
any specific
terms or
requirements.

Apply to the affiliate programs of individual stores in a network by clicking the store link in the network's dashboard. Expect to hear back within a few days most of the time.

Here are some tips for selecting stores:

✔ Stick with stores that fit well with your blog and that you would mention on your blog organically. If your traffic is low but your content is very relevant to a store, say so on the application form for the store. This may help get you accepted.

✔ Think about stores that will interest your readers, even if you might not shop there. This is particularly relevant if your blog is a shopping or review blog.

After you're accepted into a store's program, you get access to the affiliate program assets, such as ads and text links, and that's when it starts to get confusing. A lot of material is provided, and until you've worked with a program and a network a while, it can be overwhelming.

Without being specific to a particular program, for each advertiser or store program that you get approved for, you have access to advertising assets for campaigns of both long and limited duration, prebuilt text links to insert in posts, and special programs. Some programs also allow you to build your own links to specific products that you can use in your posts. Figure 6-24 is a glimpse into this for one advertiser on Google Affiliate Network.

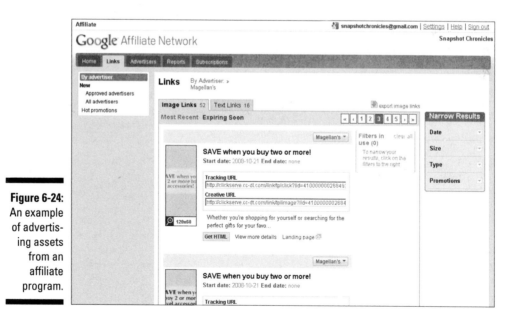

Figure 6-24:
An example of advertising assets from an affiliate program.

Your best bet is to start simple. Don't join too many programs all at once. Get a handle on the flow of things with a few stores first. Pick a few ad sizes that work well in your sidebar. If you want to easily rotate advertisers in and out, use the same sizes for all the programs you participate in.

For more best practices for affiliate marketing, read the nearby sidebar "Want Not: Building blog success with affiliate marketing" about shopping blogger Mir Kamin.

Affiliate ads look like ads, but links do not. Don't forget to disclose affiliate marketing links in posts, as I discuss in Chapter 3.

Want Not: Building blog success with affiliate marketing

Mir Kamin started her shopping blog Want Not (www.wantnot.net) as an offshoot of her personal blog Woulda Coulda Shoulda to share her *shopping ninja* skills with her readers. She loves to shop, but more important, she loves to find deals. As her masthead says, it is all about "having it all with less." The blog has since grown into a full-time endeavor that earns about 90 percent of its revenue from affiliate links.

She didn't start Want Not with the intention of making a living from it, but within a few months, she realized that it had the potential to earn "real money rather than pocket change." She had only joined two affiliate programs at the beginning: Amazon and Overstock.com. After she realized the potential, she joined many, many more programs. Initially she joined programs of the stores she shopped, but as she got to know her audience, she added stores that appealed to her readers, even though she doesn't shop there.

She pays a great deal of attention to customer service. She doesn't join, or she leaves, programs where the customer service has been awful. When she does make an exception, for a particularly good deal — "the prices are so good [she's] willing to gamble, knowing a return

might be a pain" — she makes sure to tell her readers so they can make an informed decision.

If you're going to invest your energy into working with affiliate marketing programs, Mir recommends setting up a master list of programs you belong to and identifying which network each program is with. She says:

> *"There have been times in the past when I've found a great deal that I know is going to sell out quickly and I'm scrambling around trying to figure out where I need to go to get my affiliate link. That's dumb."*

She says it's also useful to add the name of your point person or program manager for each affiliate program to your list in case you run into issues. Make sure to note how helpful the person is likely to be. Doing so can make a difference. For example, with affiliate networks that don't allow you to build links on-the-fly, some program managers will create a specific link for you, if you know, and remember, to ask.

Want Not is an influential shopping blog and gets many offers to participate in marketing programs with brands. Mir is very careful about the programs she says yes to. The first thing she considers is whether the program fits her audience. She says:

(continued)

(continued)

"When I get an offer of $90 per tube of lash-grow serum, I say no because none of my readers can afford that, and I suspect most of them would find it fussy and vain and weird. On the other hand, if it's something out of the price range of my readers but a really good/useful product, maybe I say yes. For example, I gave away a couple of Jawbone Bluetooth headsets. Generally, my readers are going to shop for something less expensive, but would be thrilled to win a top-of-the-line unit."

She also considers how well the offer fits the tone and flow of her blog. When someone offers her a product to give away as she sees fit and it's good for her readers, she's likely to do it. If the brand has all sorts of complicated rules and it sounds like it's going to be a disruption to the blog, she passes.

A big red flag is if someone requires that a giveaway include a review. She's also very wary of offers of a product for her and one for her readers. Most of the time she offers to give away both or asks that the brand just send one. In her opinion, an implicit obligation exists when you accept free product. She says:

"I don't review stuff I don't like, so I never promise a review. Also, sometimes a review just doesn't make sense. In general, it's simpler for me to say, 'I have this cool new thing to give away!' than to share my opinion."

If you plan to use affiliate marketing links to make money on your blog, Mir says the most important thing is to establish yourself as a trusted, helpful authority by linking to things your audience will find useful, regardless of whether you have an affiliate relationship with the store. She says:

"I link to plenty of stores that either don't have affiliate programs or for whatever reason haven't accepted me into their programs. The minute your linkage is all about the dollars, traffic will plummet because people will immediately be able to tell you're more interested in making a buck than in helping them."

Chapter 7

Getting Paid for Your Words

In This Chapter

▶ Discovering how to get paid for your words

▶ Earning money with pay-per-post

▶ Getting a traditional media job

▶ Writing a book

- -

*W*riting for others is an obvious option if you want to diversify your blogging revenue stream. Not surprisingly, writing for others is one of the most common revenue sources for professional bloggers. However, there's a big difference between writing to meet your objectives, as you do on your own blog, and writing to meet the requirements of someone else, whether it be an advertiser or an editor. Writing for someone else isn't for everyone. This chapter takes a look at the alternatives so you can decide whether writing for hire makes sense for you.

This chapter is about paid blogging as part of your blogging revenue mix. If you want to make your living as a freelance writer, consult specialized resources on the profession. Many books, Web sites, blogs, and online forums can give you targeted, specific advice to meet your professional goals.

Discovering the Ways to Be Paid for Writing

After advertising, freelance writing is the most commonly reported source of revenue by bloggers in the survey I conducted for this book, reported by nearly 50 percent of all bloggers (see Figure 7-1) and nearly 60 percent of the bloggers who earn 100 percent of their revenue from blogging.

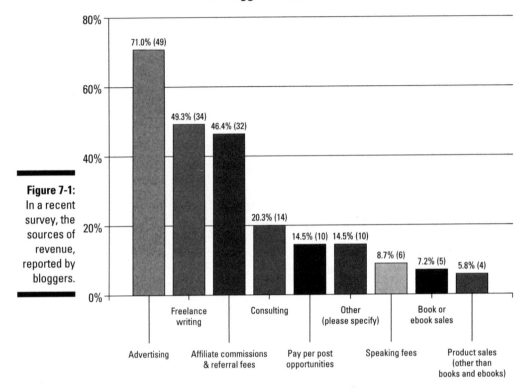

All Bloggers: Sources of Revenue

Source: Professional Blogging For Dummies survey, Susan Getgood, 2010

Figure 7-1: In a recent survey, the sources of revenue, reported by bloggers.

Freelance writing is also one of the top opportunities that bloggers get as a result of their blogs, cited second after participation in marketing programs by all bloggers, as shown in Figure 7-2. Freelance writing ties for third with consulting, after participation in marketing programs and speaking, for full-time bloggers.

If you want to get paid for your words, in order of relative difficulty, your basic options are

✔ Paid posts on your blog

✔ Writing for other blogs and Web sites

✔ Writing for traditional media, such as newspapers and magazines

✔ Publishing a book

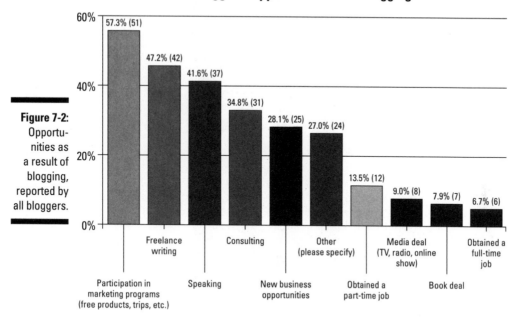

Figure 7-2:
Opportu-
nities as
a result of
blogging,
reported by
all bloggers.

Source: Professional Blogging For Dummies survey, Susan Getgood, 2010

Making Money via Pay-Per-Post

Common terms for paid posts include *advertorial* (that is, a blend of editorial and advertising), pay-per-post, and the more subtle sponsored conversation. All these terms mean pretty much the same thing; you're paid to write a post on your blog on a topic chosen by the advertiser. For simplicity, I use the terms pay-per-post and paid post in this chapter unless I refer to a specific network's branded opportunity.

Pay-per-post is different than a sponsored blog. With a sponsored blog, the named sponsor pays an advertising fee to associate its company name or products with the blog, and the sponsor usually runs advertisements on the blog but doesn't dictate editorial content or post topics.

Most pay-per-post opportunities are offered by networks that represent many companies rather than directly by the advertisers, but there are exceptions. The networks make their money by brokering the relationship between the advertiser and the bloggers. Blogger compensation is often, but not always, cash.

Depending on the advertiser, you may have detailed requirements, such as including specific keywords, promotional announcements, or links in the post; however, reputable networks and advertisers don't dictate content or tone. The blogger can write what he wants within the constraints of the topic.

You can find paid post opportunities on networks that specialize in the paid post model, such as IZEA (www.izea.com), Blogsvertise (www.blogs vertise.com), and SponsoredReviews.com (www.sponsoredreviews. com). You can also find these opportunities on broader advertising networks, such as BlogHer and Federated Media. Typically, paid post networks are pretty easy to get into, requiring just a simple registration, whereas the more selective ad networks limit participation in their programs to their members. (Read more about ad networks in Chapter 6.)

Paid posts look like editorial content, and as such, they carry an implied endorsement that advertising space doesn't. That's why the Federal Trade Commission (FTC) requires that bloggers disclose paid posts. You can read more about these requirements in Chapter 3.

Here are two examples of paid posts:

- An Electrolux campaign on the BlogHer network. Figure 7-3 shows the BlogHer post that explains the campaign and links to the participating blogs. Figure 7-4 is one of the member blogs that participated in the promotion.

- A post from Wendy Piersall, one of the bloggers who participated in a well-known pay-per-post promotion from Kmart on the IZEA network in December 2008 (see Figure 7-5). To read more about this campaign, which was one of the first big paid post campaigns and got a lot of coverage on blogs at the time, just search *kmart izea* in your preferred search engine.

Figure 7-3:
On the
BlogHer
network,
paid post
campaigns
are called
sponsored
conversa-
tions.

Self-proclaimed baking enthusiast, Kélly Ripa and Electrolux are teaming up with a virtual campaign that offers Americans a sweet way to make a difference. As the head of her kids' school bake sale committee, Kelly knows how a sweet treat can show someone you care. Now, she's got a way to care for a cause that's close to her heart: the Ovarian Cancer Research Fund (OCRF).

Visit Kelly's Cakery at www.Kelly-Confidential.com to decorate and send a special virtual cake to a friend, family member or loved one. For every cake sent, Electrolux will donate $1 to OCRF. Plus, to help spread the word, everyone who sends a virtual cake will be automatically entered for a chance to win every baker's dream: a stylish new Induction Range from Electrolux.

To help spread the word, Electrolux asked these 10 bloggers to share their favorite cake memories. Read their posts below and then head on over to Kelly's Cakery where you can join in the fight against Ovarian Cancer!

- Jenny from **Jenny on the Spot** says "Let there be cake!"
- Check out **Buns in My Oven**'s yummy Chocolate Peanut Butter Cupcakes!
- **Nika's Culinaria** shares her favorite cake-baking memory.
- Try **Picky Palate**'s Carrot Cake with Cream Cheese frosting today!
- Carmen from **Mom to the Screaming Masses** makes Darned Good Chocolate Cake!
- Learn how to make a layered rainbow cake with **Stop, Drop and Blog**!
- **Oh, The Joys!** shares her grandma's cake recipe with you!
- Time to make some red velvet cake with **Home Slice**!
- **Home Grown** gives us a peek at her Grandma's cake recipe!
- **Sweatpants Mom** has a Bundt in the oven!

*Electrolux will donate $1 for every day you log in or register and vote in Kelly's Cake Off for a Cause or send a virtual cake to a friend with a minimum of $30,000 and a maximum of $40,000.

Figure 7-4:
A blog post from the Electrolux campaign.

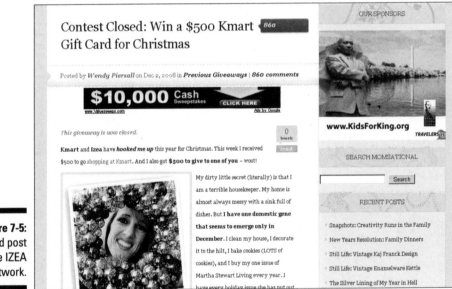

Figure 7-5:
A paid post on the IZEA network.

To join a paid post network like IZEA, fill out a profile with information about your blog, including demographics. This information impacts everything from the rates you can negotiate to the offers you're eligible for or approached about. Typically, blogs with more readers or a higher rank are presumed to have more influence, command higher rates, and get more offers.

Figure 7-6 shows part of IZEA's sign-up for its pay-per-post network (at `http://payperpost.com`), which lets advertisers offer paid post opportunities to the blogs that match the advertiser's demographic requirements.

After you're a member, depending on the network, you're either presented with offers immediately or placed in a pool from which the advertisers can select by blog name or demographic selection. Figure 7-7 shows an opportunity on another IZEA paid post network, the SocialSpark community.

One of the criticisms of the pay-per-post model is its low rates. For example, when I signed up for SocialSpark, I was offered an opportunity to write a 200-word post about SocialSpark for $5.

Very few paid blogging opportunities, whether pay-per-post or freelance writing for another blog, pay enough to truly cover the time it takes to write an original, compelling post. Balancing the value of the opportunity against the effort is critical. And the *value* that you need to keep in mind here is the value to *you;* there are no absolutes. Even a paid post opportunity that seems low paying can be useful to you if the resulting post brings new traffic to your blog through search engines.

Figure 7-6:
Adding a blog on one of IZEA's paid post networks.

Add Blog

url http://snapshotchronicles.com/roadtrip   suggest my price

description nlly travel through a slightly twisted lens

price per post 7.0

price per word 0.01

At $0.01 per word, you would make $9.00 for a 200 word post.

Link only	Link + 50 words	Link + 100 words	Link + 200 words
$7.00	$7.50	$8.00	$9.00

min adv rating 50%   allow adult content   category Travel

disclosure type In Post   preferred link type Either

next

Figure 7-7:
A paid post opportunity on the SocialSpark community.

On the other hand, your blog opens many opportunities for you. Don't sell yourself short. Editorial independence may be worth far more to you in the long run than a few paid post fees.

If you do decide to do paid posts, you need to keep your readers' expectations in mind. If they expect your experiences and opinions, paid posts might seem out of place. Stick with opportunities that are consistent with your voice and your typical content. And be sure to disclose that the post is a paid post. Your readers deserve to have this information, and the Federal Trade Commission guidelines on endorsements and testimonials require the disclosure.

Writing for Other Blogs

Many professional bloggers earn part of their living writing posts for other blogs. These opportunities take many forms — regular contributor, staff writer, columnist, or featured blogger — and range from long-term contracts (or even full-time employment) to one-time assignments.

If you take this leap, you write for someone else. That means you have to meet the editorial guidelines and deadlines of your employer. Freelance blogging is also very competitive. Although many opportunities are out there, many bloggers compete for each one.

Finding freelance blogging opportunities

Any blog (or Web site) with more than a few writers probably has some paid blogging opportunities. Big networks, such as Weblogs, Inc., Gawker Media, and About.com, resemble traditional publishing networks and operate with a similar model: some combination of full-time employees and freelancers. Compensation models vary from network to network. Independent blogs with an editorial staff (for example, MamaPop at www.mamapop.com) are also likely to use freelancers.

Community sites often are a mix of paid contributors and community member blogs. The professional blogs or posts provide a baseline of quality content to attract members to the community. For example, in the Work It, Mom! community (www.workitmom.com), freelancers write the featured blogs (see Figure 7-8).

Figure 7-8: Freelance bloggers write the featured blogs at Work It, Mom!.

Companies often hire freelancers to write articles or regular columns on a corporate or product blog. For example, menswear fashion blogger Chris Hogan, author of the Off the Cuff blog (www.offthecuffdc.blogspot.com), writes a regular column on the Nivea for Men blog, as shown in Figure 7-9. For more about the Off the Cuff blog, read the interview with Chris in Chapter 1.

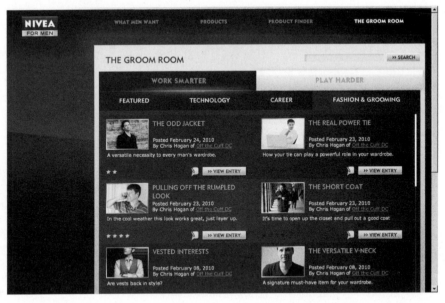

Figure 7-9:
Companies
often hire
freelance
bloggers
to write
for them.

On the other hand, paid staff members usually write blogs owned by traditional media. If the writer also writes for the print edition, the blog acts as an online extension of the work the writer does for the newspaper or magazine. But there are exceptions. Media companies will hire freelancers who offer unique content or bring new readers. For example, *Real Simple* magazine uses freelance bloggers as well as staff writers on its Simply Stated blog (`http://simplystated.realsimple.com/simplystated`). See Figure 7-10, which features a column by Kristin Brandt, cofounder of the Manic Mommies podcast, from Simply Stated.

Fees for freelance blogging vary widely depending on the blog and the topic. Expect everything from a flat-fee per post ($50 is a pretty common amount) to retainers with an expectation of a certain number of posts per week or month.

A major corporation or media outlet generally has a bigger budget than a small, independent Web site or your local paper. Set your expectations accordingly. Factor in something for the value of the exposure to you when considering the opportunity but don't give away your work too cheaply. The company hiring you will benefit from your work. So should you.

Figure 7-10:
A column
from the
Simply
Stated blog.

Positioning yourself for freelance blogging opportunities

If you're lucky and have built a solid online brand with your blog, an assignment editor may reach out to you with an opportunity, but don't count on it. You have to make your own luck. Here are some suggestions for positioning yourself for freelance blogging opportunities:

- ✔ **Write a great blog with unique and compelling posts.** You're competing with other bloggers, professional freelancers, and former journalists for paid blogging opportunities. Your voice and reputation are your most important assets.

- ✔ **If you want to write for a particular media outlet, develop your blog with it in mind.** Make sure that your blog topic fits a niche that isn't met by any of the magazine's existing columnists, online and off.

- ✔ **Get known by the blog's editorial staff.** Comment on posts. Link back to their posts from your blog. Introduce yourself at conferences and meet-ups.

- ✔ **Build a loyal, engaged audience that follows you to the new outlet.** Even if they already read the site, your column might keep them there just a bit longer. Plus, you're bound to bring along a few new readers — an attractive proposition for any editor.

    ✔ **Pitch a column (or article, if you just want a one-time assignment) that relates to the topic of your blog but has a unique spin just for the magazine.** For more about pitching to blogs and the mainstream media, read the sidebar "From blog to newsstand," later in this chapter.

Your byline has value; don't give it away for free. Opportunities to write for other blogs without any compensation aren't freelance opportunities. You may choose to accept them, but only do so if there's value in having your work appear on the site. For example, many bloggers accept the invitation to post without compensation on the Huffington Post simply for the visibility, which they then leverage into other opportunities. Be very discerning. If you do a freebie, make sure that you get what you "pay" for.

Be careful about writing on spec, too. *On spec* is when you're paid for a writing assignment upon acceptance by the editor. This is possibly worth it if it gets you in the door for your perfect opportunity. Most of the time, however, on spec isn't worth it.

You also may consider syndicating your posts. *Syndication* is when a blog network or aggregator buys the right to reprint your blog post. Here are two basic kinds of syndication:

    ✔ An aggregator, such as Newstex (`http://newstex.com`), includes your blog in a distribution package. Information companies, such as LexisNexis and Thomson Reuters, subscribe to the service and then your posts are included (via RSS feed) in their information products. Some of these information products are public Web sites, but others are subscription-only services. You're paid a royalty based on page views of your posts and get an earnings report every quarter.

    ✔ A blog network or portal syndicates an individual post based on newsworthiness or entertainment value. For example, the BlogHer network regularly syndicates posts from its community members and pays a small fee to the blogger for the right to reprint the post on BlogHer.

In addition to the financial payment, syndication gives your blog greater exposure. In fact, you may be approached about syndication opportunities that offer only exposure. You have to make the call whether the exposure offers enough value. More often than not, it doesn't.

If someone reprints your blog post in its entirety on his Web site or blog without your permission, he's violated your copyright. An excerpt or quote is okay, but the whole thing is not. Check out Chapter 3 for more on copyright and some ways you can deal with this.

Weighing the ghostwriting option

Ghostwriting is when someone else writes the content for the named author. Ghostwriting is a common form for celebrity autobiographies, and someone else ghosts more than a few bylined articles in the trade press.

The ghostwriter doesn't always get credit, and that poses a real dilemma for bloggers. Blogging is a personal medium, and readers generally expect the post to be written by the person whose name is attached.

If you decide to accept ghostwriting assignments, make sure that you know how, or whether, your credit will appear.

When I write for other blogs, I request that my posts appear under my name. Sometimes that's not the best choice for the client, in which case, I post as a function, such as Admin or Support, or under the company name. I don't allow my posts to appear under someone else's name.

Querying for contributor opportunities

Many sites — even the smaller ones — have a page that outlines contributor requirements and opportunities, such as the About.com page, as shown in Figure 7-11. If you can't find a page, e-mail the editor or site owner with a simple query. Include the following in your e-mail:

- ✔ Introduce yourself briefly.
- ✔ Express your interest in the site.
- ✔ Ask whether the site ever uses freelance writers.

Don't lead with a hard-sell pitch. Start by opening a dialogue with the site owner; let her get to know you and your work. Then when you do have an idea you want to pitch, it's more likely to land on fertile ground.

Figure 7-11:
Guidelines
for potential
contributors
on
About.com.

Getting a Traditional Media Gig

Times have been tough lately for traditional media. Editors of newspapers and magazines are challenged to fill their pages with fewer staffers and smaller budgets. Using bloggers can be an appealing alternative because they're experienced writers with a bank of post topics that can be expanded into print articles and a built-in audience of their own readers.

However, the competition is even fiercer for these opportunities than it is for Web-based ones, and every round of layoffs at a major newspaper brings new freelancers into the market. Unless you have a burning desire to be a professional writer, I don't recommend this as your main source of revenue. However, you can be opportunistic and take advantage of, or make, opportunities for yourself in print media just as you would in Web-based media.

From blog to newsstand

Kyran Pittman writes a personal Notes to Self blog (www.notestoself.us), which she describes as "a space where words have always mattered more than numbers." She counts her regular readers in the hundreds, not thousands, and is content for it to remain that way — which only goes to prove that how many readers you have isn't the goal. It's who's reading your blog that matters. In her case, the literary editor of *Good Housekeeping* was reading.

Kyran tells the story:

> "The literary editor found my blog and contracted to reprint four posts, which

opened a rapport. I then pitched a story, which became "Mommy Wears Prada," an account of my investment dressing shopping spree in New York (as shown in the following figure). The story was a big hit and led to a second feature assignment and a contributing editor spot on the masthead. A literary agent and a book deal followed. And I owe it all to a blog with a few hundred readers."

Good Housekeeping also published three articles by Stefania Pomponi Butler, author of popular blog CityMama (`http://citymama.typepad.com`), including one about her daughter's decision to become a vegetarian. All three articles were "tweaks," as Stefania put it, of posts that originally appeared on her blog.

Rita Arens is a professional writer, but her big career break came out of her blogging at Surrender, Dorothy (`http://surrenderdorothy.typepad.com`). In 2008, she published *Sleep Is for the Weak* (Chicago Review Press), a small anthology of posts from leading mom blogs. That book in turn led to freelance assignments, including one in *Scholastic Parent & Child Magazine* in November 2009, about which Rita says:

> "The editor had reviewed my book, so when I pitched her my story idea, we had a point of connection. But I still had to sell the story!"

Here are some lessons to derive from their experiences:

- ✔ **Stay true to your voice.** Those are the pitches that stand out from the others. Anyone could have gone on a shopping spree in New York. Kyran brought her unique voice to the story, and that's what made it come alive for readers.

- ✔ **After you establish a rapport or connection with an editor, don't be afraid to pitch your story.** If you don't ask, the answer is most definitely no.

Stay focused. Your point of differentiation from the other freelance writers is *your blog*. Your blog gives you a unique voice and platform that has value for the paper or magazine. Other people could write about the topic, but there's only one you.

Kyran Pittman, featured in the "From blog to newsstand" sidebar later in this chapter, offers this advice:

> *"Many new bloggers are too precious about their writing. They worry about giving 'the good stuff' away for free. Unless you already have a relationship with editors, put your good stuff on your blog. The best you've got. Give it away for free. It's not doing anything, sitting unseen in a folder, and there's always more where it came from."*

Writing a Book

Lately, every blogger seems to be writing a book, or at least talking about it. "Writing a book can't be that hard," you think. "How long can writing a book take? After all, I already write a blog." Stop right there.

Writing a book is a full-time job. And for authors working with a publisher (versus self- or e-publishing), the writing process follows a lengthy proposal and negotiating process. Among other things, publishers want to know that you have engaged, committed readers (and lots of them) who will convert into book buyers.

Pay no attention to the so-called overnight success stories about people getting book deals dropped in their lap. These are the exception, *not* the rule. Don't ignore the many years of work and positioning the author did to be in the right place at the right time.

Writing a book is by no means easy money. Proceed with caution.

Blogger Joanne Bamberger, who writes about politics at PunditMom (www.punditmom.com), is expanding the Mothers of Intention feature on her blog into a full-length book. She says:

> *"I started the feature on the blog to show that women were actively engaged in writing about political issues, even though women, especially mothers, are often portrayed in the media as being apolitical. Every week I would feature original content or syndicate an article from a woman blogger about a political topic. Now that I am expanding it into a book, I'm adding a researched narrative section to introduce each group of essays. This adds a whole new level of work to the process. If I didn't have such tremendous passion for the topic, it would have been quite easy to give up and put the whole project on a shelf!"*

If you have passion for your topic and decide to go ahead with a book, your first decision is *how* you want to publish. Will you self-publish at your own expense, or try to sell the idea to a publisher? Nearly all your other decisions about the book flow from that initial decision.

If you decide to self-publish, your next step is to select a self-publisher to help you. Why do that *before* you write your book? The publishing house has tons of experience working with authors like you and can help you avoid costly mistakes. Yvonne DiVita, president of self-publishing house Windsor Media Enterprises, says:

> *"Two of the most difficult parts of getting your book published are the cover design (both front and back) and fully understanding your audience. I read once that 'it's hard to read the label when you're inside the bottle,' and I so agree. Most new authors need a separate set of eyeballs to make sure their writing is appropriate for the market they're hoping to reach. For the cover, we've discovered all designers are not created equal. Many designers cannot work within the limitations of a book cover. New authors may think their Web designer can do their book cover, or that their brochure designer can create their book cover. Maybe, maybe not."*

You're investing your time *and* money into your book, and need someone who will be your partner in the process. Publishing a book isn't just about bindings and ink or adding another title to inventory. Publishing a book is about producing a professional title you can be proud of. Take the time to pick the right partner.

If you want to pitch your book to publishers, buy a book. Seriously. Pitching a book is a long process from your initial idea through the proposal, contract negotiations, and finally, writing it. You need to understand what you're getting into to be sure that you have the passion to see it through. I recommend these titles:

- ✔ *Getting Your Book Published For Dummies,* by Sarah Parsons Zackheim and Adrian Zackheim
- ✔ *How to Write a Book Proposal,* by Michael Larsen (Writer's Digest Books)

Part III
Building Your Blog, Step by Step

The 5th Wave   By Rich Tennant

"You can smirk all you like, but I know wearing this helps keep the entries in my Squash Lovers blog authentic."

In this part . . .

After you decide the overall strategy and objectives for your professional blog (the topics of Parts I and II), move onto the mechanics of building your blog, from creating a name and choosing your blogging software to selecting imagery and writing your first post.

This part covers the things you need to do before you can begin developing your blog. I also go over the key milestones in developing (or redesigning) your blog, including a step-by-step checklist you can use to monitor your progress.

Chapter 8

Choosing Your Blog Name, Platform, and Web Hosting

*Y*ou can change, with relatively little impact, most of the choices you make when you build your blog. Fine-tuning strategy, making design adjustments, and choosing a new advertising partner fall into this easy-to-redo category. These aren't small changes and they certainly cost time and money, but they aren't showstoppers.

In a few situations, however, changing your mind means starting all over again. You don't want to realize that you dislike your blog or domain name after you've published and promoted it. Apart from all the rework such a change causes, the Internet has a long memory. If your abandoned first try is active, even for just a little while, search engines will index it, and your old blog may turn up in searches rather than your subsequent, successful blog.

The moral of the story? Take your time over the seemingly simple decisions of blog and domain names, blog platform, and Web hosting. In this chapter, I step you through the process of naming your blog, registering your domain name, and choosing your blogging platform.

Naming Your Blog

Your blog name is one of most important elements of your blog. The name sets the stage for your words, encapsulates your strategy, and gives the readers important clues about what to expect — before they read a single post.

Your blog name is even more important than the design and graphics, both of which you can change easily in the popular blogging platforms. Often a reader's first introduction to your blog is on a *blogroll* (a list of blogs on another blog) or as a link in someone else's blog post. Having a name that catches attention improves your chances that a reader will click over to check out your blog.

Coming up with a great blog name

Because names are so important (leading Samuel Butler to once say, "*The Ancient Mariner* would not have taken so well if it had been called *The Old Sailor*"), take the time to pick the right name, one that encapsulates your strategy and creates the right atmosphere. Follow these steps:

1. **Brainstorm ideas relating to your blog.**

   Here are some places to start thinking and writing down the ideas that come to you:

   - Your main editorial topics

   - Famous quotations

   - Puns

   - Nouns that describe you, your audience, or your goals

   - Adjectives that build an atmosphere

   For example, if you're creating a blog about budget travel, you might start with words and phrases that evoke *budget,* such as *penny pincher,* and *on a shoestring;* then describe travel with words or phrases like *luxury, roughing it,* and *family friendly.*

    Write down everything in whatever format works best for you. I use big sheets of paper and mind maps. (In a mind-map diagram, you start with a central word or idea, and then link connecting words and images to the original word and to each other. You're looking for the unusual connections. The mind map helps you "see" these connections.) But don't get hung up on the idea that there is only one technique to brainstorm. If you like to think visually, imagine the look and feel you want to achieve. Imagery can lead to words. The most important thing is to generate many ideas, words, and phrases that resonate with you and your future readers.

2. **Use ideas from your brainstorming session as building blocks to create your blog name and *tagline,* a short phrase that expands upon the name.**

Some people think developing the tagline first and then the blog name is easier. For others, the name just jumps off the page. If you don't have a natural preference, start with the tagline. After brainstorming, you have many ideas to sift through. Start large and narrow your scope in stages.

You don't need a tagline, but most bloggers find that having one helps clarify the scope and sets reader expectations.

Using the earlier example of the budget travel blog, you might come up with blog names like *The Penny Pincher's Guide to Luxury Travel* and *Around the World on a Shoestring.*

In addition to providing inspiration for blog names, quotations make good taglines. I named my blog *Marketing Roadmaps* in a riff on an *Alice in Wonderland* quotation: "If you don't know where you are going, any road will take you there." In the budget travel example, you could look for quotations about voyages and travel.

3. **Search on your preferred search engine for some of your keywords and phrases to see what others have named their blogs.**

Your competitive research (discussed in Chapter 2) comes in handy here. You want a unique name that won't be confused with another blog, whether a competitor or something totally unrelated. Search engine results also give you an idea of what terms rank high in your segment, something you should definitely take into consideration. You want a name that's easy to find and remember, for search engines and people. Read more about search engine optimization (SEO) in Chapter 13.

4. **Test your proposed names on friends and family.**

Ask them what the name makes them think or feel. What kind of content will they expect to find? What would they expect to do as a result of reading a post on the blog? Their answers should match, at least roughly, what you hope to achieve with the blog. If they don't — if your name makes them think something different — go back to the drawing board. If you have very creative friends, ask them to brainstorm with you.

Avoid copyrighted material, such as song lyrics, movie lines, and show titles, in your blog name. To use the TV show *True Blood* as an example, you don't want to invest a lot of time in a True *True Blood* Fans fan blog, only to have the network ask you to rename it. Worse, your clever corporate motivational business is named Blood, and you start a True Blood Fans business blog, and the network *still* asks you to rename it. Put the band, show, or movie name in your tagline instead: *For true fans of True Blood.*

If you get really stuck and can't seem to come up with a blog name you love, put the name aside for a bit and come back to it later. Develop some preliminary designs or write your introductory post. Inspiration may strike when you're least thinking about it.

Further advice to help in your quest for the perfect blog name

Unfortunately, no magic formula exists to create the name. You just have to try different combinations of words and phrases until you find something that sticks. Here are a few tips:

- ✔ **Don't rush the process.** Creating your blog name deserves as much time as you've spent on the overall strategy. Maybe more.

- ✔ **Don't be too cute.** You'll live with this name for a while.

- ✔ **Keep it short.** Blog names with one to three words seem to work best.

Use a one- or two-sentence tagline to expand your idea rather than a really long blog name. Figure 8-1 shows how the blog PunditMom (`www.punditmom.com`) uses the tagline to further explain the blog name.

Figure 8-1:
A good
tagline
clarifies the
blog name.

✔ **Try to create an image with your words.** These blog names get to the point, even without a picture:

- Craftastrophe

- Cake Wrecks

- Lighter Footstep

- The Green Mom Review

- TreeHugger

- Dog Show Poop

- Shutter Sisters

- Suburban Turmoil

✔ **Create a new word that encapsulates your mission.** For example, eco-politology (`http://ecopolitology.org`) is a blog about the politics of energy and the environment.

For inspiration, the masthead, or header, of the blog Cake Wrecks (`http://cakewrecks.blogspot.com`), as shown in Figure 8-2, illustrates how the blog name, tagline, and imagery can come together to create just the right environment for the posts.

Figure 8-2: The blog name, tagline, and imagery create a humorous environment.

Creating and Registering Your Domain Name

Readers remember your blog's name, but technically they access it by using its Web address, the central part of which is the domain name: `www.domain name.com`.

Regardless of the blogging platform you choose (more on that in the later section, "Choosing a Blog Platform and Hosting"), you need to have your own domain name because

- ✔ **It's easier for your readers to remember than a hosted address like** **blogname**.blogspot.com. Even if you decide to use a free hosting service like Blogger (`www.blogspot.com`), you can map your domain name to your Blogspot address.

- ✔ **Your online address (URL) never changes.** You can change your Web hosting whenever you want without losing readers or search engine rankings.

- ✔ **It shows you're serious about your professional blog.** Registering a domain name isn't very expensive (about $10 per year), so even if you are just testing an idea or doing a short-term project, it's worth it to reinforce your brand.

Jetson Green: Making it easier to build green

When Preston Koerner started his environmental design blog Jetson Green (`www.jetson green.com`) in July 2006, he was working for a corporate real estate company. He was surprised that there was no sense of urgency at the firm about green construction and decided to do some research on the subject himself. The research led to a passion for green design, and then to a blog to share what he was learning with the building design community, homeowners, contractors, and developers.

Preston writes about best practices for green buildings — products, projects, and news. When I spoke to him, he was planning a blog redesign and has a firm vision for how he wants the blog to evolve. He writes about 95 percent of Jetson Green and hopes to get the community more actively involved in creating content for the blog — sharing their expertise, covering more products, and writing hands-on, how-to articles. He's even considering creating showcase projects to highlight the work of the Jetson Green community.

Preston participates on Facebook and Twitter, and has obtained speaking engagements as a result of the blog, but that's all he does on a regular basis for promotion. He says:

"I try to write the most interesting content that I can, and hope that people find and share it and the blog makes some money."

Well, people are certainly finding it. Jetson Green averages 150,000 unique visitors per month, and page views range from 300,000 to 450,000 per month. The blog has also been mentioned in numerous print and Web publications, including *The Wall Street Journal, The Washington Post,* and *USA Today* as well as top-ranked blogs, the Huffington Post and Apartment Therapy.

And he's making some money with Google AdSense and BlogAds. Monthly ad earnings fluctuate, but he says it's enough that he could rely on the blog income if he had to.

Preston says that the blog has also helped him in his career:

"Jetson Green has definitely increased my exposure in the local community and as an attorney. I've only been practicing law since 2008, but I've already had the opportunity to write two articles for legal journals on state and federal green building regulations and new laws relating to green development."

Now that he's a practicing attorney, Preston isn't as involved in the business of the building industry as he used to be. He says the most rewarding things about blogging for him are staying involved in the green building community, keeping up-to-date on innovations, and staying sharp in an area he's passionate about.

He recently helped a lawyer friend set up a blog, and the advice Preston gave him was to understand that a blog is a long-term effort:

"It's a marathon, not a sprint. Take your time and enjoy it. You're probably not going to get rich at it. But success comes in many different ways — including the new friends and opportunities you get as a result. Once you invest the time, you can get a lot out of your blog. But you have to be committed to the long-term, at least 1–2 years, before your efforts will bear fruit."

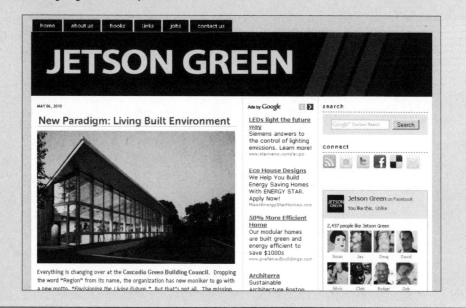

Determining your domain name

Your domain name can be the full blog name or a segment of it, depending on how long your blog name is. There's no hard-and-fast rule about whether your full blog name or a truncated version is better. You just want something easy to spell and remember; the shorter, the better. Here are some examples:

- ✔ **Woulda Coulda Shoulda:** www.wouldashoulda.com
- ✔ **Lip-sticking:** www.lipsticking.com
- ✔ **Motherhood Uncensored:** www.motherhooduncensored.net

In some cases, the availability of a domain name (more about that later) dictates your blog name. Preston Koerner, founder of environmental design blog Jetson Green (www.jetsongreen.com), explains:

> *"I wanted a name that evoked technology, progress, and modern design on the one hand, and green, sustainable, and environment, on the other. I had probably 25 different ideas, but none of the domains was available. I needed something crazy enough to be able to get a domain name, and came up with Jetson Green to evoke modern and green — like jet set, only without the wealthy connotations."*

More about Preston and Jetson Green in the nearby sidebar, "Jetson Green: Making it easier to build green," later in this chapter.

For a quick check of whether your desired domain name is available, you can do a search on the name in your preferred search engine. I prefer to use a domain registrar, such as Network Solutions, for my searches because if the name is taken, Network Solutions suggests some alternatives, which can spark your creativity. I step you through the process of looking up and registering your domain name in the next section.

Resist the temptation of using bizarre spellings, homonyms, and puns as your domain name. These are okay as part of your blog name or tagline, but you want your domain name to be simple enough that if you were telling it to someone in a noisy crowded room, she could write it down without your needing to spell it.

Registering your domain name

You register a new domain name at a *domain registrar,* such as Network Solutions, Register.com, or Go Daddy. Your hosting company may also be able to assist with registering your domain name.

Whether you register directly or with a Web hosting company's assistance, your first step is to check the availability of the domain name. For example, on the Network Solutions Search page, as shown in Figure 8-3, you can check up to ten possible names across the full spectrum of domain extensions.

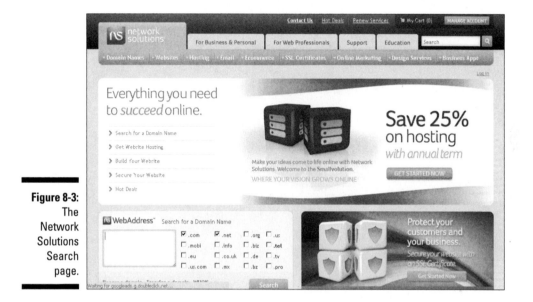

Figure 8-3:
The
Network
Solutions
Search
page.

The domain extension is the part after your domain name: `.com`, `.net`, `.org`, country extensions, such as `.us`, `.co.uk`, and so on. Generally speaking, `.com` is preferable for U.S.-based Web sites. If your preferred domain name(s) isn't available, the search results will indicate which extensions are available, such as `.net` and `.us`, as well as offer spelling variations.

The domain name you want may have been purchased by a *domain squatter,* a company or individual that purchases desirable domain names in bulk and resells them. The squatter offers you the opportunity to bid for the name you're after. Bidding usually isn't worth it. You'll pay an inflated price. Better to just find another name. If you have a defensible copyright, such as a trademark, you can legally get a squatter removed, but it'll cost you time and money. Weigh your investment in the name. A legal effort that may be worth it for a big consumer brand might not be worth it for you.

Unless the domain was privately registered, you can find out who owns a domain name by using the WHOIS lookup. All the domain registrars provide access to this query. Just look for a button or link labeled WHOIS. If the domain was privately registered, the name of the domain registrar shows in the query results rather than the domain owner.

People register domains privately, at an extra cost, to avoid their e-mail addresses from being published on the Web where spammers can get them and to keep their ownership of a domain private, such as for a confidential project.

When your search turns up a domain name that's both suitable and available, follow these steps to register it with Network Solutions:

1. **Navigate to the home page of Network Solutions (`www.network solutions.com`).**

2. **Enter the name in the Web Address field and then click the Search button.**

   The search results screen appears, showing the availability of the name across all the extensions.

3. **If the name you want is available, preferably as a `.com`, click the selection box and then click the Add to Cart button.**

   Over the next few screens, Network Solutions offers you the opportunity to purchase additional services, including

   • *The domain name with other extensions:* This isn't expensive, so you may want to take advantage of this to prevent competitors or spam advertisers buying the similar domains.

   • *Public or private registration:* As mentioned earlier, the extra cost option for private registration keeps your contact information hidden.

   • *A Web hosting package:* Later in this chapter, I cover what you need to consider when selecting a Web host.

4. **Make your choices and click through until you finally get to the My Cart Screen.**

5. **Select the number of years for the registration and then check out with your preferred method of payment.**

If your chosen domain name is available, you can register it through any domain registrar. You don't have to register it with the Web site you used to do the search. The steps on other domain registrars are similar to the ones listed earlier for Network Solutions.

As I mention in the steps for registering a domain on Network Solutions, you may want to purchase your chosen domain name with multiple extensions to avoid competitors or spam advertisers buying them and causing confusion. Doing so isn't very costly. If you're buying the `.com` extension, consider getting `.net`, `.org`, and `.biz` if they're available. You can then point all the extra domain names to your main blog address, the `.com` domain.

After you find an available domain name, you have a number of purchasing options, including multiple years and private registration; however, don't automatically purchase a Web hosting package when you register your new domain, even if the pricing looks attractive. The *Web host* is the computer that stores your blog pages and makes them available on the Internet. A *Web hosting package* is a combination of software, computer storage space, and services. Instead, choose your blog platform first (see the section "Choosing a Blog Platform and Hosting," later in this chapter) so you can purchase a hosting package that supports it. Depending on what you choose, you may not even need separate hosting.

Mark the domain expiration date in your calendar right away so you don't forget to renew on time. As a courtesy, the domain registrar usually e-mails the owner when a domain registration is about to expire, but don't count on it. If you don't renew on time, the domain name can be sold to someone else, who can then benefit from all your hard work and site traffic.

Linking your blog to an existing domain name

If you already have a Web site with its own domain name and your new blog is closely related to the topic or business of the site, you may want to link your blog to that domain name instead of registering a new one. This *co-location* makes it easier for blog readers to find (and remember) your main site, and visitor traffic to both the blog and Web site contributes to the search engine rankings for the main site. This is what I did with my blog Marketing Roadmaps; its Web address is `www.getgood.com/roadmaps`.

To link your new blog this way, set it up as a sub-directory of your existing Web site. If you don't know how to do this, the developer who built your original site or your Web hosting company can help you.

Choosing a Blog Platform and Hosting

Your *blog platform* is the software you use to publish your blog. Your *blog host* is where the files reside. You can select these independently or bundled together as a hosted service.

Many options for your blog platform and hosting are available, and new ones are added all the time. Instead of focusing on specific offerings, I go over the main things you need to consider when making your choices.

Choosing a hosted service

With a hosted service, you get the blogging software and Web hosting in a single, integrated package. If this is your first blog, a hosted service can be a good choice because everything is managed for you. No need to install software or worry about updates. To get started, you simply set up your user account on the service.

The most well-known hosted services are Blogger, TypePad, and WordPress, but they aren't the only ones. Blogger and basic WordPress are free. TypePad charges a fee but offers a free trial.

Blog hosting services are all fairly similar — a simple dashboard and a library of design templates (or *themes*) — so you can get up and running quickly. A design template contains all the files necessary for the design; it's a simple matter of following the platform's instructions to apply the template to your blog.

Some hosted services offer more add-on functionality through plug-ins and widgets than others, but all the major hosted services have fairly robust design and development communities that can support you if you need help. Check out their Web sites and do some searches on your preferred search engine for the latest information.

If you're leaning toward a hosted service for your blog, it costs you nothing to try it. Set up a simple test blog:

- ✔ Do you like the dashboard; is it intuitive for you? Figure 8-4 shows the editing window for a Blogger blog.
- ✔ How easily can you change the blog design after you set it up?
- ✔ Check out the support forums. How responsive is the company? How supportive is the community?
- ✔ How easily can you customize the blog with widgets and plug-ins?
- ✔ How easily can you map your domain name to the blog address assigned by the service? Hosted services assign a URL address on their domains, such as `catblog.blogspot.com` or `catblog.typepad.com`. You want to use your own domain name, as I discuss earlier in this chapter.

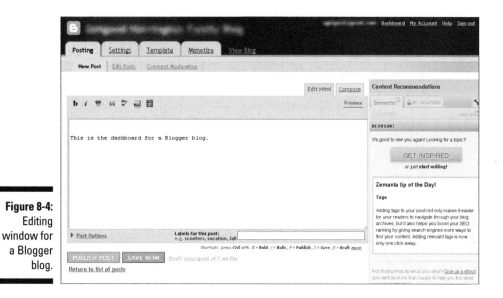

Figure 8-4:
Editing
window for
a Blogger
blog.

You can't use a hosted service if you want to integrate your blog into your existing Web site. Hosted services also may not have the software options or flexibility you need to execute your professional blog plan. In particular, customization may be limited. Also, if you choose one of the free services, you may have to live with a text or small display ad for the service on your blog.

If you do decide to use a hosted service, make sure that you map your blog to your own domain name rather than publicize the hosted service URL. Putting your own domain name front and center helps build your brand. Also, if you decide to switch platforms down the road, you won't lose your search engine ranking and your readers can still find your blog.

Hosting your blog yourself

The other option is to unbundle the software from the Web hosting and host your blog yourself. In this case, you have to select your blogging *platform* (or blogging *software*) and a Web hosting company separately.

Hosting your own blog is the better long-term choice for a professional blog, and it's your only choice if you plan to add the blog to an existing Web site. You have to do more work on background technical tasks, such as installing software, but you have more options and control over your site.

Select your blogging platform first, and then pick a hosting company that can support it (see the following sections).

Choosing your blogging platform

Two of the most popular blogging platforms for self-hosted blogs are WordPress, which is free, and Movable Type, which is not. Another option is a full-featured content management system, such as ExpressionEngine or Drupal, which adds functionality, but also complexity.

When choosing your blogging platform, find out what platform is used by the blogs with design and functionality that you like. This isn't as hard as it sounds. Here are some ways to discover which platform a blog uses:

- ✔ **Look at the browser interface and URL.** Blogs with hosted services are easy to identify because they have the icon of the hosted service in the address bar and on the tab in your browser; in Figure 8-5, the B icon stands for Blogger. Often, but not always, the URL shows the hosted service domain, such as `www.blogspot.com`, `www.typepad.com`, or `http://wordpress.com`. In Figure 8-5, however, the domain is mapped to the blog's domain name, Mom-101.

- ✔ **Look at the footer and sidebars.** Many bloggers indicate the platform and even the design template or designer in these spots. Figure 8-6 shows a footer that specifies the WordPress platform — as well as the design template — and a sidebar that lists the Movable Type platform.

- ✔ **Ask.** Very few bloggers are offended by an e-mail complimenting them on their blog. Most are happy to tell you what platform they use. Also ask how easy the blogging platform is to use and whether they'd choose it again.

Research the blogging platform Web site. Does your preferred platform have the functionality you need to execute your blog strategy? Ask friends and acquaintances about their experiences with the platform and check out the support forums.

If your blog is fairly straightforward with the standard elements — posts, comments, a blogroll, archives, a Really Simple Syndication (RSS) feed, some advertising, and so on — any one of the popular blogging platforms will do everything you need . . . and then some. Let your budget and referrals from friends and acquaintances guide you.

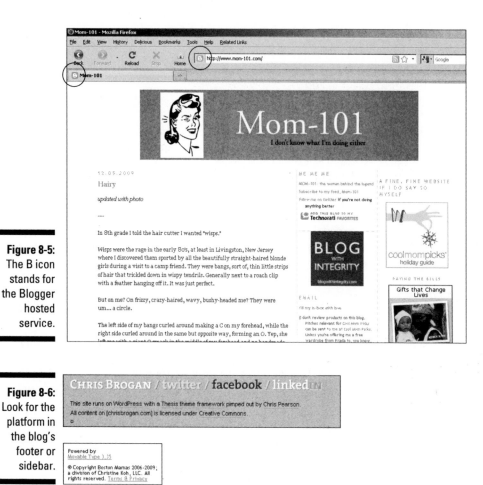

Figure 8-5: The B icon stands for the Blogger hosted service.

Figure 8-6: Look for the platform in the blog's footer or sidebar.

If, however, you want to include more complex functionality, do more homework before you choose. To save time, you may want to consult a professional blog consultant or designer. These professionals usually specialize in one or two blogging platforms, and keep on top of the latest widgets and plug-ins. They can also help if you're seeking to develop some special functionality just for your blog.

Choosing your hosting company

After you select your blogging platform but before you purchase any software, select a Web hosting company that supports the technical requirements of your software.

Most blogging software uses a LAMP (Linux/Apache/MySQL/PHP) environment:

- ✔ **Linux** is the Web server operating system.
- ✔ **Apache** is the Web page serving software.
- ✔ **MySQL** is database software. Among other things, MySQL stores your blog posts.
- ✔ **PHP** (Hypertext Preprocessor) is a programming language that the blogging software uses to connect all the parts.

A hosting company offers a number of Web hosting packages. Select the one that supports the environment your blogging platform requires. Also consider how much storage space you need for things like photos or podcast files. Everything the server environment needs to operate properly is installed and supported as part of the hosting package.

If you include a podcast or video blog as part of your site, you have additional technical and storage requirements beyond the basic ones I list here. If that's the case, I suggest that you buy a book about podcasting (such as *Podcasting For Dummies* by Tee Morris, Chuck Tomasi, and Evo Terra) or a video for an up-to-date checklist of technical requirements.

Web hosting is a very competitive business. Hundreds of firms are in the United States, and offerings, service quality, price, and reputation are all over the map. Here are a few well-known hosting companies:

- ✔ **Web.com:** www.web.com
- ✔ **Go Daddy:** www.godaddy.com
- ✔ **Network Solutions:** www.networksolutions.com
- ✔ **BlueHost.com:** www.bluehost.com
- ✔ **DreamHost:** www.dreamhost.com

Don't select your Web hosting company based solely on price. Ask around before you sign on the dotted line. Find out the company's customer service reputation. How much support will the company provide if you have problems installing your blogging software? Does the company offer 24/7 support? How much downtime has the company had in the last year? Does the company offer backup? Finally, look carefully at the Control Panel you'd use to manage your Web hosting account; is it easy for you to use?

Some Web hosting companies offer a blogging software package as an option. This may be a good deal, but don't confuse it with a hosted service. You may still have to install and manage the blogging platform yourself. Read the fine print.

If you already have a Web site and like your Web hosting company, don't change unless the company can't support your platform requirements, which is unlikely. You may need to change your hosting package options to support the new blog; the hosting company can help you through that process.

Setting up your blogging platform

Setting up your blogging platform is much easier than it used to be, and you only have to do it once. Some Web hosts even offer one-button installs for certain platforms. However, if that's not an option, you need to know that a manual install isn't as simple as running an installer to load a program on your PC.

However, setting up your platform isn't rocket science either. If you want do it yourself, I highly recommend getting the *For Dummies* book for your chosen platform. For example, *WordPress For Dummies* by Lisa Sabin-Wilson has nice, clear instructions for installing WordPress on your host.

But, if you're leery about installing it yourself, retain a professional. Here are some options:

- ✔ **Blog consultants:** A blog consultant manages the entire project for you, soup to nuts. He probably doesn't perform all the tasks personally, but he sources everything and manages the resources.

- ✔ **Blog designers:** A blog designer develops a custom design to your specifications and usually installs the blog platform. Many blog designers also help you install and modify a design template.

- ✔ **Your Web hosting company:** Many Web hosting companies offer software installation services for an extra fee.

- ✔ **Your blogging platform company:** Check with your preferred vendor to see whether it offers this service.

- ✔ **Your Web site developer or designer:** If you have an existing Web site and plan to link the new blog to the existing site, such as www.old site.com/newblog, involve the designer or developer who supports that site. She can also help you with the software installation.

If you're just looking for someone to install the software, you're better off asking your hosting company, the blogging platform company, or your Web site developer. A blog consultant or designer typically prefers to be involved in the whole project. On the other hand, if you're planning to work with a designer or consultant, she needs to be willing to do this as part of the service.

Chapter 9

Designing Your Blog

· ·

· ·

Good design is like a nice suit. The clothes don't make the man, but they sure can make him look good.

That's what your blog design does for your content: It makes it look good. Good blog design provides a framework that displays your content for maximum effect and reader engagement.

Because of the way blogging platforms work, it's really easy to try on a number of "suits," and easily change your design when you need (or want) to.

In this chapter, I explain how your blogging platform and design work together, provide an overview of your design options (including when it makes sense to hire a designer), and wrap up with an outline for pulling together all the design elements.

Discovering How Blogging Software Incorporates Design

Before picking a design option for your blog, it helps to have a basic understanding of how your blogging platform works. A *blogging platform* is a lightweight content management system. It uses a limited set of standard design elements, such as post title, byline, headline, sidebar, default text, block quote, and so on. As shown in Figure 9-1, the platform stores the design of your blog in one place (the CSS files) and the content of your blog — your posts — in another (the database). When someone visits your site, a set of instructions (PHP scripts) combines the design and the content, and renders the blog on the screen.

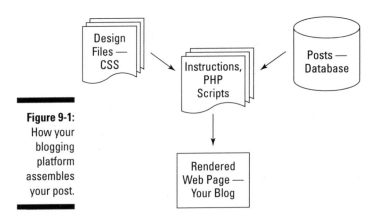

Figure 9-1:
How your
blogging
platform
assembles
your post.

Because the blogging platform works with the content separate from the
design, you can develop blog designs *independent* of the content. Simply tell
the software which design you want to use. You can easily get started with a
template or a wizard to develop your layout and formatting, and you can just
as easily change designs.

After your blog is set up, you don't need to know anything about Cascading
Style Sheets (CSS), Hypertext Preprocessor (PHP), HyperText Markup
Language (HTML), or databases to write and post your articles through your
dashboard (see Figure 9-2).

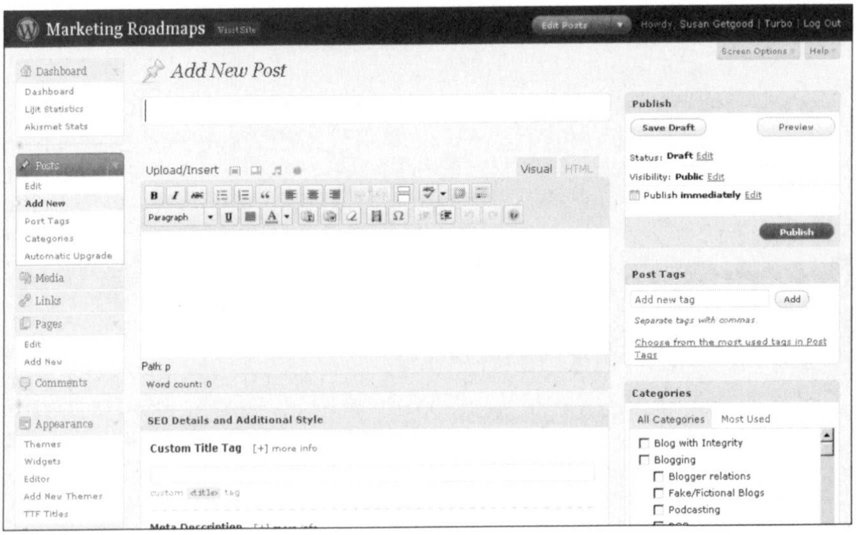

Figure 9-2:
Write and
publish
a post
with your
software's
dashboard.

If, however, you want a more custom appearance for your blog, even if it's just a design modification to a template, you have to know a little about CSS, PHP, and HTML. Or hire someone who already has the knowledge to do it for you .

Understanding Your Design Options

The easiest way to understand and choose how you're going to design and develop your blog is to break it down by how much technical knowledge is required, how much customization you want, and how much effort you're willing to put in.

No matter what blogging platform you're using, here are the three basic choices for designing and coding your blog:

- **Use a standard template (or theme)** *as is.* Some software packages also offer a wizard that builds a simple design for you. No knowledge required. This is very easy, but the resulting designs tend to look pretty generic.

- **Customize a template.** Some HTML, CSS, and PHP required. How much depends on how much you want to tweak. This option is a good middle ground, especially when you're just getting started. The most important change you can make is to customize your header with a *masthead,* a graphic that combines an image with your blog name.

- **Code your blog from scratch.** Experts only. This gives you the most custom look, but it's more expensive because you probably need to hire a consultant or designer to help you.

The questions you have to answer are: How much work do you want to do? And how much do you have to do to stand out from all the other blogs in your segment? Generally speaking, I don't recommend using a standard template without customization for your professional blog. You need to do a little customization.

Regardless of how you decide to develop your blog, you may want to have a professional designer create your masthead. The masthead combines your blog name, tagline, and usually an image and sets the tone for everything that follows. Check out the difference between the text-only masthead in the WordPress Classic template and the professionally designed masthead I use on the Marketing Roadmaps blog, as shown in Figure 9-3.

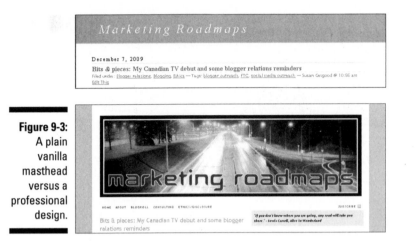

Figure 9-3:
A plain
vanilla
masthead
versus a
professional
design.

Deciding Whether to Do It Yourself or Hire a Designer

Setting up a blog is a fairly mechanical task. The tools make setting up a blog easy enough for anyone to do it, even a total computer novice, and the design templates (or *themes*) available on all the popular blogging platforms make it relatively easy to set it up yourself.

A design template contains all the files necessary for the design; it's a simple matter of following the instructions of your platform to apply the template to your blog. Some templates — including the ones built into your blogging software — are available for free; others cost a nominal fee, usually around $100. Some of the built-in templates for Blogger are shown in Figure 9-4.

You usually can find third-party templates for your blogging software on the company's Web site. Figure 9-5 shows an extensive directory of templates available for WordPress. Another good source is to use your preferred search engine to search for *blog design templates* — or add the specific platform to your search phrase, for example *custom design for blogger.* Figure 9-6 shows the results of searching for Blogger designs through Google.

Good design makes content more accessible. Most people read blogs on the site, versus in a Really Simple Syndication (RSS) reader or by e-mail. Also, if readers want to leave a comment, they have to go to the blog site. Good design makes readers' interactions easier and the blog a nicer place to be.

Figure 9-4:
Blog tem-
plates on
the Blogger
hosted
service.

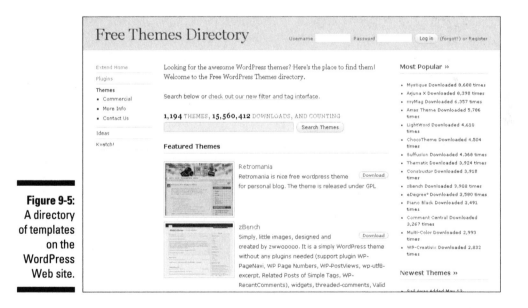

Figure 9-5:
A directory
of templates
on the
WordPress
Web site.

You can go quite far with a template, particularly if you have some skill with your blogging software and can do simple things, such as changing the colors and adding elements to the sidebars. For example, I recently switched my Marketing Roadmaps blog (http://getgood.com/roadmaps) to the popular Thesis template (http://diythemes.com/thesis) and was able to make most of the simple design changes I wanted without too much trouble. However, I spent the better part of a day getting things *mostly* the way I wanted, with a few things I couldn't quite figure out. Luckily, a friend who is a Thesis whiz helped me with the final tweaks. (See Figure 9-7 for how my blog looked before converting to the Thesis template; see Figure 9-8 for how the blog looked midway with the same design color scheme and masthead from the previous design; finally, see Figure 9-9 for the finished product.)

A professional blog designer can create a completely custom design to your specifications, help you tweak a template, or simply create a masthead and other graphics to spice up your blog.

From my experience, a unique design — one that's tailored to your blog and its objectives — created by a professional designer may make the difference between a good blog and a great one. And an excellent blog isn't that easy to create. You need a good topic, a solid strategy, the commitment to write, and a deep understanding of your readers. Adding a good design really helps get across the message.

Figure 9-6:
Use your preferred search engine to search for templates and designers.

Figure 9-7:
Marketing
Roadmaps
prior to con-
version to
the Thesis
template.

Figure 9-8:
Marketing
Roadmaps
after con-
version to
Thesis
template.

The good news is that custom design for a simple blog isn't that pricey. You can get exactly what you want, and the designer can help you with other blog-related tasks as well (for example, setting up your blog platform or creating custom graphics to promote it). If budget is an issue, some designers also help you tweak a template.

Figure 9-9:
Marketing
Roadmaps
after profes-
sional help.

The following sections go over some of the things you need to consider when deciding whether to use a blog designer or do it all yourself.

Design elements a pro can help with

Designers can help with a variety of tasks related to your blog, and you don't have to retain one to do everything to benefit from professional design. As noted earlier in this chapter, hiring a designer to create a masthead for your blog is a good idea even if you do all the rest yourself. I list some of the other ways a designer can help you in the following sections.

Making your blog match a Web site or brand

If your blog needs to match a Web site or a brand, invest the time and money to hire a professional to create a custom design that complements the Web site without copying it.

If your Web site or brand has recognizable graphic elements that you want to extend into the blog, either as part of the design or in your sidebar badges and widgets, you need custom graphics. Although you can create graphics with a graphics package, it will probably *look* like you did them yourself. Is that the image you want to project?

Making your blog unique

Unless you make significant modifications, a template is still a template; other sites are bound to be using it, especially if the template is a particularly flexible one. With a custom design, you get a unique look and feel for your blog that helps tell *your* story more effectively because it was created *for* just that purpose.

I highly recommend a unique blog design if

- **Your topic is visual or relies heavily on photography.** For example, cooking, gardening, photography, or arts and crafts all require adequate illustration.

- **You're in the marketing or graphic arts field.** As the saying goes, "Eat your own dog food."

- **Your competition made the investment in custom design.** You want the reader experience at your blog to be better, richer.

- **You have an unusual or humorous topic.** What better way to highlight your uniqueness than with a unique design?

Tweaking a template

Blog designers are generally willing to help you tweak a standard template, and many of them create their own library of designs for sale.

Creating a logo

Even if all you do is go to the occasional chamber of commerce meeting or *tweet-up* (an in-person meeting of people who know each other through the Twitter social network), you need business cards. For that, you need a logo — not cute pictures or stock art from a vendor. Although you can use a graphics program or an online logo design site to morph type and add graphics to create a logo, don't. You're developing a professional blog. Brand matters.

If your budget is really tight, you can purchase stock art from a stock house, such as iStockphoto (www.istockphoto.com), or use free images licensed under a Creative Commons license (explained in Chapter 3). Then use the image as a basis for your logo. Be aware, though, that other people have access to the same images. To really stand out, you need something unique.

A good professional designer digs into what your business and blog are about to create a graphical representation that summarizes your story in a subtle way. If you can find the dollars ($500–$1,500 on average, depending on where you're located and what you need), a professional designer is well worth the investment.

If you're using a designer just to develop a logo, it isn't critical that she's a blog or Web site designer. Work with someone who has solid branding and logo experience for the best results.

Working with a professional

Although nearly all professional designers now have some online experience, not every designer is familiar with the blog form. Many have a lot of experience creating designs and graphics, but very little experience actually building a Web site or a blog. They don't know how to actually set up and code your blog. You need a designer or design team that can do both. When interviewing blog designers, ask to see blogs they've developed from scratch. Failing to do so can add cost and delay your blog while your expert uses your project (and budget) to educate himself on your blogging platform.

Managing costs

Professional Web design used to be really, really expensive, and it still can be, if you aren't careful. Rates are all over the map, from the kid just out of high school who charges $25 per hour to designers at the top interactive agencies who bill hundreds of dollars per hour. The solution for your blog is somewhere in between these two extremes. Depending on where the designer lives, expect to pay in the range of $75–$150 per hour.

The best way to control costs is to develop a blog specification (see Figure 9-10) at the beginning of your project that outlines your goals, templates, and key blog elements that must be included. Use a specification document even if the designer is simply creating your masthead or tweaking a template. Your designer can then quote to those specifications. Some designers quote a fixed fee, whereas others work hourly. If your preferred designer works on an hourly basis, still ask for an estimate. You can also stipulate a not-to-exceed amount. That way you'll get a heads-up if you're about to go over budget.

An experienced designer working on a fixed-fee basis tells you how many review/revision cycles are included in each design phase. If you think you need more, negotiate this upfront. After the project starts, extra work (often referred to as *out of scope*) costs you extra money.

In your specification, don't forget to require a test of the design on the common operating systems and popular browsers to make sure that it looks good to all your visitors. Your designer needs to build time for testing into the proposal. If you're doing the work, Browsershots.org (`http://browser shots.org`) is a great, free resource for checking compatibility.

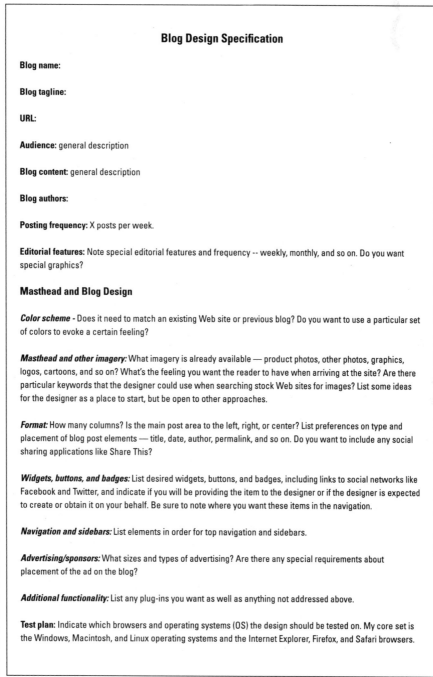

Blog Design Specification

Blog name:

Blog tagline:

URL:

Audience: general description

Blog content: general description

Blog authors:

Posting frequency: X posts per week.

Editorial features: Note special editorial features and frequency -- weekly, monthly, and so on. Do you want special graphics?

Masthead and Blog Design

Color scheme - Does it need to match an existing Web site or previous blog? Do you want to use a particular set of colors to evoke a certain feeling?

Masthead and other imagery: What imagery is already available — product photos, other photos, graphics, logos, cartoons, and so on? What's the feeling you want the reader to have when arriving at the site? Are there particular keywords that the designer could use when searching stock Web sites for images? List some ideas for the designer as a place to start, but be open to other approaches.

Format: How many columns? Is the main post area to the left, right, or center? List preferences on type and placement of blog post elements — title, date, author, permalink, and so on. Do you want to include any social sharing applications like Share This?

Widgets, buttons, and badges: List desired widgets, buttons, and badges, including links to social networks like Facebook and Twitter, and indicate if you will be providing the item to the designer or if the designer is expected to create or obtain it on your behalf. Be sure to note where you want these items in the navigation.

Navigation and sidebars: List elements in order for top navigation and sidebars.

Advertising/sponsors: What sizes and types of advertising? Are there any special requirements about placement of the ad on the blog?

Additional functionality: List any plug-ins you want as well as anything not addressed above.

Test plan: Indicate which browsers and operating systems (OS) the design should be tested on. My core set is the Windows, Macintosh, and Linux operating systems and the Internet Explorer, Firefox, and Safari browsers.

Figure 9-10:
A blog specification document that I use on client projects.

Also, if you're working with a designer on a fixed-fee basis, don't be any less succinct on your instructions or feedback than if you were paying for every hour. It's not professional.

Expect the same professional behavior from your designer. Set deadlines upfront, meet your obligations, and require the same from your designer.

How to find designers

If you have a particular blogging software platform in mind, a good place to start looking for a designer is the software company's Web site. At a minimum, the company's site has a section showcasing blogs with that platform and often includes a directory of approved blog developers and designers, such as the TypePad Services page, as shown in Figure 9-11, which includes a link to blog designers and developers that specialize in the TypePad platform. Your preferred search engine is also a good source.

The best way to find a blog designer, though, is to find out who designed the blogs you love. Look in the blog's sidebar or footer. If you can't find a link for the designer, e-mail the blog owner and ask. Bloggers are normally willing to share information with colleagues.

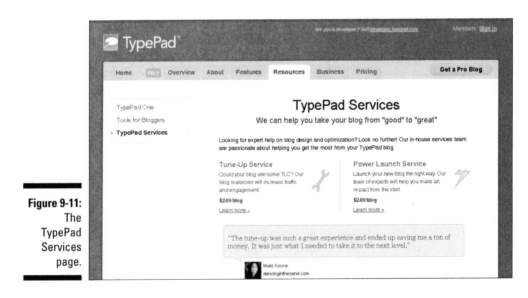

Figure 9-11: The TypePad Services page.

TypePad Services
We can help you take your blog from "good" to "great"

Looking for expert help on blog design and optimization? Look no further! Our in-house services team are passionate about helping you get the most from your TypePad blog.

Tune-Up Service
Could your blog use some TLC? Our blog makeover will increase traffic and engagement.
$249/blog
Learn more »

Power Launch Service
Launch your new blog the right way. Our team of experts will help you make an impact from the start.
$249/blog
Learn more »

"The tune-up was such a great experience and ended up saving me a ton of money. It was just what I needed to take it to the next level."

Maile Keone
dancinginthesand.com

Pulling Together the Design Elements

A blog design has four basic components: the masthead, the post, the navigation, and the sidebar(s). The masthead and the post have a pretty standard set of elements. The navigation and the sidebars, on the other hand, are more complicated because you can include numerous elements in either component. Also, you have to make decisions about the elements to include based on your objectives (as I discuss in Chapter 1) and monetization plan (as I discuss in Part II). Figure 9-12 breaks down the main elements of a blog design.

As you move through the different elements of the blog design, divide them into two categories: *artistic* decisions, such as colors, typography, and graphics, and *logistical* ones, such as where certain elements are placed in the design. The artistic decisions are about how your blog looks, whereas the logistical ones are about how it functions. You want your blog to be welcoming and easy to navigate.

Your design creates an entry point into your content for your readers. In the design, you want your readers to easily find what they're looking for, whether it's your posts or an advertisement. Your content dictates design, not the other way around.

Knowing that you need blog specifications

Before you start developing your blog, create a blog design specification document that outlines the key elements of the blog and any design preferences you have. If you're handing off your blog design to a professional, as I note in the previous section, the designer uses this document to quote your project and then as a working document. If you add or change the scope during the project, expect additional fees; it's very important to nail down as much as possible in your design specifications.

The template I use for blog design specifications (refer to Figure 9-10) covers the general information about the blog and its positioning. This document also outlines the preferences or requirements that the blog author has, going into the process. Be sure to include some examples of blogs you like and why!

If you're creating your blog, you have more leeway because you can experiment with many different layouts at no out-of-pocket cost. However, don't minimize the cost of your own time. The discipline of a written specification is useful even if the person you're handing it off to is yourself.

Blog content

Sidebar   Sidebar   Top Navigation

Widget   Logo   Post   Ads   Masthead
Badge

Figure 9-12:
Anatomy
of a blog
design.

Deciding on a basic blog format

The first thing you have to decide is your basic blog format. Two and three columns are the most popular layouts, with the main post column to the left, right, or center. Figure 9-13 shows a two-column blog, Snapshot Chronicles Roadtrip (`http://snapshotchronicles.com/roadtrip`), and Figure 9-14 shows a three-column blog, Z Recommends (`www.zrecommends.com`).

Figure 9-13: The Snapshot Chronicles Roadtrip blog with a two-column format.

Figure 9-14: Z Recommends is a three-column blog.

You also need to decide about typography and placement of blog post elements, such as date, author, *permalink* (the permanent URL that links to the post after it moves off the main page), tags, and categories as well as whether you want to include social sharing applications such as Share This (see Figure 9-15), which lets you share posts with friends on popular social networks and aggregators as well as through e-mail.

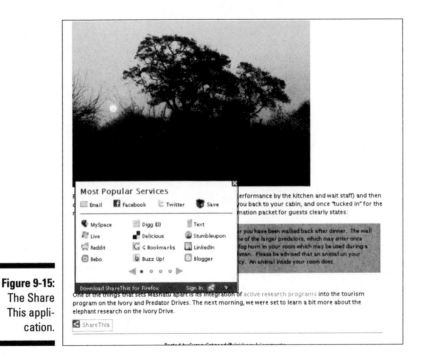

Figure 9-15:
The Share
This appli-
cation.

Before you create your masthead, you need to make some basic decisions about color scheme. Here are the key considerations:

- ✔ **Do you need to match an existing logo or Web site?** If so, use its fonts and colors as a point of departure.

- ✔ **Are particular colors more evocative (or to be avoided) for the theme of your blog?** For example, if you're a financial planner or CPA, avoid using red.

- ✔ **What are competitors using?** Stay away from a color scheme that looks too similar to your competitors' blogs to avoid confusion for your audience.

Creating your masthead

In your masthead, the blog name, tagline, and an image come together to set the visual stage for your blog content. The masthead is both the anchor and the introduction to your blog. Even if you're developing your blog design or using a design template, you may want to have an artist or professional designer help you with the masthead.

Your options range from the simplest text-only masthead to custom photography or illustration:

- ✔ **Text** is the simplest alternative and ranges from the simple do-it-yourself text on a plain background to elegant text treatments that use the font to tell the story as eloquently as any image.

- ✔ A **simple graphic background** can set the tone for a blog, even without an image or photograph. See Figure 9-16, which displays the masthead for The Green Mom Review (http://thegreenmomreview.com).

- ✔ **Photography and illustrations** are the most commonly used graphic elements in blog mastheads. The key to success is how well the designer integrates the masthead image with the name, tagline, and blog design. You can use stock images from sources like iStockphoto and Getty Images or, budget permitting, you can use custom photography and illustration. Figure 9-17 shows how three popular blogs — Notes from the Trenches (www.notesfromthetrenches.com), Shutter Sisters (http://shuttersisters.com), and PR-Squared (www.pr-squared.com) — have integrated image, tagline, and text to successfully set the stage for the blog content.

Figure 9-16:
The masthead for The Green Mom Review uses a simple graphic background.

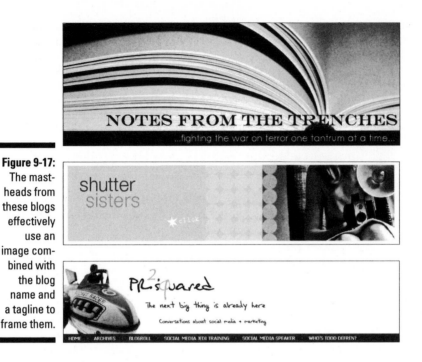

Figure 9-17:
The mast-
heads from
these blogs
effectively
use an
image com-
bined with
the blog
name and
a tagline to
frame them.

Organizing your navigation and sidebars

How you organize your navigation and sidebars is the heart of your specification document. An important step in the design process is deciding which elements you want on the blog home page and which elements can exist on separate, "inside" pages. I use the following terms for blog elements throughout this book:

- ✔ The **sidebar** is the commonly used term for secondary columns; in the case of a one-column blog, the sidebar is beneath the main post column.

  Anything that's critical and needs to be seen immediately needs to be in the sidebars and toward the top. Advertising, links to social networks, comments, and categories for posts usually fall into this critical and need-to-be-seen group.

- ✔ The **navigation** elements are links that connect you to other parts of the site or external content. You can have navigation at the top or in the sidebars. Most blogs use a combination of both.

  Any link that is critical to navigate the site needs to be in a top navigation bar or at the top of a sidebar. These include subscription links and information about your blog, such as the About page and your Disclosure policy (see Chapter 3).

Everything else can go wherever you want! I usually put the blogroll and archives on separate pages with just links from the main page. Sometimes in the sidebar, sometimes in the top navigation. Other things you may want to include in your navigation or sidebar include a Contact Us link, credits, and a privacy and copyright notice.

Sorting buttons, badges, widgets, and feeds

You can put lots of stuff in your sidebars that go beyond the standard blog elements of recent posts, comments, archives, and categories. I start with some definitions:

- ✔ **Buttons** are small, clickable graphics that link to Web content either on your site or elsewhere on the Web. Often these are used for links to your RSS feed and presence on social networks like Facebook, Flickr, LinkedIn, and Twitter.

- ✔ **Badges** are really just bigger buttons. They're also commonly used as a promotional tool. A site provides the code to display the badge, and you just copy and paste it into your sidebar, as shown in Figure 9-18. No need to download the image.

- ✔ **Widgets** typically contain functionality. These are options such as a search feature, friends and fan lists, blogrolls, recent visitors, shared links, Twitter posts, and RSS feeds. Badges don't change; widget content does.

To add any of these elements to your blog, follow the instructions of your platform to edit the sidebar file. Some blogging software makes adding elements easy, for example, with drag-and-drop widgets. In other software, you have to roll up your sleeves and edit the sidebar file directly.

Figure 9-18: Display badges in your sidebar, using simple Web code.

GET THE BADGE

To place a Blog With Integrity badge on your site, simply copy and paste the below code (125 or 150 pixel square button) into the desired location of your HTML.

For bloggers:

BLOG WITH INTEGRITY
blogwithintegrity.com

```
<a href="http://www.blogwithintegrity.com/"><img
src="http://www.blogwithintegrity.com/badges/BWI_125sq.jpg"
border="0" alt="BlogWithIntegrity.com"/></a>
```

Here's some general guidance for working with badges, buttons, and widgets:

- ✔ **Create badges and widgets that others may download to promote your blog.** You can easily create content widgets by using Widgetbox (`www.widgetbox.com`). (See Figure 1-1 in Chapter 1.)

- ✔ **Think carefully about the external badges and widgets you include in your sidebar.** This is valuable real estate. Does the badge really belong in your neighborhood?

- ✔ **Organize by categories if you can.** For example, in the blog Meal Makeover Moms' Kitchen (`http://mealmakeovermoms.com/kitchen`, refer to Figure 9-12), the buttons, badges, and widgets in the left sidebar are generally about connecting with the authors, other bloggers, or the blog itself, and the ones on the right are mostly about looking for things, whether it's content on the blog or other food blogs.

- ✔ **If you're active in public social networks (Twitter, Facebook, LinkedIn, Flickr, or YouTube), include links to your presence on your blog.** Often, you have a choice among button, badge, or widget. A good rule of thumb: If your content on the social site changes frequently, a widget that displays recent content can be very effective. Otherwise, stick to a badge or a button.

Adding additional functionality

You can add functionality, such as shopping carts, polls, and discussion forums, to your blog with software programs that integrate with your blogging platform. These can be widgets that display on your blog or programs that operate in the background. You can also add functionality with custom applications.

Your blog specification document needs to include any special functionality you want on your blog. If you're working with a blog developer, just outline what you want to accomplish in the specification; she can find the appropriate tool or connect you with a developer who can create it for you. If you do your blog on your own, check out the developer forum and plug-in or widget directory for your platform.

Adding additional functionality can get complicated. Even if you do your blog development, you may want to consult a pro.

Be sure that custom development benefits merit this path before going down it; it's generally less expensive if you can accomplish your goals with supported programs that will be updated when your blogging software is. When you do custom development, you're responsible for keeping it compatible with your blogging platform. This adds cost down the road.

Incorporating advertising

The final consideration when outlining the contents of your blog sidebars is advertising. For instance, what kind of advertising — graphic, text, or some combination of both? Do you need to install widgets on your blog that connect to an advertising network and automatically download ads in the appropriate spot? If you're part of an advertising network, does it have special requirements for participation; for example, requiring that its advertising appear in a certain place on your blog? If you're selling ads directly, you need a page with your advertising rates. You may also want to run *house* ads for your own products, services, and content.

Online display, or graphic ads, could come in any size, but the industry has standardized the sizes and positions, as I cover in Chapter 6. When designing your blog, the important consideration is how the advertising will affect the overall look of it. The Z Recommends blog (refer to Figure 9-14) and the Boston Mamas blog (www.bostonmamas.com, see Figure 9-19), show how two popular blogs resolve this question. For instance, the Boston Mamas blog runs an ad banner over the masthead and two sidebar columns of ads on the right.

Figure 9-19:
Boston
Mamas runs
ads over
the top and
at the right
side.

Chapter 10

Developing Your Blog Content

· ·

· ·

*I*n Part I, you discover how to sketch a preliminary plan (see Chapter 1) and an editorial mission (see Chapter 2) for your blog. Part II covers monetization options so you can plan your blog design to accommodate the right advertising choices for your business. Finally, in the first two chapters of Part III, you explore the technical nuts and bolts of blog design and development.

Now you're ready to write. Almost. First, you have to put the final touches on your strategy. After all, the best-designed and positioned blog is ineffective unless the content meets the readers' needs. Readers appreciate your efforts to make the blog look good and function well, but they come to read what you have to say about your topic and then discuss it with you — in your comments, on social networks, and on their own blogs. Good blog content tells your story in a compelling, interesting way, and that's what gets the conversation started.

In this chapter, I help you complete your blog by offering you a framework for developing and presenting your blog's content. I go over finding your *voice* (the subtleties of presentation that distinguish your writing), developing an editorial calendar for your blog, building a *blogroll* (a list of recommended blogs that you promote on your site), setting a commenting policy, and writing your first few posts.

Putting the Final Touches on Your Strategy

If you're reading this book in order, you probably noticed that I chunk the development of your blog into relatively discrete sequential steps:

1. **Outline your business strategy.**

   Start by setting your objectives, identifying your audience, and analyzing the competition to develop a unique niche for your professional blogging effort.

2. **Determine your editorial mission.**

   The editorial mission is your charter; it simply states what you're going to write about, why readers will care, and why you're the best person to do it.

3. **Establish a monetization plan.**

   There are a number of ways to make money with a blog. To choose the right methods for your blog, you have to consider your objectives, your audience, and how hard you want to work at your blog.

4. **Decide on site development and design.**

   These are the mechanics of building and presenting your blog so your story can shine through.

This presentation isn't accidental, or just because it matches the *For Dummies* book format. Although all these earlier steps relate to your ultimate goal of creating a successful professional blog, they're stand-alone tasks that can and should be done in order, as each one flows logically into the next phase of blog development.

After you complete the design phase, however, you're ready to pull together your business and editorial strategies, execute your monetization plan, and put your exceptional design to its best use. You do so with your content — your posts, links, and comments — which appear together on the page.

Your voice is the glue that holds together all the elements of your blog. And defining your voice is the essential final phase that fortifies your strategy.

Finding Your Voice

In the simplest terms, your *voice* is your writing style. Everything in written form has a voice. Even academic writing, dull as it may seem, has a voice; it's just not a particularly exciting one.

Don't get hung up on style and think that you need to follow a bunch of rules and regulations regarding how you should write your blog — except for basic grammar and spelling, which are really important. Nothing says *unprofessional* like typos, spelling mistakes, and bad grammar.

Your voice on your blog is *your* writing style that lets *your* personality and passions shine through. Elements that help define your voice include

- ✔ **The passion that inspired your blog in the first place:** Let your excitement about sharing your topic with your readers show.

- ✔ **The topics you choose to cover:** Your topics are the crucial starting point for the conversation.

- ✔ **The theme and name you give your blog:** These elements establish an entry point into your content that your readers can identify with.

Setting appropriate boundaries

To some degree, your authentic voice defines itself as you write, but think about the persona you want to present online. How much of yourself are you willing to share? Personal experiences? Political leanings? Religious views? What are your boundaries for sharing information with your readers? Where do you draw the line?

There is no single right answer. You need to let your own comfort level, and that of your friends and family, guide you. For example, if your spouse is a very private person, she may not want to appear on your blog under her own name — or even at all. Many women bloggers with husbands who are sensitive about this issue blog under a maiden name, even if they've legally changed it. Likewise, older children may be uncomfortable having you tell stories about them.

You can use pseudonyms for friends and family members; however, I don't recommend that you blog anonymously or mask your own identity on your professional blog. Doing so limits your opportunities because companies may be less likely to work with someone they can't check out. More about that in Chapter 12.

Here are some things you can do to navigate this challenge:

- ✔ **Use a different last name from your family.** I use a different last name than my husband and son. That protects their privacy to some degree, although the connection isn't really hidden.

- ✔ **Think before you write.** My son is ten. I talk about him on blogs, and he is a central part of my family travel blog, but I am careful to avoid telling stories that might embarrass him when he gets older.

✔ **Save some material for your personal blog.** I don't hide my political or religious views, but I don't write about them on my professional marketing blog.

Coordinating voice for a multiple-author blog

Setting a consistent voice is particularly important if you have multiple authors. You need to set some editorial guidelines for your writers so you can create a distinct voice that reflects both your authors and your brand. These guidelines don't have to be rigid or complicated, but everyone needs to know how much of themselves to reveal.

At a minimum, editorial guidelines for a multiple-author blog need to address the following points:

✔ **Voice:** Should each author have his own personality, a consistent single voice for the blog, or some blend of the two? Give some examples, so your writers know what to do.

✔ **Format:** Define a standard format for posts. Posts of the same type (review, opinion, and narrative) need to have the same elements, formatted in the same way. Your blog design can carry some of this burden, but a few elements are always at the author's discretion.

✔ **Comments:** Who responds to comments? The editors, the individual authors, or both?

✔ **Editorial process:** Is the post edited prior to publication? For content, for grammar and typos, or not at all?

Creating the Editorial Calendar

Your *editorial calendar* is the itinerary for your blogging journey; it lends structure to the voice portrayed in your written word. Creating your editorial calendar is like making a road map for your content to follow and is very similar to what a magazine editor does when planning an issue.

If your blog is a personal narrative, it's tempting to think that you don't need a framework and schedule for your posts. However, most blogs — even personal stories — benefit from a little discipline. If you blog without an editorial calendar, you start from scratch every day. Make it easier on yourself with a little structure.

Wading through the creation process

Your editorial calendar provides consistency for your blog and lets your readers know what to expect; it also helps you manage your time. Some post types are short and pithy; others are a long, thoughtful exposition. When you're busy, you can write one of the shorter types and save the longer posts for when you have more time.

The editorial calendar is just a guideline to help you write your blog. The calendar isn't set in stone. You can always swap things around if you need to; after all, it's *your* blog.

Creating an editorial calendar is a two-step process:

1. **Construct an editorial framework that identifies the type of posts you intend to write.**

   You can have more than one type of post on your blog. In addition to type, the framework you construct includes information such as *frequency* (how often you post), length, author qualifications (for multi-author blogs and guest posts), art and multimedia requirements, and any special requirements related to the subject matter or external considerations. Table 10-1 gives examples of some common types of posts and their potential characteristics. Use this table to outline the type of posts you'll have on your blog every week.

2. **With your framework, outline (or schedule) your editorial calendar of specific posts.**

   For a single-author blog, you can probably create your editorial calendar weekly and adjust the schedule as necessary if news breaks that you want to cover instead. For a multi-author blog, schedule posts for at least a month at a time, and have a backup plan in case someone doesn't meet a deadline. Here are the key things you need to include in your editorial calendar:

   - *Date of post:* Proposed posting date

   - *Post type:* From your framework

   - *Proposed topic/title:* Description of the post contents and title

   - *Author(s):* The assigned author(s)

   - *Art:* Any art needed and source

   - *Multimedia:* Any mutimedia needed, source, and schedule

   - *Deadline:* Due date (guest posts and multi-author blogs)

Unlike a print magazine, which is subject to printing and distribution time-lines, your blog publishes instantaneously, allowing you to make adjustments and changes up to the last minute. For instance, if you scheduled a review for Tuesday but something happens in the news that you want to comment on, you can change your type of post on-the-fly. You can also schedule posts for a specific time, which is very helpful if you publish multiple posts in a single day and want to spread them out, or are going to be away but want the blog to stay active.

Table 10-1	Type and Characteristics of Blog Posts			
Type	*Typical Length*	*Author Qualifications*	*Art or Multimedia Required*	*Special Considerations*
Daily narrative	Any length	None	Optional (graphic, audio, or video to support narrative)	
Structured essay	Long	Topic expertise	Optional	Cite sources and include outbound links. Fact check.
Review (for example, product, restaurant, or travel)	1–10 paragraphs	Experience with item/service reviewed	Yes; photo or video	Include outbound links and disclosure statement. Include buying information and affiliate links. Fact check.
Opinion/ criticism	Any length	Topic expertise	Optional	Cite sources and include outbound links.
Podcast/ video — summary, with links to multimedia content	Short, 1–4 paragraphs to summarize the multimedia content	Production skill for audio or video	Yes; podcast or video	

Type	Typical Length	Author Qualifications	Art or Multimedia Required	Special Considerations
Promotion or contest	Any length but preferably short; 1–4 paragraphs to explain the contest	None	Yes; photo or graphic	Terms and conditions for contest must be included in the post.
News and analysis	Any length but typically short; 1–4 paragraphs	Topic expertise	Yes; graphic, photo or embed a video from the news source	Cite sources and include outbound links. Fact check.
Recipe or instructions	Varies depending on topic	Topic expertise	Yes; photos or video demonstrating steps	Include buying information for ingredients or materials and affiliate links.
Roundup or top ten lists	At least 4–5 items with 1 short paragraph each for a roundup; 10 items in a top ten list	None	Optional	Roundups of posts from your blog or other blogs, and top ten lists are good space fillers.
Buying guides	Long	Usually multi-author	Yes; product photos or videos	Include outbound links and disclosure statement. Include buying information and affiliate links. Fact check.

The framework sets out what kind of posts you plan to have on your blog. The editorial calendar is a specific schedule.

For example, the Meal Makeover Moms' Kitchen (`http://mealmakeover moms.com/kitchen`), a food and recipe blog that focuses on healthy eating written by registered dieticians Janice Newell Bissex and Liz Weiss, runs the following types of posts:

- ✔ Podcast
- ✔ Recipe
- ✔ Narrative
- ✔ Review
- ✔ Promotion or contest

They post twice a week, usually on Mondays and Wednesdays. Their podcast and podcast post are the centerpieces of their site and are published every Wednesday. The other post for the week usually appears on a Monday and is a recipe in their "Healthy Meals with Kid Appeal" series, a recipe makeover, a product review, or a narrative about an event or trip. They mix up posts pretty well; typically, one of each runs every month. They also do a contest or promotion post every month.

Having a framework like this makes planning each month easier. Instead of worrying about what type of posts they'll write, Janice and Liz can focus on choosing interesting topics and writing compelling posts.

Mixing it up without mixing up your readers

While creating your framework and calendar, don't forget about special features that you may want to post a few times a year. For example, on review site Cool Mom Picks (`http://coolmompicks.com`), you normally find product reviews mixed in with the occasional longer essay about an event or an issue. But a few times a year — for the holidays, back to school, Mother's Day, and so on — the site posts buying guides, as shown in Figure 10-1.

I don't have a "right" answer when it comes to how many types of posts you need to write on your blog. That decision depends on your subject, your audience, and your personal preference. You can make your framework as loose or as rigid as *you* want.

For example, on her popular personal blog The Pioneer Woman (`http://the pioneerwoman.com`), author Ree Drummond covers a wide spectrum of topics including personal stories, photography, cooking, and home schooling. Each topic has its own tab (which links to a section) within her site to make it easier for readers to find the topics they're most interested in. (See Figure 10-2.)

Figure 10-1: For variety, schedule special features, such as holiday gift guides and top ten lists.

Figure 10-2: The Pioneer Woman blog uses sections to organize the author's many topic areas.

Organizing your blog into sections, like The Pioneer Woman, is one way to help your readers identify your types of content. Another is to use categories (more about categories in the later section, "Using categories and tags") to classify your posts, combined with simple cues in the post title. Using categories is particularly helpful to readers if your blog covers a single topic but you post different types of information.

For example, the blog Inside Facebook (www.insidefacebook.com) mixes news and analysis about the Facebook platform with regular features that update readers on the platform's demographics — top applications, games, pages, and overall users. Figure 10-3 shows a list of emerging apps, posted weekly, that makes it easy for Inside Facebook readers to keep up with changes in the popular social network.

Figure 10-3:
Regular features help keep regular readers informed.

Building a Blogroll

A *blogroll* is a list of blogs that a blog author likes and recommends. You can find a blogroll on a blog's sidebar like the Mom-101 blog, as shown in Figure 10-4. Or you can find the blogroll on a separate blog page — usually dubbed Blogroll or Links — as shown on the Diva Marketing blog in Figure 10-5. The blogroll includes a hyperlink to each blog on the list.

The blogroll serves two very important purposes for your blog; it

- Helps establish your *blog neighborhood* (the company you keep). Knowing the blogs you read and enjoy gives your readers very important clues about your blog content even before they start reading.

- Contributes to the process of *discovery* (getting your blog discovered). When you link to another blog, whether in a post or on a blogroll, the other blogger probably learns about your link when checking his Google Alerts (using the Link option) or other tracking mechanism.

LIKE I HAVE TIME TO
BE READING ALL THIS:

[+] NotBlogs

[-] Blogs

alpha mom
amalah
baby on bored
the blogfathers
blogs are stupid
blueschild
bread 'em and weep
citymama
cheeky lotus
chicky chicky baby
cocktails with kevin
crouton boy
cynical dad
daddytypes
design mom
fairly oddmother
finslippy
fussy
gingajoy
gray matter matters
greek tragedy
her bad mother
girl's gone child
halushki
the happiest mom
i am bossy

Figure 10-4:
Mom-101
shows the
blogroll in
a sidebar
on the main
blog page.

Diva **Marketing** *Blog*

An approach to marketing that's fun, bold and savvy...
but always strategically aligned with your brand's objective

Home   About   Contact   Diva's Blogroll

More links for you to visit Darling

- Working Solo
- Wild Woman Fundraising
- Vitamin IMC
- VITA
- Virtual Woman's Day Celebrations
- Unsolicited Marketing Advice
- The Keyhole: Peeking at 21st Century Brands
- The Association Blog
- Sparxoo
- Social Media Group
- SoCal AMA Talkshop
- Six Figure Moms Club
- Rick Short's Blog
- Resonance Partnerships
- ProBlogger
- Pandemic Blog

Blog Strategy:
The Diva Marketing Blog Approach To
Blog Strategy GO »

On The Road
Looking for a presentation or
workshop on blogs, eMarketing,
marketing for non marketers? GO »

Quote
The most exciting, challenging and
significant relationship of all is the
one you have with yourself. And if
you find someone to love the you,
you love, well, that's just fabulous.

Carrie, "Sex and The City"

Figure 10-5:
Diva
Marketing
puts its
blogroll on
a separate
page.

Creating a blogroll is pretty easy. The popular blogging platforms offer this capability as an option, usually for posting directly on a sidebar. Or you can create your blogroll as a separate page. Doing so gives you more control over the blogroll's appearance and organization, but you have to create the page and the links manually.

More important than how to create your blogroll is what you include in it and how you organize it. Your blogroll is a reflection of you — your tastes, your knowledge, your friends, and so on. You want to be sure to include a mix of sites you love and read regularly as well as sites you consider role models.

Deciding on links to include in your blogroll

To build your blogroll, start with the blogs you like best in your interest or topic area. These are the ones that you read every day. Next, be sure to include a few highly influential blogs in your sphere, even if you read them less frequently. Also, if you belong to any associations or affinity groups, consider adding links to their blogs or Web sites. Blogs about complementary topics or products are also excellent candidates for your blogroll.

Don't be afraid to include blogs that compete for the same readers. People have time to read more than one blog, and the very best blogs in your interest or topic area are exactly the neighborhood you want to be in.

In addition to the blogroll you create for your site, you may also want to include a community blogroll in your blog sidebar. Figure 10-6 shows two such community blogrolls for food blogs, BlogHer Food and The Foodie BlogRoll. These blogrolls are delivered through widgets. The easiest way to add this type of blogroll to your site is when you find a blogroll widget you like, click the Get Widget (or similar) button. This takes you to a Web page where you can download the code to install on your sidebar. If you can't find a similar Get Widget button, click in the lower left of the widget. You can also find blogrolls (and lots of other widgets) at Widgetbox (www.widgetbox.com).

Organizing links to help readers navigate

If you have many sites on your blogroll, organize your blogroll into categories. The blogroll (or links) functionality in most popular blogging platforms allows you to easily categorize your links for display on the blog sidebar, as shown in Figure 10-7.

Figure 10-6:
Food blog-
roll widgets
from The
Foodie
BlogRoll and
BlogHer.

Figure 10-7:
Blogroll
organized
into
categories.

To organize your links into categories, using the links functionality in the WordPress blogging platform, follow these steps:

1. **Log in to your blog dashboard and click the Links menu item.**

   The Edit Links screen opens.

2. **Click Link Categories.**

   The Link Categories page opens, as shown in Figure 10-8.

3. **Type your Link Category name in the Link Category Name box.**

   You don't have to enter anything else.

4. **Click the Add Category button to save your changes.**

5. **Repeat Steps 3 and 4 to add as many categories as you need.**

6. **To add and categorize a new link on your blogroll:**

   a. Click the Add New link under the Links heading.

      The page in Figure 10-9 appears.

   b. Type the required information, select a category from the Categories section, and then click the Add Link button.

   c. Repeat for as many links as you want to add.

7. **To categorize existing links:**

   a. Click the Edit link under the Links heading to return to the Edit Links screen.

   b. Select the link you want to categorize.

      A screen just like the one in Figure 10-9 appears, except the link information is already filled in.

   c. Choose the category and then click the Update Link button.

   d. Repeat for as many links as you want to categorize.

Many blogging platforms default to post the blogroll on a sidebar, and that may not suit your design. On my Marketing Roadmaps blog, as shown in Figure 10-10, the blogroll is created manually as a separate blog page.

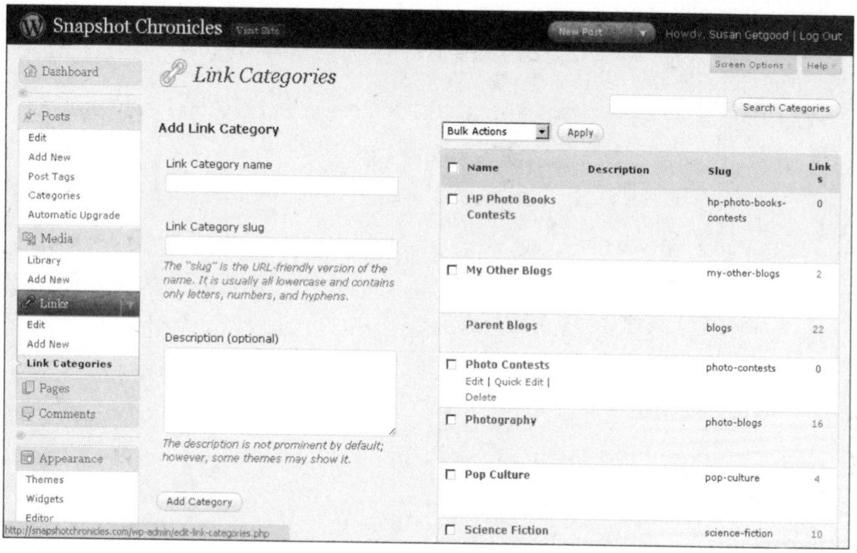

Figure 10-8:
Link cat-
egories in
WordPress.

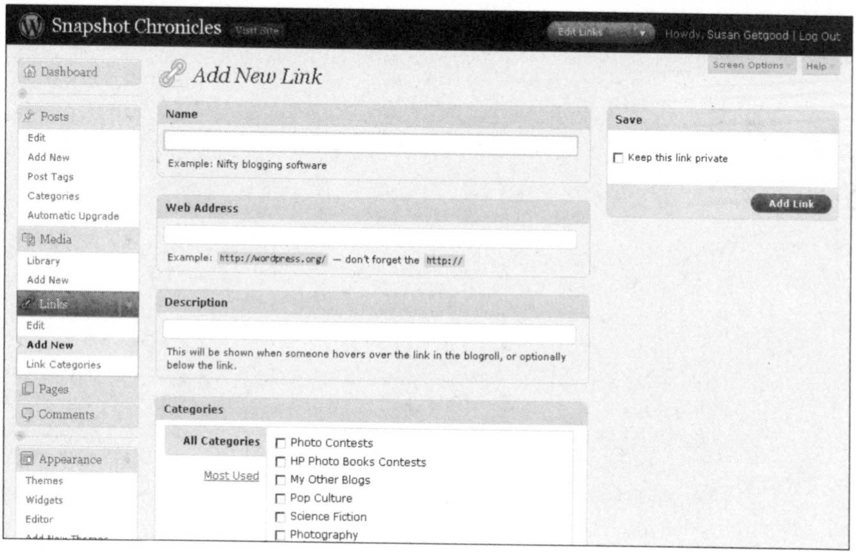

Figure 10-9:
Adding and
categorizing
a new link in
WordPress.

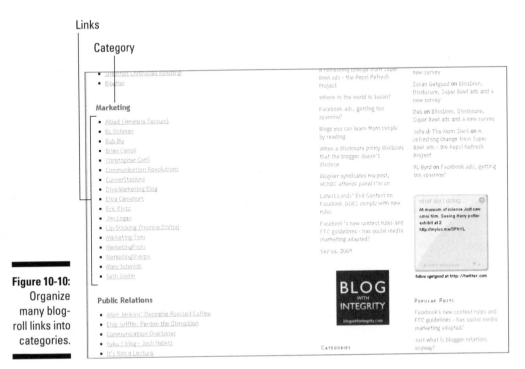

Figure 10-10:
Organize many blog-roll links into categories.

Setting Your Editorial Policies

Setting blogging policies is a best practice that helps your readers understand how you handle things like reviews, privacy, comments, and disclosure. Your policies are the embodiment of transparency.

The two crucial editorial policies are a general editorial policy and a comment policy. I cover both of these in this section. In addition, your blogging policies need to address privacy and compliance with Federal Trade Commission (FTC) disclosure requirements. I cover those, along with other legal issues like copyright and fair use, in Chapter 3.

Establishing a general editorial policy

Your general editorial policy explains the editorial practices on your blog. This policy outlines how you handle reviews and marketing offers, and helps companies understand how they might best work with you.

Things to include in your general editorial policy are

- ✔ **How you handle reviews:** Do you accept free products or services? If so, outline the kinds of products you're interested in. Explain how you handle reviews if you don't like a product.

- ✔ **That you don't guarantee to review a product:** This is especially important if you decide that you will only post positive reviews. If you hate a product, it's very annoying when the public relations rep keeps sending follow-up e-mails.

- ✔ **What you do with products after the review is complete:** Do you keep, return, or give away to readers?

- ✔ **A statement that participation in a marketing program doesn't guarantee a post on your blog:** If you participate in marketing programs with companies and brands.

- ✔ **Whether you write paid posts on your blog or participate in link exchanges:** See Chapter 7 for more on writing paid posts.

- ✔ **The best way to contact you about doing a review or participating in a program**

I also recommend that your policy include any information about you that would help your readers more easily understand your point of view. For example, business relationships, biographical information, and affiliations.

For a good, and amusing, example of a general editorial policy, read the disclaimer at the review site Cool Mom Picks, `www.coolmompicks.com/disclaimer.php`.

Be careful when using generic policy templates. Writing your own policy is always best, but if you use a template, consider it a starting point, not the finished product. Review the policy carefully and modify it to fit the policies you practice on your site.

Creating your comments policy

Although you don't have to allow reader comments on your blog, I strongly recommend that you do. Readers expect to make comments, and really, without comments — or reader interaction — a blog is nothing more than a Web site.

You have to sort out your commenting policy. Consider the following points:

- ✔ **To moderate comments, or not:** Moderating comments allows you to review and approve each comment before it's posted. Moderating comments also helps minimize spam and overly promotional comments; however, it adds latency. Because of this latency, some authors prefer to allow the comments to go up without moderation and deal with any problems afterward.

TIP

The blogging platform I use (WordPress) offers a nice compromise: The first comment is moderated, but after I approve a commenter, subsequent comments are posted automatically. This allows me to filter garbage that the spam filter doesn't catch but lets my regular readers comment immediately. If you like this idea, check for a similar compromise on your blog platform.

✔ **To restrict comments, or not, and how:** You may want certain restrictions on how people may comment, including no profanity, no negativity, no HTML hyperlinks within comments, and so on. For example, the author of style and fashion blog What I Wore (`http://whatiwore.tumblr.com`) asks only for positive feedback in the comments (see Figure 10-11).

There's no one right answer. You have to decide what fits your blog and community when setting your comments policy. A popular rule of thumb is the *living room doctrine* — before you post a comment, make sure that it's something you'd say to someone directly if he was sitting in your living room.

Post your policy on your blog so readers understand the rules of the road. Keep your policy simple, and tell your readers how you handle comments and what you expect from readers when they comment on your site. See Figure 10-12 for two more examples.

Figure 10-11:
The comment policy of style blog What I Wore.

photo by Jamie Beck

Oh hello, my lovely ladies (and gentleman). I should have done this at the beginning, but here's a quick little outline on the code of conduct for the comments queue.

1. Keep comments positive! If you wouldn't have worn it the way I did, that's fine! But I'm not looking for pointers! Everyone has a unique sense of style and I like mine just the way it is!

2. No back and forth. Short hair! long hair! Sexier! Sweeter! Bolder! Badder! Uht uhh. Drop it.

3. Weight is not up for debate. Mine, yours or that girl over there.

4. If you have personal issues, please e-mail me instead of airing your complaints to the world.

UPDATE: In reference to point #1, imagine you were walking down the street, hallway or in an elevator and someone came up to you and said "OH! I LOVE YOUR SHOES… but the rest of your outfit isn't really that great" and hopped on her way. That is how I feel about sassy comments that aren't positive. I'd rather no one stopped me in the street than to be stopped by half insulting comments. I opened up comments because so many people gave me *feedback* that they'd like to see them. And I welcome feedback! Last week I asked for pointers for the blog and I got (and answered) over 200 e-mails plus over 100 comments . But there is a difference between *feedback* and being *critical* (and I don't mean constructively critical). I'm not a fan of the later from comments on What I Wore or in real life. I am a real person, this is not a fashion magazine and if you're truly attempting to be helpful and constructive, you'll send me a private e-mail.

December 12 2009 Comments

Share On Twitter | Share on Facebook

Code of Ethics

Marketing Roadmaps is my opinion, based on my experience. Your mileage may vary. I will be respectful of my readers' views, and expect the same courtesy.

- When I have an opinion, I will be completely clear about it. You won't have to guess.
- I won't delete posts unless the content proves to be completely off base, in which case I will leave a placeholder that explains what happened so search engines won't perpetuate any mistakes I have made. Typically I will annotate the original post with new material rather than delete the post.
- I will not blog information learned offline or in private conversations unless I am absolutely certain that it is public information or I have obtained permission from the person who shared the information. When in doubt I will err on the side of caution.
- I will not delete comments unless they are spam or off-topic. Ditto trackbacks.
- I will link and trackback to other blogs appropriately, and always endeavor to add to the conversation.
- I will say thank you, replying to emails and comments promptly and pleasantly, even when I disagree with you.
- I will be honest about my clients and relationships so my readers will understand my loyalties.

Figure 10-12: A Code of Ethics and a Comments Policy.

COMMENTS POLICY

Lorelle VanFossen and the administrators and contributors to Lorelle on WordPress have the right to edit, delete, and block any and all inappropriate or unnecessary comments on this blog, as they see fit. Commenting is a privilege. Play fair and play nice.

For more information on comment policies and standards, see How NOT to Comment on Comments, Comments on Comments, Editing Your Blog Comments, Mean Spirited Comments and Blogging, and I Love It When You Say Nice Things About Me.

Grabbing and Holding Readers' Attention

Three seconds. That's about what you have to grab someone's attention and get her to start reading your post. Your headline is critical in those crucial first moments, but headlines don't keep the readers. Your whole post has to live up to the promise of the headline for the readers to stay engaged.

And if the readers can't find your content in the first place, it's all moot. That's where categories and tags come in. They make it easier for readers to find what they need on your blog and for the search engines to find you in the first place.

Finally, images can enhance your stories, so I give you a few tips on how to get started with photos and multimedia on your blog.

Making good use of your headline

Your *headline*, or title, sets the tone for your post. Your headline is an important element in a search engine's evaluation of your post, and the first thing a visitor will read. You need to strike a balance between establishing tone and using the keywords that make your post more attractive to the reader and discoverable by the search engine. Think about the terms that prospective readers might be searching on and make sure that those words are in your headlines.

As with so many things in the blogging game, there's no "right" way to achieve the tone versus keyword balance. However, the more descriptive your headline is, the better, but don't worry about using every possible keyword in every headline. Instead of using the title "Blog Roundup" for a post about different unrelated things that interest you, call it "Blog Roundup: *Topic, Topic, Topic*."

For example, "BlissDom, Disclosure, Super Bowl Ads and a New Survey" isn't the sexiest headline in the world, but the title (see Figure 10-13) gives the reader a good idea of the post content and includes terms that casual searchers might be using on February 8, the day after the Super Bowl and the end of the BlissDom blogging conference.

Figure 10-13:
This headline uses keywords to describe the contents of the post.

> BlissDom, Disclosure, Super Bowl ads and a new survey
> *by* SUSAN GETGOOD *on* FEBRUARY 8, 2010 • 2 COMMENTS   [EDIT]
> *in* BLOG WITH INTEGRITY, BLOGGING, ETHICS, PROFESSIONAL BLOGGING FOR DUMMIES, SPEAKING

Keeping readers after you catch them

Your headline is important to attract readers (and search engines) but your content is what keeps them. I can't tell you how or what to write, but I can give you a few tips for engaging your readers:

- ✔ **Write in a conversational tone, use first person, and avoid the passive voice.**

- ✔ **Add video, pictures, and graphics when appropriate** but don't overdo it — unless of course the images are the topic of your blog! More about this a bit later in this chapter.

- ✔ **Ask questions to involve your readers.** Surveys are a great way to get input from your readers and also are fodder for a subsequent blog post.

- ✔ **Liberally use hyperlinks to other sites and bloggers.** Doing so makes your posts more interesting, shows good blog citizenship, and helps other bloggers discover your blog (through their Google Alerts and ego searches). But beware of making posts just links only. That starts to resemble a black-hat practice — *link farming.*

- ✔ **Proofread. Then proofread again.** Use spell check, even if you're a decent speller. Double-check spell check for typing transpositions, such as *from* and *form.*

- ✔ **Respond to comments left on your blog,** especially if the commenter poses a question.

- ✔ **Stick to a regular posting schedule.** You don't have to post every day, but you do have to post often enough for your readers to get used to you. Two or three times per week is a good goal in the beginning; you can adjust the amount as your blog matures, depending upon what you and your readers need. I've been writing my marketing blog for more than five years, and I average about two posts per week. Some weeks, that's one long post, and others, three or four short ones.

- ✔ **Pay attention to posts that get lots of comments.** This is a good thing! Your topic struck on a popular topic that spurs strong opinions. You probably should revisit it, perhaps from a different angle.

- ✔ **Check out your analytics to see which posts were the most popular.** Especially look at page views and inbound links. And then write more of the same! More about how to use your analytics in Chapter 13.

- ✔ **Don't be afraid of controversy, but don't write solely to create controversy.** Having an opinion is a good thing. Being a bully is not.

Bank at least six posts on your blog before you announce it. Nothing is more frustrating for a reader than to discover a new site with an interesting topic, only to arrive and find nothing but the introductory "Welcome" post. Make sure that your prospective readers have enough to really sink their teeth into before you start promoting your blog.

Using categories and tags

You can use categories on your blog to organize your content and make it easier for your readers to find older posts that might be of interest. For example, on a post I wrote in early February called "Blissdom, Disclosure, Super Bowl Ads and a New Survey," I use five categories to classify the post for my readers (refer to Figure 10-13). Two of the categories — Blog with Integrity and Professional Blogging For Dummies — are specific to my blog. The other three — Blogging, Ethics, and Speaking — are more generic, but all the categories serve both an internal and external purpose for the post. Internally, they classify the post on the blog. Externally, they serve as keywords for search engines.

Figure 10-14, from Meal Makeover Moms' Kitchen (`http://mealmakeover moms.com/kitchen`), shows how you can list categories on your sidebar to allow readers to search for all the posts in a specific category. You can do this in a simple list or a *category cloud,* which increases the size of the type of a category in the list based on the number of posts. The bigger the word in the list, the more posts in the category.

Figure 10-14:
A category
cloud in a
blog side-
bar.

You can use *tags* — keywords that further define the content of your post — as another way to organize content. Search engines use the tags to index your content, and this is the most important reason to get in the habit of using them. But you can also display them on your blog, either in the post or in a *tag cloud* (a grouping of your tags that displays the most often used ones in larger type) on your sidebar, to help your readers dig deeper into your content.

If you use tags, be sure to use terms that are likely to be used broadly as search terms rather than special names that only have meaning for you. Save the special names for your categories.

For example, on my Snapshot Chronicles Roadtrip travel blog, I use fairly broad categories such as countries (Botswana), regions (Africa), and types of travel (Airlines). I only add tags when I want to indicate specific places (Pete's Pond), attractions (Stoneham Zoo), or organizations (National Geographic) that I don't mention often but which might be common search terms (see Figure 10-15). This can improve the search engine discoverability of the post, and ultimately, my blog.

You add tags and categories to your posts in the editing dashboard of your blogging platform, as shown in Figure 10-16.

Many of the popular blogging software programs also let you use your categories as tags. If you go this route, be sure to use at least one category on each post. If you don't, you've missed an opportunity to provide keyword information to the search engines.

Figure 10-15:
On my travel blog, a category is used many times, whereas a tag may only be used once or twice.

	Post	Author	Categories	Tags
☐	Blissdom was wonderful, but there's no bliss in winter air travel	Susan Getgood	Airlines, Blogging	No Tags
☐	Viva Las Vegas – My trip to the Consumer Electronics Show	Susan Getgood	Airlines, Las Vegas, Nevada	CES, Southwest
☐	Happy New Year	Susan Getgood	Holiday	No Tags
☐	Lilac Breasted Roller	Susan Getgood	Africa, Birds, Botswana, Mala Mala, Mashatu, South Africa	No Tags
☐	Mala Mala, South Africa	Susan Getgood	Africa, Botswana, Mala Mala, Mashatu, South Africa	No Tags
☐	Pete's Pond	Susan Getgood	Africa, Botswana, Mashatu	National Geographic, Pete's Pond
☐	Leaving Mashatu	Susan Getgood	Africa, Botswana, Mashatu	National Geographic, Pete's Pond

Figure 10-16:
Tags are added to your posts during the writing process.

You can use tags on your posts without actually displaying the tags on your blog. This is the functional equivalent of using the tags as keywords for search engine optimization. Just make sure that your blogging platform offers functionality that presents the tags to the search engines as keywords. For example, in WordPress, the All in One SEO Pack plug-in application (http://semperfiwebdesign.com) converts tags (and optionally, your categories) to keywords.

I use this method on my blogs because I want to make sure that the search engines find the relevant keywords and send new readers to my posts that might interest them, but I don't want to clutter the presentation of my blogs with lots of tags at the bottom of each post or in the sidebar.

Showing while telling: Using pictures and multimedia on your blog

I don't know if a picture is really worth a thousand words, but pictures, audio, and video can enhance your story. Here are some tips to get you started.

Adding pictures

You can add your own images to your blog posts or purchase stock images from photo services, such as iStockphoto (www.istockphoto.com). If you do reviews, you can also get image files from the company.

If you use your own photos, the easiest way to do this is to upload your photos to a Web service, such as Flickr (www.flickr.com), and then link to the photos. Follow these steps to upload and link photos with Flickr:

1. **Open a Flickr account and then follow the instructions on the Flickr site to upload your photos.**

   A Flickr account is free, with limits. Or you can pay $24.95 per year for unlimited use.

   An added benefit of using Flickr, or a similar photo service, is that the service acts as an additional backup for your images.

2. **Find the photo you want to add to your blog post and then click the All Sizes button in the menu just above the image.**

3. **Select a size that fits in your blog column, as shown in Figure 10-17.**

   Small (240 x 160) or medium (500 x 333) works for most blogs.

4. **Copy the HTML and paste it into your post.**

   Be sure to paste the code into the HTML of your blog post (as shown in Figure 10-18), not into the visual representation. If you paste the code into the visual representation, the blogging platform interprets it as text, not as HTML code.

You can also upload photos directly to your blogging platform, using the functionality in your software. This is your only option if you use stock photos from a service like iStockphoto or image files from a company. With the stock photo service, you have to purchase and download the image. After you have a copy of an image on your computer, upload the image to your blog by using your blogging platform's graphic uploading functionality.

If you do a lot with your own photography, you probably want to invest in simple photo-editing software like Photoshop Elements (www.adobe.com/products/photoshopelwin/?sdid=EPZYQ) and *Photoshop Elements 8 For Dummies,* by Barbara Obermeier and Ted Padova.

Figure 10-17:
Linking to your Flickr account is an easy way to add pictures to your blog.

Figure 10-18:
To add video or photos, embed code in the HTML view.

Another option for adding photos is to use a browser plug-in, such as Zemanta (www.zemanta.com), that feeds you appropriate, copyright-cleared photos from stock sources and sites, such as Flickr, based on your post content. Zemanta also suggests hyperlinks to Web and blog content based on your post, making it a very cool addition to your blogging arsenal.

Embedding video

Embedding video from Web sites, such as YouTube, or television networks is as simple as the earlier Flickr example. Just find the code to embed for the video and copy/paste it to your blog post in the HTML code view.

Creating your own video or podcast

If you decide to add your own video or a podcast to your blog, you definitely need some help, whether a book or professional consultant, to get you going.

When I started doing a podcast for a client a few years ago I turned to *Podcasting: The Do-It-Yourself Guide,* by Todd Cochrane (Wiley). I also bought a book to help me use my sound-editing software more effectively. I only use about four to five pages of it on a regular basis, but I use those pages *every* time I edit a sound file for the Internet, making it worth every penny I spent. I use *Sound Forge 8 Power!,* by Scott Garrigus (Course Technology PTR), which, of course, is only good if you use Sound Forge 8. I'm certain there's a book for your platform, whatever you use.

I don't do much personally with video on my sites. I'm still working on my photo skills. That's enough of a challenge for now, so when I use original video for a client, I leave it to the pros. However, the equipment and software available to amateurs has gotten so good, there's no reason not to experiment if you have the interest in mastering the skill. Here's a book recommendation for you: *Get Seen: Online Video Secrets to Building Your Business,* by Steve Garfield (Wiley). I haven't read that yet (although I plan to), but Garfield has an excellent reputation. You can check out his Web site at http://stevegarfield.com.

Don't buy too many platform- or software-specific books. Features constantly change, and if the book is too tied to a particular version, it may not be as useful when the next version of software is released. Buy books that offer advice on strategy or technique. They have a longer shelf life because they help you understand the underlying principles. If you do feel you need version-specific help, stick to one or two titles at most and use online resources, such as support forums and wikis, to fill in what the books don't offer.

Part IV
Maximizing Your Blog's Success

"We weren't getting the traffic we'd hoped for on our blog, so we're adjusting the server's feng shui and adding a chant in our SEO."

In this part . . .

After you build your blog, get the word out and start building your community of readers.

The chapters in this part cover blog promotion strategies, search engine optimization, working with marketers, and measurement. And because launching the blog is only the beginning, I offer some suggestions for how to grow your blog and keep it fresh.

Chapter 11

Getting the Word Out about Your Blog

Remember the quotation, "If you build it, they will come"? In a Hollywood movie maybe, but not in the blogosphere. For people to read your blog, they have to know about it, and the only way to make that happen is to tell them. You don't need a megabucks advertising budget, just a simple promotional plan.

This chapter outlines a number of ways to promote your blog. A few of them, such as commenting on other blogs and using your social networks appropriately, are musts. The others are up to you, your inclinations, and in some cases, your budget. The more tools you use, the more people are likely to be exposed to your blog.

Keep your perspective. Just as no amount of marketing will save a poor product from failure, your content is the key to your blog's success. Promotion gets people there, but your unique voice and compelling posts keep them coming back.

Telling Your Friends, Family, and Business Contacts

When your blog is ready for readers, tell people whom you already know.

Sending an e-mail

E-mail your friends, family, customers, and business contacts. Personal notes are better than mass e-mails, but if you already have an established newsletter list that complies with the *CAN-SPAM Act* (a law that regulates commercial e-mail in the United States; see Chapter 3), definitely send it.

Promoting your blog on your Web site

If you have an existing Web site, include your blog in your top or side navigation menu to make it easy for visitors to find your blog from any page on your Web site. Also include a small graphic on the home page to call attention to your blog. You can also use a simple text link on your home page, but that's less noticeable.

Using the traditional marketing toolkit

Promote your blog in any traditional marketing efforts, such as advertising and direct mail, that you use in your business. Here are just a few ideas:

- ✔ Include the blog and its address on your business cards and in your e-mail signature.
- ✔ Add information about your blog to any secondary pieces, such as brochures, direct mail, and ads, you produce. Even include blog info at your trade show booth if you have one.
- ✔ If you have a customer or prospect newsletter (via print or e-mail), announce the new site.
- ✔ If your local chamber of commerce or business association has a newsletter, include an announcement there as well.

Informing the local press

If you regularly issue news releases about your products and services, be sure to add information about your blog to your *company boilerplate,* the brief company description at the end of a news release.

Even if you don't have a public relations (PR) program already in place, still let your local paper, industry publications, and alumni magazines know about the blog. You don't have to have an official press release. In fact, unless your blog is truly breaking new ground in your field, you're better off just sending a brief personal note to the appropriate editor.

Keep your news release simple and resist the temptation to use PR jargon, such as "*Company X* is pleased to announce that it has introduced a ground-breaking new communications vehicle, blah blah blah." Just tell them about the new blog — what topics the blog covers, where they can find it online, and who would find it most useful. Include a little information about you so the recipients better understand your unique expertise and perspective on the topic.

Be realistic about your PR program. If you're the first business of your kind in your community to launch a blog, it may be news. Reach out to the local paper (and possibly even your local TV and radio stations). Reach out to the newspaper editor whose beat most closely matches the topic of your blog. For a personal blog, try the lifestyles editor; for movie reviews, the entertainment editor; for business topics, the business editor; and so on.

In larger metropolitan areas, however, unless you have something really unique, a new blog is far less likely to be newsworthy. Focus your attention on industry publications, niche outlets, and your alumni magazines and don't forget to reach out to both offline and online vehicles.

It's called a *news*paper for a reason. Your story has to be new, fresh, and compelling to capture a reporter's attention. Overly promotional marketing speak won't get a second look.

Just be yourself, keep it simple, offer to be a resource on your topic, and keep in touch with any reporters who do contact you, even if they don't use the material the first time around. There may be a next time.

Making New Friends

Making new friends is another way of describing *discoverability* — how easy it is for people who share your interests to find, or discover, your blog. Discoverability embraces a wide range of tactics, from simply commenting on blogs to search engine optimization.

Building your blogroll for maximum exposure

Your *blogroll*, or list of links to recommended sites, tells your readers the company you keep — the bloggers and blogs you read, respect, and recommend. The blogroll is also a simple way to let those bloggers know about your blog.

Tracking who mentions and links to you

Most established bloggers set up *ego searches* on a variety of search engines to let them know anytime their blog is mentioned or linked to by others. You can set up the search on your name or your blog name, and can also be notified anytime someone links to your blog. Figure 11-1 shows the results of a Google search for mentions of my name on blogs. Figure 11-2 is an e-mail alert from a day within the same time period and includes mentions on the Web, not just blogs.

To monitor a specific topic in Google, follow these steps to set up a Google Alert:

1. **Go to www.google.com/intl/en/options and click the Alerts link.**

   The Google Alerts page appears.

2. **In the Search Terms box, enter the topic you want to search.**

   For example, enter your name or blog name.

3. **Specify what type of search you want to set up.**

   Your options are News, Blogs, Comprehensive (default), Web, Video, and Group.

4. **Fill in the rest of the options to specify how often you want to be notified, whether you want up to 20 or 50 results, and where to send the notification (e-mail or your feed).**

5. **When you're finished, click Create Alert.**

   That's all there is to it.

You don't need a Google account to set up alerts, but if you sign in to Google first, you can go back later and change your alerts. For example, if you want to get an alert more frequently or narrow one to Blogs only.

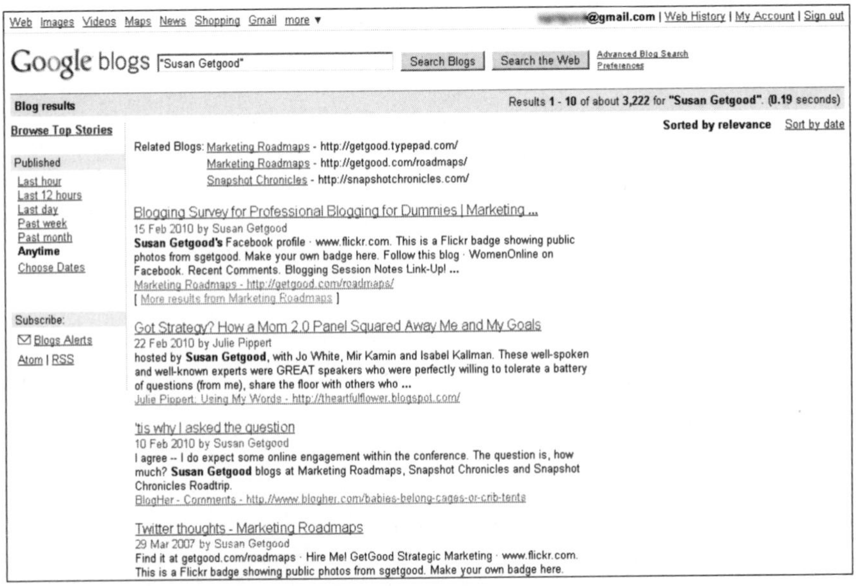

Figure 11-1:
The results
of a Google
blog search
on my name.

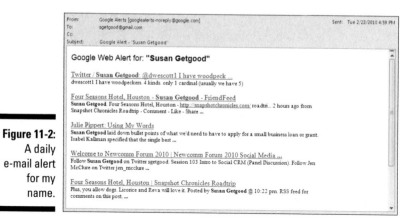

Figure 11-2:
A daily
e-mail alert
for my
name.

Taking stock of analytics

Experienced bloggers also use their analytics to understand which sites drive traffic to them. The Traffic Sources report in Google Analytics, shown in Figure 11-3, shows the sources of traffic to the Web site for the grassroots ethics initiative Blog with Integrity (www.blogwithintegrity.com).

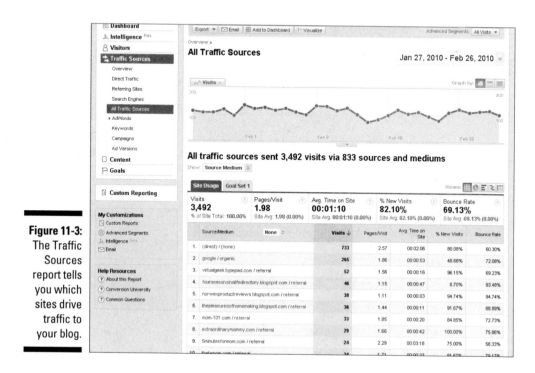

Figure 11-3:
The Traffic
Sources
report tells
you which
sites drive
traffic to
your blog.

When bloggers see your new blog in their alerts or analytics, they're pretty likely to check you out. You can also accelerate the process by sending a short e-mail telling bloggers about your new blog and letting them know that you've added them to your blogroll. For the lowdown on analytics, page ahead to Chapter 13.

If you send e-mails to the bloggers you've added to your blogroll, do *not* ask for a link in their blogroll; it's very bad form. And most definitely do not send a link exchange request, "I'll link to you, if you link to me."

Choosing the blogs for your blogroll

To build your blogroll, start with the blogs you like best in your interest or topic area. These are the ones that you read every day. Next, be sure to include a few highly influential blogs in your sphere, even if you read them less frequently. Also, if you belong to any associations or affinity groups, consider adding links to their blogs or Web sites. Blogs about complementary topics or products also are excellent candidates for your blogroll.

Don't be afraid to include blogs that compete for the same readers. People have time to read more than one blog, and the very best blogs in your interest or topic area are exactly the neighborhood you want to be in.

If you end up with a really big blogroll, divide it up into multiple lists or categories. All the popular blogging platforms have easy ways to do this, and it makes the blogroll much easier for your blog readers to use.

Writing posts with links

I mention this throughout this book: Include links to other blogs in your posts. When you link to someone else, as I describe in the preceding section, the blogger is notified of the link through a search engine alert or his analytics. That blogger will then probably check out your blog.

Linking is also part of what makes you, and your blog, part of a community. When you share and build upon the thoughts and experiences of others in your posts, you become far more interesting to people than if you just write about yourself.

You don't have to include links to others in every post, but it's good practice to do so on a regular basis. Here are some of the ways you can include links to other blogs:

✔ Link to a specific post that relates to or expands upon a point you're making in your post, as shown in Figure 11-4. This also lets you credit the other person's idea.

✔ Link to the blog's home page when referring to it in general or to a blogger by name; for example, in a post describing a recent event you attended with the person, as shown in Figure 11-5.

✔ Include the blog in a *roundup,* a post that collects a number of different posts on a single theme, or a top ten list, such as My Favorite Blogs about Gardening or Favorite Posts about the Olympics.

If you quote from another blog or significantly paraphrase it in your post, you must cite your source. Also including the link to the original is a best practice that will be appreciated by the other writer.

You don't have to agree with someone to link to them. Just don't engage in *link baiting,* which is disagreement solely to provoke and harvest inbound links to your blog. Be as sincere and respectful in disagreement as you are when you agree with someone. A good way to make sure that you aren't inadvertently creating a link bait post when you disagree with someone is to reread your post as though someone else wrote it about you. If you'd be offended, it's a good chance the other party will be. Rewrite.

Figure 11-4: Link to specific posts, such as the recommended reading on PunditMom.

Links to posts

Link to blog home page

Figure 11-5:
A link to a blog's home page rather than a specific post.

Trackbacks

Another way bloggers might be informed of your link to their post is through a trackback. A *trackback* (or *pingback*) is an automatic notification from your blog to theirs informing them that you linked to their blog. Trackbacks appear in the Comments section or in a special Trackbacks section at the bottom of the post on the blog you linked to, with a link back to the originating blog, as shown in Figure 11-6.

Most of the popular blogging software packages support trackback functionality; however, trackbacks are used less and less often lately, largely because they aren't as necessary as they were in the early days of blogging. Improvements in discovery tools, such as search alerts and analytics packages (discussed earlier in the chapter), give you the tools to find out who links *to you* without relying on trackbacks. You can then decide whether you want to link to the blogger in one of your posts.

Similar links are created in your Comments section by newer products, such as Chat Catcher (`http://chatcatcher.com`), that notify you if one of your blog posts is referenced in a tweet on Twitter. Weigh the benefits of these new products as they come along and then decide whether you want to spend the moderation time deleting the inevitable spam tweets.

Figure 11-6:
Three types
of comments
you run into
on a blog:
a normal
comment
posted on
the blog by
a person,
a track-
back, and
a comment
imported
from a
social
network.

Imported from Twitter   Link to post

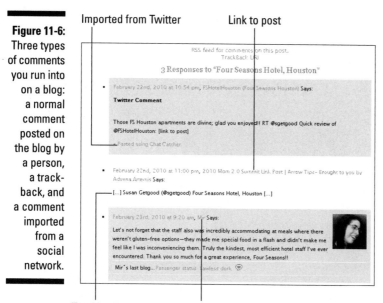

Trackback   Posted on blog

The effort is probably worth it if your blogging community uses a social net-work to discuss your post, versus commenting directly on your blog. On my professional blog Marketing Roadmaps, I'd miss about half of my comments if I didn't use Chat Catcher, and as shown in Figure 11-6, a short post on my travel blog, Snapshots Chronicle Roadtrip, managed to get one of each: a Twitter comment, a trackback, and a normal blog comment.

Commenting

Commenting on other blogs is one of the top ways bloggers promote their blogs (see Figure 11-7). To see the full results of how people promote their blogs, check out the complete survey results at my blog Marketing Roadmaps (http://getgood.com/roadmaps).

When you leave a comment on a blog post, you identify yourself as part of the community. Assuming that what you say in the comment is smart and rel-evant to the conversation, other readers of that blog may want to check out your blog to see what else you have to say.

Most blog commenting systems create a hyperlink to your blog URL in the comment, usually linked to your name, which makes it easy for people to click over to your blog. In Figure 11-6, the circled commenter name is a link to the person's blog.

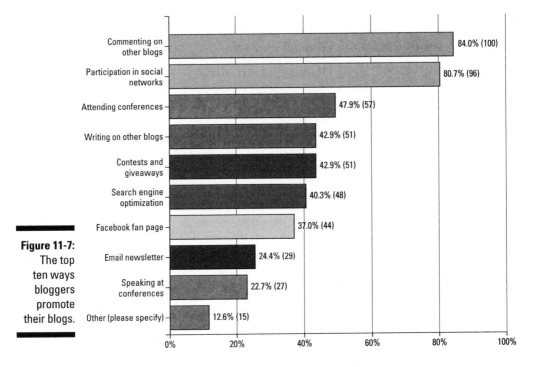

Top Ten Ways Bloggers Promote Their Blogs

Commenting on other blogs — 84.0% (100)
Participation in social networks — 80.7% (96)
Attending conferences — 47.9% (57)
Writing on other blogs — 42.9% (51)
Contests and giveaways — 42.9% (51)
Search engine optimization — 40.3% (48)
Facebook fan page — 37.0% (44)
Email newsletter — 24.4% (29)
Speaking at conferences — 22.7% (27)
Other (please specify) — 12.6% (15)

Figure 11-7:
The top ten ways bloggers promote their blogs.

Source: Professional Blogging For Dummies survey, Susan Getgood, 2010

Here are some guidelines for successful commenting:

- Make sure that your comment is relevant to the post, not simply a commercial for your blog. Saying something like "This blog is really great. Lots of good stuff. Be sure to check out my SEO tips at blah blah blah" is spam, not a comment.

- Don't simply agree or repeat what other commenters have said. Try to add something new to the conversation that highlights your knowledge and expertise — without being too commercial.

- If you're commenting about something in which you have a personal or material interest, be sure to disclose it.

- Check the other comments on the blog to make sure that the blog will link your URL to your name. Some don't, in which case, you want to include your blog name and URL in the text of the comment. If HTML isn't allowed, delete `http://` from your URL address, and the URL will probably be accepted.

✔ If HTML is allowed and you want to include a link to another blog post or Web site, don't include more than two URLs in your comment. Some spam filters assume that comments with lots of URLs are spam comments. For good reason; they usually are.

✔ Comment twice as much about things of interest to the community that have nothing to do with your blog or business as you do about things that are relevant directly. Answer questions or provide information when there's no immediate or direct value to you.

✔ Reread your comment aloud before you click the Send or Submit button. The Internet is (basically) forever, and your words have to convey both tone and meaning, especially in the beginning when the author and other readers don't know you very well.

✔ If you think your comment may be too promotional, it probably is. Take the safe route and e-mail it directly to the blog author. He can decide whether to share the information with the other readers.

Contests and giveaways

In the early days of blogging with the first crop of companies reaching out to bloggers with offers and free products, simple contests and giveaways were fairly effective tools for building an audience.

Now, the blogosphere is far more crowded than it used to be. More blogs. More companies. More products. More competition for the reader's attention. Contests and giveaways may still be a good idea for your blog to build readership and reward loyal readers. Especially if you get lots of products for review and would rather give them away than keep them. When weighing your promotional options, however, consider the following things.

Increasingly, companies are holding contests directly, either on their own blogs or Facebook (read more about that in the section "Getting the Most Out of Your Social Networks," later this chapter). This gives the company more control over the contest.

Furthermore, contests and sweepstakes must meet specific legal requirements, which vary country to country and state to state. Companies spend thousands of dollars just making sure that their contests meet these laws. That's why you sometimes see exclusions in the terms on a consumer contest entry form: U.S. only, not valid in Nebraska, and so on.

Keep in mind the important distinction between a contest and a sweepstakes. In a *contest,* the winner is selected on merit. In a *sweepstakes,* the winner is selected at a random. The rules are different and complex.

Comments and links

Comments and links to other bloggers are what create the conversation in the blogosphere. They're also the two elements that most clearly distinguish a blog from a static Web site. Blogs have comments and bloggers link to other bloggers. Web sites don't.

You need to know, however, that not all blogging communities comment and link in the same way. Or as much.

In some blog communities, such as personal narratives and parenting blogs, the conversation is fueled by blog comments. The comments form an integral part of the community. In my experience, these communities with comment-intensive blogs tend to link to each other much less frequently than other communities — which makes sense. If the blogger tells her story, there's probably less reason to link to other blogs. That doesn't mean these bloggers don't link to other blogs; they just don't do it as often as you might find in other groups.

In other communities, such as tech and marketing, the action — the *conversation* — seems to happen between blogs or on social networks like Twitter and Digg (http://digg.com). The bloggers write their own posts building upon and linking to the ideas of others or submit the post to the community for discussion on sites like Digg and memeorandum (http://memeorandum.com). That doesn't mean the blog posts don't have any comments. Or even lots of comments. Linking to each other is just more important than it is in the more comment-intensive blog segments.

Try to strike a balance with your professional or small-business blog. On your blog, link to others and encourage your readers to leave comments. To promote your blog, develop a habit of regularly reading and commenting on other blogs in your area of interest, even — and perhaps, especially — in segments that don't have many other comments.

I'm not a lawyer and this is not legal advice, but simply an observation. When the stakes are fairly low — inexpensive or moderately priced consumer products given away on blogs — the regulators aren't too concerned about the giveaways. As the stakes get higher and the value of the prizes increases, the authorities *might* decide to enforce the contest and sweepstakes laws — especially for high-value goods. For this reason, combined with the fact that giveaways are time consuming to administer and possibly less effective given the market noise, many bloggers don't run their own contests.

If you decide to use contests and giveaways on your blog, get legal advice so that you set up the contest properly. Your lawyer can also help you with any revenue or tax implications of the contest or giveaway. If your budget permits, companies that specialize in setting up contests and sweepstakes also can help you, but this can be pricey.

Getting the Most Out of Your Social Networks

You belong to any number of social networks, online and off, and you need to promote your blog, appropriately, in them all. Participating in online social networks, such as Twitter and Facebook, is another key way bloggers promote their blogs, just a bit less than comments (which I discuss earlier in this chapter).

In this section, I mostly refer to Twitter and Facebook because those are likely to be the most relevant social networks for the largest number of readers. However, be aware that online sites can change their designs and policies at any time. In fact, Facebook is (in)famous for it. Use these examples as a guide to what you need to look for on *any* network or online community.

Here are two principal types of social networks:

- ✔ **Public social networks, such as Twitter, Facebook, LinkedIn, and MySpace:** These require registration but offer no barrier to entry. Some public networks offer members the ability to create special interest groups, such as Facebook Groups, within the network.

- ✔ **Communities built around a common interest:** These can be public or private, and are often established by organizations as an extension of offline membership or ownership. Some require membership approval. Here are some examples:

    - *Travel Blog Exchange:* A community for new-media travel writers with more than 2,500 members (see Figure 11-8). (`http://travelblogexchange.ning.com`)

    - *PROpenMic:* A social network for public relations (PR) practitioners, students, and teachers with more than 6,000 members worldwide. (`http://propenmic.ning.com`)

    - *BlogHer:* A community for women bloggers (but men can join, too) that has more than 83,000 registered users. (`www.blogher.com`)

Like any group or community, with social networks you benefit in proportion to what you invest. If you're an active, engaged, and helpful community member who gives before she gets and adds more value than she receives, the community will be receptive to the occasional promotional post or mention of your product. However, if you treat the network like a broadcast channel and do nothing but promote yourself, well, let me just say that your friend and fan numbers will likely start moving in a negative direction.

Figure 11-8: Home page for a social network for travel bloggers.

Promoting your blog with your personal accounts

First and foremost, list your blog in your community profile wherever it's appropriate. On Twitter, include your blog URL in your profile (see Figure 11-9). On Facebook, you can include your blog address in your Contact Information section of the Info tab and the left display box under your profile picture (see Figure 11-10).

Find out whether you can link your blog content to your account on the social network. Facebook lets you link your blog to the Notes tab (see Figure 11-11), and you can also link to individual posts in your status updates.

To link your blog to the Notes tab in Facebook, follow these steps:

1. **Choose Account⇨Application Settings.**

2. **Click the Notes link.**

3. **Click the Import a Blog link on the right side of the page.**

4. **Enter the URL of your blog into the text box and then select the check box underneath to agree to the Terms of Use.**

5. **Click Start Importing.**

   Your previous posts appear as notes, and any new posts you make display automatically.

Blog URL

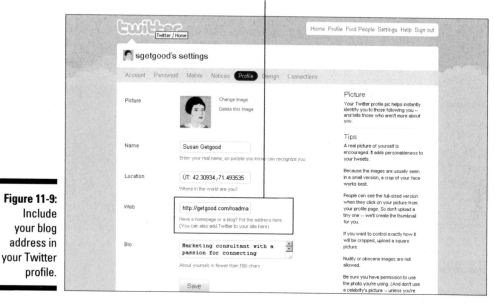

Figure 11-9:
Include
your blog
address in
your Twitter
profile.

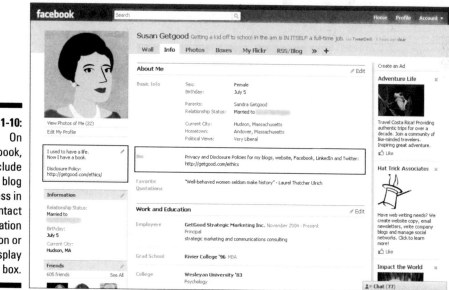

Figure 11-10:
On
Facebook,
include
your blog
address in
the Contact
Information
section or
the display
box.

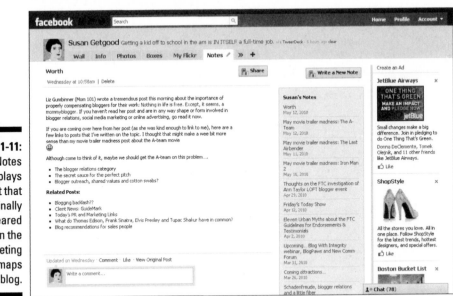

Twitter doesn't have anything comparable. However, you can change your background image, and many people promote their blog in this graphic. The downside is that this image isn't a hot link.

To change your background graphic in Twitter:

1. **Create a graphic with the desired information in your preferred graphics program (or have a designer do it for you).**

   The final file must be smaller than 800K and saved on your computer as a JPG, GIF, or PNG file.

2. **Open the Settings tab, located in the top-right menu bar on Twitter.**

3. **Click Design in the menu bar.**

4. **Click the Change Background Image button at the lower left and then click Choose File to browse to the file you want to import as the new background.**

5. **Import the file and then save your changes.**

For more on creating a custom Twitter background or to find a designer who will create one for you, just search *custom twitter backgrounds* in your preferred search engine. A simple custom background costs less than $100.

If you belong to membership communities, they probably offer similar ways to promote your blog within the community. I can't begin to cover every possible community, but at a minimum, here's what to look for:

- ✔ A place to list your blog in your profile
- ✔ A public membership blogroll

Join groups within the community that share your interests, and comment or post within the group on a regular basis. You can also start your own group, but if you do, you have to maintain it. Most communities name the owners of public groups, and an abandoned group reflects badly on your brand.

On Facebook, start groups based on interests, not on the name of your company or blog. Use the Facebook Like page for that.

Finally, promote your posts in your status alerts but don't overdo it. If you're an active participant in the social network, a few alerts every week with links to posts are just fine. In fact, your friends probably expect and rely on it. People have a hard time keeping up with everything; Twitter and Facebook updates with links to interesting posts help them stay informed.

What you want to avoid is the impression that you're broadcasting your news rather than conversing with others. I don't have any magic formula, but the rule of thumb I follow is about five to one. I try to post *at least* five responses to other people or informational links not related to my work for every one tweet or Facebook post about my blogs.

If you prefer to use Twitter but also have lots of friends on Facebook, or vice versa, use an application that sends your Twitter tweet or Facebook status update automatically to the other service. To show your tweets in your Facebook status update, install Twitter's Facebook application (www.facebook.com/apps/application.php?id=2231777543&b&ref=pd_r) or use a Twitter client, such as TweetDeck (www.tweetdeck.com), that can be configured to send your tweets to multiple accounts and social networks.

To go the other way, use a Facebook application — *Tweet* — that sends your Facebook status updates to Twitter: (www.facebook.com/apps/application.php?id=2231777543&b&ref=pd_r#!/apps/application.php?id=37869243997&ref=ts). Just remember when going from Facebook to Twitter, that Twitter has a 140-character limit; longer messages are truncated.

Model your behavior on other people in your community. If your community is link-averse, post fewer links to your own work on the network. If your community is promo-friendly, you can probably post more often about your blog or your products.

Facebook for marketers

As of May 2010, Facebook had nearly 500 million active users, according to estimates by the Inside Facebook blog (www.insidefacebook.com). Without a doubt, some, even many, of your potential readers engage on Facebook every day. You want to be there to engage with them and invite them to your blog.

The Facebook page

The Facebook page is the equivalent of the personal profile for companies. You can do many of the same things on the page as on your personal profile, including linking your blog so that posts appear on the Facebook wall for your fans. Figure 11-12 shows the Facebook wall for the review site Cool Mom Picks.

The two biggest differences:

✔ The page automatically accepts people's requests to "like" the page. You don't need to approve them as you do with your personal Facebook friends.

✔ The page has analytics to help you understand the traffic to your page.

Many professional bloggers set up pages so that they can grow their audience while limiting their personal Facebook profile to real-life friends. That's a reasonable approach, but like any Web site, you have to update it regularly for it to have the intended promotional effect.

Figure 11-12: A Facebook page is a great way to promote your blog.

Use your Facebook page to promote your blog posts, your fans' posts and activities, and Web links and stories that match your (and your customers') interests. For maximum engagement, post unique content on the Facebook page whenever you can. The perfect candidate for this is links to posts and sites that interest you but about which you are *not* going to post on your blog.

Make sure that you pick the right category for your page when you create it (see Figure 11-13). The options for your Info tab are different, depending on the initial category you pick, and you can't change your category later.

To get started with your Facebook page, scroll to the very bottom of your personal Facebook profile and click the Advertising link. On the page that appears, click the Pages tab. You can then choose to follow the step-by-step tutorial or start creating your page right away.

When you set up your page, you can invite your personal Facebook friends to "like" the page.

The Facebook like box

You can also create a like box to post on your blog or Web site that links back to the Facebook page. This closes the loop between your blog and the page, allowing readers to flow back and forth between the two and giving you further leverage for your investment in the Facebook platform.

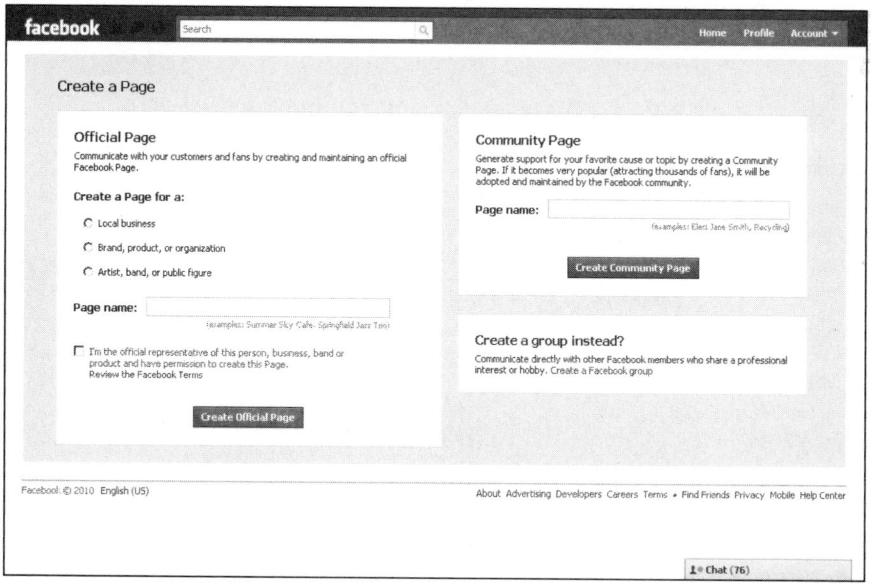

Figure 11-13: When you create a Facebook page, make sure that you select the right category because you can't change it.

When you set up your like box, you can share your Facebook wall updates, fans, or both on your site (see Figure 11-14). Readers can like your page with one click, if they're already logged into Facebook.

Facebook Like button

The Facebook Like button was introduced in April 2010. This button lets your readers share your blog content with their friends on Facebook with one click.

To put a Like button on your blog, you create a small snippet of code at the Facebook Developers Social Plugins page (`http://developers.facebook.com/docs/reference/plugins/like`) and then copy it into your blog's code where you want the button to appear. You can see what this looks like on Marketing Roadmaps, as shown in Figure 11-15.

The Like button was still very new when I wrapped up the writing of this book, but I'm sure that the major blogging platforms will develop plug-ins and add-on widgets to make it even easier to add a Like button to your blog by the time the book is published.

Figure 11-14:
Use the fan box to promote your Facebook presence on your Web site or blog.

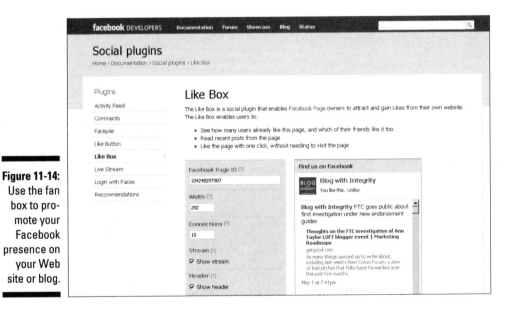

Facebook Like button

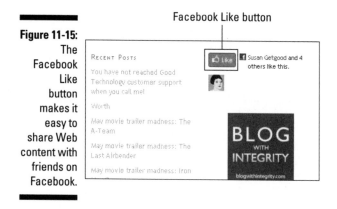

Figure 11-15:
The
Facebook
Like
button
makes it
easy to
share Web
content with
friends on
Facebook.

Facebook ads

Facebook ads can be a cost-effective way to reach a targeted demographic audience with a marketing message about your blog. Like any ad, however, you have to have a solid value proposition and a call to action. A flat announcement won't attract new readers. You have to give them a good reason to click over to your blog, such as special content, a contest or giveaway, an exciting event, and so on.

Facebook contests

Holding a contest on Facebook can be an excellent way to spread the word about your blog or product. However, because Facebook has very strict guidelines for contests and sweepstakes administered on the Facebook platform (`www.facebook.com/promotions_guidelines.php`), contests can also be pricey, putting them out of reach of most individuals and small businesses.

Contests must be approved by Facebook in advance, meet the requirements in the guidelines, and be administered by using a Facebook tab or application (not on the Facebook wall or through any standard Facebook functionality, such as the photo wall, video uploads or messaging).

As a result, you need to work with a Facebook application developer to set up your contest. The results may be well worth the cost, but I recommend starting with simpler (free) strategies before moving up to the costlier options. Only do a contest if you have something really exciting or unique that will attract enough new blog readers to justify the cost.

Facebook application developers that specialize in contests and promotions, such as Votigo (`http://votigo.com`) and Wildfire (`http://wildfire app.com`), can also help you meet the legal requirements for a contest.

Facebook applications

Many of the social tools associated with Facebook, such as games (Farmville, anyone?) and quizzes, are actually third-party applications that extend the Facebook platform. You can find hundreds of free ones that you can install to personalize your Facebook profile, and many are product or brand promotions.

A smaller but ever-growing number of applications are developed for Facebook pages. Although applications for personal profiles tend to be for games, socializing, and personal productivity, the page applications are more about customizing the appearance and experience on the page. Some of these professional applications are free but many of the ones most useful for promoting your brand or company aren't. For example, Facebook application company Involver (www.involver.com) allows you to use two of its applications for free on your page but excludes the more robust promotional tools from the free offer.

When you first launch your blog, engaging with your friends and fans on Facebook is more important than adding bells and whistles to your Facebook page, so focus your attention on the conversation, not the customization. As your blog matures, you can shake up things by adding functionality to your Facebook page with an application or two.

Facebook is an engaging social network that offers many opportunities for personal and professional connections. Facebook has also changed its privacy policies multiple times in the past few years. Be aware that Facebook may share information you post in your profile, including the brands and companies you like, with third parties.

If you really want to dig into the Facebook platform, check out *Facebook For Dummies,* 2nd Edition, by Leah Pearlman and Carolyn Abram.

Taking Full Advantage of Search Engines

No matter how popular your blog or Web site, some portion of your visitors will always come from the search engines, especially from the mammoth Google. Ideally, a new reader finds you through a search and keeps coming back because your content is relevant and well written.

Here are the two opportunities for readers to discover your new blog through search: natural (or *organic*) search and paid search engine advertisements. Figure 11-16 and 11-17 show search results for bird feeders from the Bing and Google search engines, respectively.

Natural search results appear in a central column. Paid search engine advertisements, if there are any for the keywords, appear on the top and to the right of the organic results. Google also lets you narrow your search results to specific types of content, as shown in Figure 11-17. For example, to search blog posts only, click More in the left column of the search results to expand the menu list. Then select Blogs.

Search engines calculate natural search results, using proprietary algorithms that factor in things like keywords, keyword frequency, and inbound links to determine relevance and site importance. To prevent manipulation, the algorithms are hush-hush, although an entire industry, *search engine optimization,* exists solely to pierce the veil of secrecy through analysis. (You can read more about that in the following section.)

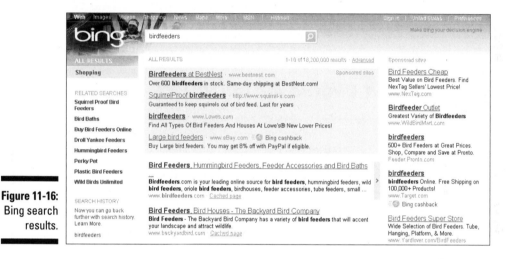

Figure 11-16: Bing search results.

Figure 11-17: Google search results narrowed down to blogs.

Very generally, the *importance* of your site is based upon how many other sites link to you and how important those sites are. *Relevance* is based upon how well the content of the page or post matches the search term. The more important and relevant your blog is, the higher it appears in the organic search results for a term. The higher a site appears in the results, the more visitors it's likely to get from the search engine.

If people search on your name or blog name, you'll probably do okay in organic search without too much effort, but that's only going to get you the readers who are already looking for you. You want new readers to discover your new blog; people who are searching for information by using more general terms. Unless your blog topic is both rare and specific, and people are using the same terms that you use on the blog in their searches, you aren't going to turn up on page one or two of search results without a little effort. That's when search engine optimization comes in.

Search engine optimization

Search engine optimization (SEO) is exactly what it sounds like: It's making changes to your site to improve your position in organic search. Here are the two parts to optimization:

✔ Changes you make to the underlying HyperText Markup Language (HTML) code of a site to make it easier for the search engines to index your site properly

✔ Writing your blog or Web site with the keywords that people are commonly using to find sites or content like yours

Your blogging platform may have plug-ins or add-on products that handle simple SEO code changes in the background. For example, I use the All in One SEO plug-in (available from `http://semperfiwebdesign.com`) on my WordPress blogs to make things, such as post titles and tags, search engine friendly without making them reader unfriendly.

I focus on the task of writing your blog posts with relevance. If you want to know more about SEO techniques, start with *Search Engine Optimization For Dummies,* by Peter Kent.

Jaelithe Judy (`www.jaejudy.com`), the SEO expert who helped me with my sites, describes SEO as

"A two-way street and a tool for building relationships online. It's not just about driving traffic, any traffic, to a site — it's about connecting real people who need something with other real people who can provide it. Good SEO helps my clients find people who are already looking for them — people who are already out there on the Internet, searching for information, products, services, or even just good conversation that my clients are able to provide."

Jaelithe says that the most important thing is to think like a searcher. For instance, what would you type in the search engine if you were looking for your content? You want to use those terms — the ones that people search on — in the text of your blog posts, post titles, categories, and tags.

Use a keyword suggestion tool to get ideas about what people are likely to search for and then incorporate those words into your post titles, categories, tags, and body text. See Figure 11-18 for one such tool: the Google Keyword Tool at (`https://adwords.google.com/select/KeywordToolExternal`). Developed for advertisers to pick the keywords they want to buy for paid search engine marketing on Google, this tool is equally useful for picking effective keyword terms for your posts.

Just type in your blog URL or some keywords and phrases, and Google returns a list of suggested keywords, along with data on monthly search volume. The default is to sort them by relevance, which is the best choice for your purposes. Use the list to pick the best terms to try. For example, in the search shown in Figure 11-18, the phrases *botswana safari, holidays south africa,* and *kruger lodges* all seem to be good choices.

But don't overdo SEO. Remember that you're writing for people, not search engines. To quote Jaelithe:

"There is no point in getting a first page spot on Google if no one stays at your site once they arrive there. Write good, engaging, useful content that also happens to be optimized for search, and you will not just attract new visitors — you'll create regular readers."

Here are Jaelithe's top tips for SEO:

✔ **Track your traffic with an analytics program.** What search engines are driving new visitors to your blog? What keywords are people already using to find your content? Figure 11-19 shows some of the top keywords people have used to find my professional blog, Marketing Roadmaps.

✔ **Identify your target audience.** Who would be most interested in your content? Who do you most want to attract to your site? Try to think like those people. What would you search for?

✔ **Make sure that you include the words people are likely to type into the search engine in multiple places on your page.** If a search term isn't on your site, a searcher can't find it.

✔ **Don't underestimate your ability to figure out the basics of SEO to promote your blog.** Jaelithe recalls the many times she's taught someone beginner SEO, only to have them say, "I never knew this was so easy."

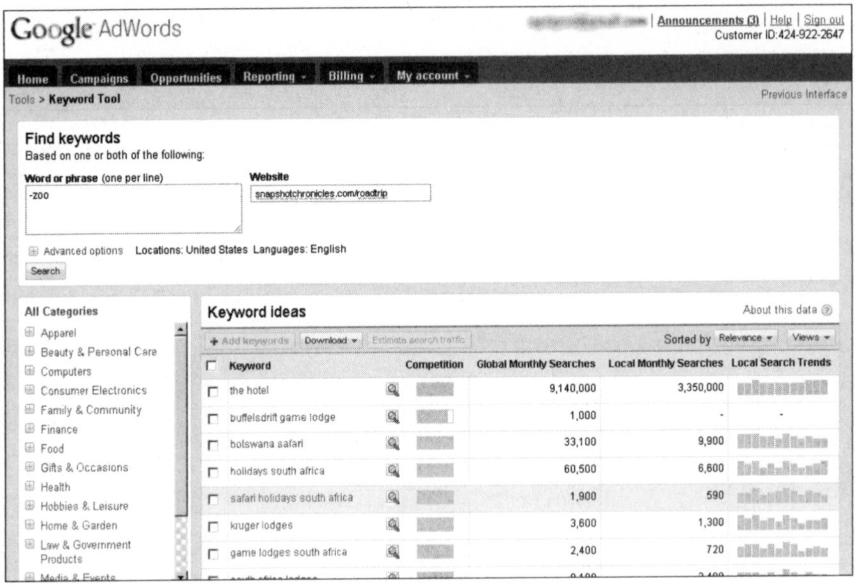

Figure 11-18: Use Google's Keyword Tool to get ideas about what people are likely to search for, and then incorporate those words into your posts.

Figure 11-19: Your analytics can tell you the keywords people already use to find your blog.

	Keyword	None	Visits
1.	what is blogger relations		34
2.	marketing roadmaps		31
3.	susan getgood		23
4.	crystal ball predictions		13
5.	marketing pitch examples		9
6.	new facebook contest rules		8
7.	blogger relations		7
8.	facebook fan page contest rules		7
9.	facebook contest rules		6
10.	facebook is a drug		5

You got here from that? The quirks of search engines

The quirks of search engines are why nearly every blogger, at one time or another, looks at the keyword searches that sent people to his blog and shakes his head: *You got here from that?*

For the most part, search engines parse Web sites and blogs pretty accurately. But these search engines aren't intelligent. The secret formulas are based on algorithms, proximity, frequency, page rank, and who knows what else. SEO specialists spend hours each day analyzing results, evaluating keywords, and making recommendations to their clients who are trying to rise in the search engine results to the mecca of page one.

So, people optimize their sites to improve their chances that people interested in their topic or product will find their blogs. And of course, they do. However, they also arrive from far stranger places. Although some of the people who took my blogger survey for this book reported no weird search terms and others said they didn't track that sort of thing, most had found a few weird search terms in their analytics reports. One person commented, "*I don't know off the top of my head. But I have learned the Internet is filled with freaks. Weird, weird, freaky freaks.*"

The following is a list of some of the odder search terms people remembered:

✔ *Kosher clowns*

✔ *Why do children lick the bottom of their shoes?*

✔ *Does Smart Food make me smart?*

✔ *Sister prettier than me*

✔ *Ghetto chicken head*

✔ *Girls are trouble*

✔ *Book devil will get you if you sing in bed*

✔ *Bangkok bicycle*

✔ *Black nail polish*

✔ *Pregnant man*

✔ *Nose in a parking lot*

✔ *Labrador retriever eat chicken marsala*

✔ *Yellow balloon cake*

✔ *Stinky sandals*

✔ *Hot moms in swimsuits*

Here's the thing: Optimize for search, but not at the expense of telling a good story or making your point. Search engines are robots. They "read" the words, not the tone. Write your blog for your readers, not the robots.

Some so-called SEO experts promote shady techniques to manipulate inbound links and create false relevance, such as link farms and spam blogs, which often scrape (or steal) legitimate content to provide a context for the links. Other black-hat techniques include using competitors' trademarks as your keywords and stuffing keywords, relevant and not so relevant, in hidden text in the footer of a site. All these tactics are frowned upon; if you succumb to the temptation and are caught, you might find your blog deleted from the search engines.

Paid search engine advertising

In paid search engine advertising, or search engine marketing (SEM), you bid for keywords based on how much you're willing to pay-per-click. The higher your bid, compared to other competitive bids, the higher your advertisement appears in the search engine results. The Google Keyword Tool, discussed in the preceding section, gives you an idea of the competition for your keywords. If you need fast results, paid search can get you to the top of the search engine results right away, but it'll cost you, especially if you're trying to rank on a popular keyword that many other established sites compete for.

And if you don't invest in some search engine optimization, you'll have to keep paying to stay there. Search engine expert Jaelithe Judy advises that bloggers try search engine optimization before spending money on paid search ads:

> *"SEO, if you do it yourself, is free. If you make a mistake and pick the wrong keywords, it won't cost you anything but your own time. Even if you decide to hire an SEO consultant to help you, if you are willing to do some of the long-term maintenance SEO work yourself, SEO is almost always cheaper than SEM over the long term."*

Chapter 12

Responding When Companies Come Calling

▶ Discovering why companies reach out to bloggers

▶ Figuring out best practices for working with marketers and PR reps

▶ Staying focused on your objectives

*T*he media landscape is a very different place now than it was even four or five years ago. People used to rely on TV, newspapers, magazines, and even media Web sites to deliver the news. Now, people rely on each other as much as on the mainstream media, possibly even more. People read blogs, chat on Twitter and Facebook, and trust the recommendations of online friends.

In this chapter, I cover how blogger relations evolved out of the public relations function and give you some tips on how to evaluate the offers, or *pitches,* that you may get from organizations that want you to write about them on your blog. I also suggest some best practices that you can use to attract the attention of companies you're interested in.

Understanding Public Relations and Blogger Relations

Blogger relations is the business practice of contacting bloggers with company or product information in the hope that they'll write about it. Blogger relations is also referred to as *influencer relations,* to reflect the fact that some online influencers are active on social networks like Twitter and Facebook, and not on blogs. Another term, *blogger outreach,* is used to emphasize that a company is reaching out to the blogger. The terms are interchangeable; I use the terms blogger relations and blogger outreach depending on the context.

Seventy-three percent of bloggers in a recent survey reported getting additional opportunities (such as participation in marketing programs and freelance writing gigs) as a result of their blogs, and offers to participate in marketing programs was the number one opportunity (see Figures 12-1 and 12-2). (To see the complete results from this survey, check out my blog Marketing Roadmaps at `http://getgood.com/roadmaps`.)

After you launch your blog, marketers *will* reach out to you, hoping that you'll endorse their product or service on your site. You may only get a few pitches; you may get hundreds. The bigger your traffic numbers, the more pitches you're likely to get, but bloggers with smaller audiences still get pitched, especially if your topic is very narrow or specialized. You need to understand the process, your role in it, and if you choose to participate, the best practices for working with companies.

For the most part, *blogger relations* is patterned after the public relations (PR) process. The main elements of the PR process are the list of reporters who cover a topic, the press release that summarizes the news, and the pitch. (The press release has the facts, and the pitch tells the reporters — in the case of blogger outreach, you — why they should care about the company's product, service, program, or story.) In practice, the process isn't that simple, but this is close enough for your purposes.

Unfortunately, the PR model was developed to meet the needs of mass media and isn't a perfect fit for reaching out to customers, and outreach to bloggers isn't always as targeted or relevant as it needs to be.

Has Your Blogging Led to Other Opportunities for You?

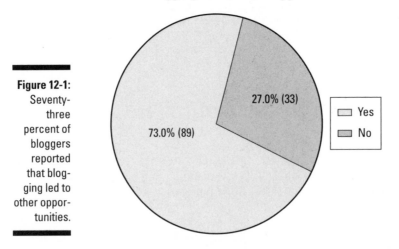

Figure 12-1: Seventy-three percent of bloggers reported that blogging led to other opportunities.

Source: Professional Blogging For Dummies survey, Susan Getgood, 2010

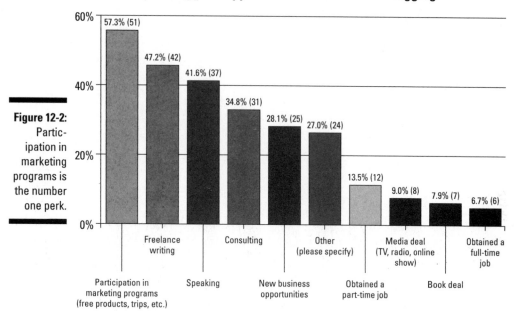

All Bloggers: Opportunities as a Result of Blogging

Figure 12-2:
Partic-
ipation in
marketing
programs is
the number
one perk.

Source: Professional Blogging For Dummies survey, Susan Getgood, 2010

Sometimes the PR process goes awry, and you wind up with

- Pitches e-mailed to Dear Blogger or Dear *<insert name here>*
- Pitches for products that aren't even remotely relevant to your topic area
- Pitches that offer zero added value to you, which are tantamount to a request for free advertising
- Pitches that ask you to do a tremendous amount of work in exchange for "exposure" or free products that you probably don't want anyway
- Pitches that don't even include a pitch, just a press release, as though you could magically divine why this news might be important to you

Luckily, some brands and companies get it right. These companies want to build long-term, mutually beneficial relationships with bloggers and will bother to learn your name, read your blog, and reach out appropriately.

My focus is to help you figure out which of these pitches are good and which ones aren't.

Telling a good pitch from a bad pitch

There are no absolutes. Assuming the company got your basic contact information right, a pitch isn't good or bad in and of itself. The yardstick is whether the pitch is good *for you*.

Pitches don't always have a press release attached. In fact, some of the best ones don't. They can be short, personal e-mails that quickly tell you about the product or program, why the company thought it was a match for you, and your next step if you want to participate.

When you get a pitch, here are some things to consider:

- ✔ Is it relevant to your blog topic? If you write about baking from scratch, it doesn't matter how good the packaged cake mix is; it's not a fit.

- ✔ Is it interesting — to you, to your readers? There's a big difference between products that you might purchase and products that interest you enough to spend time writing about them.

- ✔ Is it something you'd normally write about? For example, if you don't write product reviews, a pitch offering a product to review isn't a match even if you might like or buy the product.

- ✔ If you're being invited to an event, is it relevant to your blog and is it convenient and affordable for you to go?

Find out what other bloggers in your niche do. What's the accepted practice? For example, restaurant critics in traditional media dine anonymously and always pay for their meals. They'd never accept an invitation for a free meal from a restaurant; this has become best practice among food bloggers as well.

I also recommend that you post an editorial policy on your blog that outlines how you handle reviews and marketing offers. This disclosure is a best practice and helps companies understand whether their product is a fit for your blog. I include some examples later in this chapter.

Here are some of the pitches you might get from companies and their marketing or PR agencies:

- ✔ Product announcements, often with a contest or special offer, such as a coupon for your readers, are the most common.

- ✔ Products for review or to give away to your readers are also quite common.

- ✔ If you live in a major metropolitan area like New York or Los Angeles, you might get invitations to press events and promotional events held just for bloggers.

- ✔ If you have a very popular blog or a unique expertise, you might get invited to a multi-day blogger event, either at the company's headquarters or a resort facility. Usually the company pays your travel expenses.

The bottom line: You have to balance the value between what you're being asked to do in the outreach program — attend an event, try a product, write a review — and its value to you and your blog. If the value you get is worth it to you, it's a good pitch. If the value isn't worth it, it's not a good one; it might be for someone else, just not for you.

Doing blogger outreach that works

Why do some blogger outreach efforts resonate with bloggers and others — even for excellent and worthy products — fall flat? The mechanics of the pitch have very little to do with a successful blogger outreach, although these are important to get an e-mail opened and read. If the PR person doesn't spell someone's name correctly or addresses the e-mail to Dear Blogger, chances are slim that the recipient pays much attention. Relationships between marketers and bloggers, although important and worth nurturing on both sides, are no guarantee either.

Success starts with understanding the crucial differences among reaching out to a journalist, an objective third-party observer, and a blogger. A blogger is a customer *and* a reporter. What really matters is how well the pitch connects with what you write about on the blog and care about in your life.

The basis for the connection isn't in the product's features, benefits, or even the product's usage. The real connection is emotional, and it's forged in the shared values between a company and its customer.

This book isn't about blogger relations, but I briefly step you through the process I use to find these shared values. You may find this process useful if you ever decide to do outreach to other bloggers or directly to firms, and it certainly can help you evaluate the pitches you get.

Figure 12-3 shows my Model for Finding the Mutual Value mind map. The key to using this model is stepping away from the features and functionality of the product. Look for issues that both the company and the customer care about, and then build a program around these mutual or shared values.

I show you how to use this mind map in the following steps (which feature an example of cotton swabs, which is essentially a commodity product):

1. **Start with how the customer uses the product.**

   Family care, particularly ear care, is a key market segment for cotton swabs. The popular cotton swab brands don't even need to remind people of this. In fact, a main concern is to make sure that people don't poke the swab too far into their ears.

   A blogger program for cotton swabs could be broadly aimed at families and ear care; however, narrowing in on a smaller demographic makes it easier to find a common issue among the members.

For this example, step into the shoes of a parent of a younger child, 1 to 4 years old.

2. **Move on to the emotional.**

   What do customers care about when they use the product? What other things do they care about?

   During the toddler years, ear infections are an issue at the top of parents' minds. How do they protect their children? If their children are prone to ear infections, how can parents keep them healthy? Should they opt for surgical intervention or hope that it runs its course?

3. **Link these things to the product.**

   Start with features, but also include *attributes,* the intangibles people associate with products, and corporate values. Focus on the values shared by the company and the customer.

   To reach these bloggers — a very active parent blogging segment — I'd recommend that the cotton swab company develops a Web site and program devoted to education and information about ear infections and surgical intervention. This is valuable information that bloggers will want to share with their friends and readers.

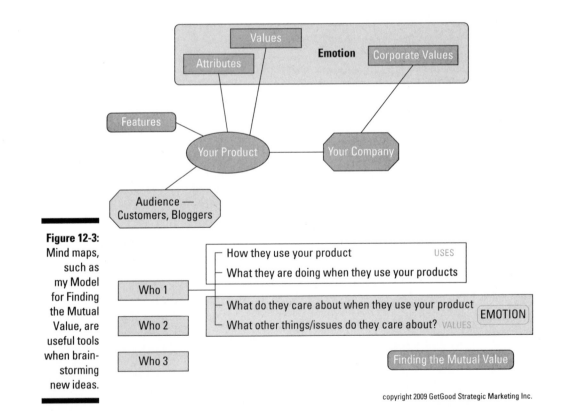

Figure 12-3:
Mind maps, such as my Model for Finding the Mutual Value, are useful tools when brainstorming new ideas.

copyright 2009 GetGood Strategic Marketing Inc.

The blog doesn't discuss the product specifically, but it sits squarely in the shared values of ear care and family:

- *Relevant:* Check.
- *Blogworthy:* Check.
- *Consistent with brand:* Check.

Developing Best Practices for Working with Marketers and PR Reps

You're probably going to get pitches from marketers and PR reps, no matter what. If you want to get some of the more interesting offers and invitations from companies and brands, however, you need to work at it.

Blogger relations is a two-way street. You need to balance the value before you accept an offer, and the company needs to make sure that the bloggers it contacts are the right ones for its brand.

Positioning yourself to get offers

After your topic, a company looks at your traffic and the level of reader engagement. Do you have lots of comments or inbound links? How many people follow or friend you on social networks? What's the tone of your posts and reader interactions?

The best-case scenario for a company, according to Todd Defren, principal at SHIFT Public Relations is

> *"a blogger who has been around for a while, has a good reputation and a fair bit of reliable traffic, and who seems to be a lucid, reasonable, respectful person."*

David Wescott, social media VP at APCO Worldwide, agrees and says that although traffic is important, he wants more than that when thinking about building a relationship with a blogger:

> *"I want to know where you have real influence, and I want to know how you measure that. Are you prominent in a specific community? It could be any community — moms, environmentalists, doctors, scientists, academics, gamers, stock traders, political activists, you name it. [I] want answers to some very specific questions. Do you have a day job that puts you in a*

public spotlight? Does a relationship with you bring with it the possibility of crossover into mainstream media channels? Do you have a relationship with a specific person or people that might be valuable to me, like a political leader or a CEO? It's called social networking for a reason."

Beyond your monthly blog traffic, think about who you might like to work with, and then write about the category and the company. The fact that you're interested in the product on your own goes a long way. Laura Tomasetti, managing director of public relations firm 360 Public Relations, says:

"We look for bloggers who have already posted or tweeted about a brand and topic of importance to the brand — such as healthy or green living — to ensure an authentic connection, especially if we want to identify a blogger to contribute content to a brand Web site, provide insight, or participate as an expert spokesperson in a brand campaign."

Laura and Kami Watson Huyse, COO of social media firm Zoetica, advise getting to know the PR reps and marketing people from the companies you're interested in. Kami suggests:

"Follow or friend the person responsible for social media. Send links if you see someone has written about the company or on a topic that is related to that company's interest. Write about the company on your blog and be constructive. In other words, you have to give a little and have some humility, too. If you do this, it won't be too long before you become a trusted part of that company's social circle."

Consider adding information to your blog about the sort of company outreach you're interested in receiving. Here are some examples:

- ✔ **Christine Koh** has a very detailed page that tells companies how to best work with her site Boston Mamas (see Figure 12-4).

- ✔ **Liz Gumbinner,** the author of Mom-101, clearly states on the sidebar that she doesn't do reviews (see Figure 12-5).

- ✔ **Amy Oztan** uses her Twitter background @SelfishMom to publish links to her editorial policies (see Figure 12-6). This is a good place to publish your policies if you plan to tweet about products.

Finally, be realistic. If you like to use strong language on your blog, don't expect family-friendly companies to contact you: You don't fit their brand. If you develop a reputation, through your blog or on the social networks, for being highly negative and critical about companies you do business with, don't be surprised if they're a little leery about working with you. Engaging in social media is risky enough for the average organization; it doesn't need the deck stacked against it. For more red flags that make a blogger less attractive to a company, read on.

Figure 12-4:
The editorial policy of Boston Mamas is on a dedicated page.

Figure 12-5:
Mom-101 doesn't do reviews (unless it's a new wardrobe from Prada), and it says so in the sidebar.

Figure 12-6:
Your Twitter
background
is a good
place to
publish your
editorial
policies.

Being aware of red flags
that mark you as trouble

According to some PR and marketing pros, here are some red flags when considering whether to work with a blogger:

- **Bloggers who don't pay attention to details:** Spelling a brand name wrong or getting other key information incorrect.

- **Profanity**

- **Excessive negativity:** For example, every post is a flame against corporations.

- **Canned outreach:** Everyone likes to feel special. A cut-and-paste e-mail in which text is various sizes and fonts is a dead giveaway.

- **Unkind or arrogant behavior, online and off**

- **Asking to be paid for posts**

- **Bloggers just looking for free stuff**

- **Super-demanding tweets or e-mails bragging about who you are**

- **Lying:** Especially hiding or misrepresenting your identity

- **Sharing too much detailed personal information on Facebook**

Saying no without saying never

Sometimes you get a pitch from a company that you want to work with, but the particular offer or program doesn't appeal to you. You need to gracefully say no without saying never.

The best way to do this is to send a short e-mail to the PR or marketing rep, declining the particular offer but expressing interest in the company and its products in general. Explain why this offer doesn't fit your blog and tell the rep about the sort of programs you are interested in. The more information the company representative has about you and your blog, the better she can target her outreach.

If you know other bloggers the offer is a good fit for, offer to introduce the PR rep; it's good karma. And not only that, but you get to help your fellow bloggers, and a good PR rep will remember your help and keep you top of mind for future programs.

If you sell advertising on your blog, you can certainly mention this as an alternative for the company. However, in most companies, different departments, with separate budgets, handle public relations and advertising. The person pitching you with a PR program probably has no influence on or input to the advertising budget. In your e-mail, be clear that you understand this but wanted the company to know that your readership could also be reached through advertising.

Understanding and meeting your obligations

If you decide to accept an offer from a company, behave in a professional manner. You may not be a journalist, but you're now acting in an editorial capacity. Strive to meet, or exceed, the standards and quality of the mainstream publications in your segment or niche. What working with you is like is as important as what you write when the company decides who to reach out to the next time.

Know what's being asked of you

Make sure that you understand exactly what's being asked of you, and what you'll receive from the company *before* you agree:

- If you're getting a product to review, does the company expect you to return it, and if so, is it paying for the return shipping?

- Does the company provide all the supplies or tools you need to review the product? If not, what do you need to provide? Is what you're providing something you already have or do you have to buy it?

✔ If the company offers products to give to your readers, who ships them? You or the company? Shipping costs can add up quickly.

✔ What are the company's expectations of you? A post — on your blog or on theirs? A series of tweets? Unless you agree *in advance* to a specific deliverable, you aren't obligated to write anything but don't run the risk of a misunderstanding. Make sure that everyone's on the same page.

✔ Does the company expect to approve your post? This is a giant red flag if the company wants to approve or edit something you post on your blog. If the company asks you to write something for their site, expect some editorial process but make sure that you understand the requirements.

✔ If you're invited to an event, who's paying the expenses? You may decide to go to the event even if you have to pay some or all the costs, but you need to know upfront to make your decision.

And get the agreement in writing.

Be cautious of pitches that offer you the so-called amazing opportunity to write about a product, for free, and then provide specific language or keywords for your posts. This type of pitch is an effort to improve the ranking of a product in the search engines, and the resulting posts sound forced and generic. Your readers deserve better!

Be accurate and fair

Be honest, accurate, and fair. If you don't know something about the product or company, ask for clarification. Don't be afraid to be critical because nothing is perfect. A balanced post that points out both positive and negative is far more useful to your readers. After all, if the company just wanted your audience, not your opinion, it could run an ad and control the message. For example, Liz Gumbinner writes about a terrific press trip to the Atlantis Resort in the Bahamas on Cool Mom Picks but cautions readers about the cost (www.coolmompicks.com/2010/02/atlantis_resort_bahamas.php).

If the story really *is* all good, don't think you *must* find something negative. At the risk of sounding cliché, the best rule of thumb is to be true to yourself.

If you get something for free, disclose

Don't forget about disclosure. As I cover in Chapter 3, the Federal Trade Commission (FTC) guidelines for endorsements and testimonials require that you disclose if you're compensated, in cash or in kind (such as free product or a trip), when you blog, tweet, or otherwise spread the word. You also have an obligation to be accurate, and if you make a mistake, the company must try to correct the inaccuracy.

Approaching companies you want to work with

As your blog evolves, you may want to reach out to a company about one of its products or services. This is a very different proposition than responding when a company reaches out to you. You may be writing about the company or one of its products and need a few facts for a post. In this case, however, you're acting as a reporter, and that's how you need to reach the company. Contact the company with a clear and professional request for information and be sure to state your deadline.

Don't wait until the last minute to reach out with your request. A PR person may take a little time to get the answer for you.

You can usually find the name of the public relations contact on a company's Web page in the News or Press section. Sometimes, that contact is just a dummy (not to be confused with *For Dummies*) address, such as news@ company. In that case, go ahead and send the e-mail, but also reach out to your own networks on Facebook, LinkedIn, and Twitter to see whether anyone you know has a contact at the firm.

The process is a bit more involved if you want to establish a long-term business relationship, for example, as a brand ambassador. You have to make a business case for why you and your blog make sense as a channel for the company's story.

In your pitch to the company, be sure that you

- ✔ **Outline your relevant background and expertise.** Tell the company who you are and why you're a credible resource for the community. Mention any mainstream media coverage you or your blog have received.

- ✔ **Tell about your readers.** Blog traffic, unique visitors, monthly page views, length of visit, RSS subscribers, and other stats help the company understand how many people are regularly reading your blog. Read more about analytics in Chapter 13. You might also want to do a demographic survey using a tool like SurveyMonkey (www.surveymonkey.com) or Zoomerang (http://zoomerang.com) to get demographic data such as gender, age, education, income level, and so on.

- ✔ **Explain how your blog is a good fit for the brand.** Expect that the company will do some research on you to determine how well your public persona fits its brand.

✔ **Present your creative ideas for how your blog can advance the marketing mission of the brand.** My Model for Finding the Mutual Value mind map for blogger relations (see the section "Doing blogger outreach that works," earlier in this chapter) is a useful tool for brainstorming ideas.

✔ **Have an idea of how you want to work with the company.** This may be as a brand ambassador, sponsorship, spokesperson, and so on, but be flexible. Find something that works well for both parties.

Communications professional Ike Pigott suggests you treat your blog like a résumé:

> *"Your blog represents you. It is often how people will form first impressions of you. If you are approaching a company about working with them, be aware that what they see first will go a long way in eliminating you from consideration.*
>
> *Make sure your blog posts are on topic. Put your recipes and children's pictures elsewhere (unless what you are selling is recipes and family values). If you are pulling Tweets into your site, keep them appropriate and focused."*

Don't approach this process with a sense of entitlement, even if the company has reached out to you in the past for one of its programs. This time, you're asking the company for something. You have to make the professional business case. That means have your facts and figures in order to show the company why you and your blog are uniquely qualified to help meet its goals.

Don't be discouraged if you aren't immediately successful in your outreach, especially if your blog is fairly new. However, I suggest waiting until your blog has an established, loyal following before reaching out to companies. Todd Defren from SHIFT elaborates:

> *"If the blog is brand-new or only has a few subscribers, I am sorry to say that there is rarely enough time to respond to that writer. If [his] requests and style seem in keeping with the clients' goals, we might respond positively later and we certainly start to keep tabs on [him] to see [whether he's] building up a good track record."*

Focus on building a long-term relationship with the company. Even if you don't have an immediate opportunity when you first contact the company, staying in touch helps make you an invaluable resource, and perhaps partner, for the brand.

Here's an example. Of late, a glut of bloggers has asked brands to sponsor their trips to conferences. Understandable given the economy, but realistically, what does the brand get for the somewhat random investment in your travel? A mention on your blog? A few tweets? Pretty superficial, and not very interesting or unique.

Now think about a deeper engagement in which the brand and the blogger get to know each other. As a result, they can work together to create a sponsorship that adds value to the company as well as defrays the trip cost for the blogger.

An example of one such sponsorship involves the folks at e-commerce site Alice (`http://alice.com`), which sells household products in bulk directly from the manufacturer. The folks at Alice got to know Kristen Chase, author of Motherhood Uncensored (`http://motherhooduncensored.net`) and cofounder of Cool Mom Picks (`http://coolmompicks.com`), and subsequently sponsored Kristen's trip to the 2009 BlogHer conference.

During the conference, Kristen did short video interviews with bloggers, with fun questions — like what household product you resemble the most to who's the cleaner in your house. The videos were then posted on the Alice Web site. The questions were consistent with Kristen's light, somewhat irreverent style and tied in well with the Alice products without being in-your-face product promotion. The company got some great promotional material featuring well-known women bloggers (some of whom also mentioned the interview on their own blogs), and Kristen got her expenses paid. A win for everyone.

Avoiding Burnout and Staying Focused on Your Objectives

If you have a popular blog, you're going to get a lot of offers. Perhaps too many to accept them all, and guaranteed, some are more relevant to you and your blog than others. Don't burn out trying to do every last one; it's okay to say no. Getting invitations and offers from companies is a nice perk, but they aren't why you started your blog.

Of the 119 bloggers who offered a detailed reason for why they started their blog in my survey, only one specifically said it was to get discounts and free products. Most mentioned personal discovery, sharing with family, a love of writing, or professional objectives as the reason they initially started a blog.

I know it's tempting to take advantage of all the offers and invitations, especially in the early days when your blog is new and unknown. However, if you want to build a successful blog, you must stay focused on *your* objectives and not get distracted by someone else's marketing goals.

More advice about working with brands from PR and marketing pros

Here are some final pointers from people who've been there:

- "Social media has blurred the professional and personal more than ever. That doesn't mean you should censor yourself so much that you can't express what makes you unique, but being online means you're always being watched." — David Wescott, APCO

- "If you are a blogger that is 'all that' on Twitter, your blog, and more, the company you are trying to reach might not know it. Yes, they can be out-of-touch with your reality, but being nice gets you a lot further than an entitled attitude. If they mess up badly, you may have the power of the pen but reserve it for the truly bad situations. Otherwise, you will get a reputation as being difficult and companies informally share this information when they meet up at conferences and other events." — Kami Watson Huyse, Zoetica

- "Be yourself. What you are selling is you. Don't try to be someone you're not because you'll never be able to deliver. Keep your writing style personal and individual. Don't get sucked into the trap of feeling like you must write in a buttoned-down corporate style. Companies have too many people who write that way already." — Ike Pigott, Occam's Razr

- "Be interesting. Bring your own unique viewpoint to whatever you do. Perspective and analysis is a useful commodity, speed is not. You are better off selling what you can own than trying to be the next Mashable or Lifehacker. You can't compete with that pace, and a week later who cares what was there anyway?" — Ike Pigott, Occam's Razr

- "There is no need to be a Tier One blogger as we certainly recognize that a Tier One blogger commonly reads the B through Z blogs and thus might be influenced by an article in a lesser-known outlet. Today's Z blogger could be tomorrow's kingpin. We aim to be respectful to all." — Todd Defren, SHIFT Public Relations

- "At the end of the day, the best bet for working with brands is to focus on making your blog the best it can be. Carve out an area of expertise; for example, as a regional blogger or a blogger who writes for a particular segment of moms or foodies. That will build and engage readers, and attract the brands to your blog." — Laura Tomasetti, 360 Public Relations

 Filter the offers from the very beginning. Accept if the offer or program adds value to your blog, the deal is fair and balanced for both you and the company, and your readers will enjoy the resulting post. If not, do yourself a favor and just say no.

If you don't say no, you run the risk that your blog never captures your true voice and unique positioning. Instead, your blog will just be one more of hundreds of blogs that sound much the same.

Chapter 13

Monitoring and Measuring: Why They Matter

. . . .

. . . .

Can you have a successful blog if you don't monitor who links to you and measure your blog traffic? Sure, you can. The key to building readership is writing an interesting, compelling blog, not obsessing over your stats.

However, when you get a handle on your metrics, you have a much better idea of whether, and how well, you're achieving your objectives. Knowing the most popular posts, common keywords, and most productive advertisers can help you improve your blog and your revenue stream.

In this chapter, I explain the difference between monitoring and measurement, and discuss why both are important. I then dig into your blog analytics as well as advertising and affiliate reports, including how you can use the data to forecast future results.

The most important thing about metrics, though, is to keep them in perspective. Metrics help you improve your blog, but they don't attract and engage your readers. You do.

Monitoring and Measuring Your Blog Activity

Monitoring and measurement are often confused because some of the same tools are used to do both; however, they are two different — but related — tasks. The best practice is to use them in combination to maximize results.

Monitoring

In terms of blog activity, *monitoring* is *tell me everything you know*. Monitoring is simply listening to what's being said, or written, about you, such as who's linking to your blog, or talking about you and your ideas. Monitoring is more than an ego search; it's critical to managing your brand and personal reputation as well as protecting your copyrights and trademarks. Monitoring also helps you understand reader and community attitudes about your blog or products.

Because most experienced bloggers monitor, you can take advantage of this to promote your blog by linking to them or commenting, as I discuss in Chapter 11.

Your main sources of monitoring data are

- ✔ **Alerts from monitoring services:** The most commonly used free tool is e-mail alerts from search engines. I prefer Google Alerts (see Figure 13-1), but the Yahoo! (www.yahoo.com) and Bing (www.bing.com) search engines also offer e-mail alert services for Web content. (See Chapter 11 for the lowdown on setting up a Google Alert.) Set up e-mail alerts to notify you whenever your name or blog name are mentioned, or whenever your blog is linked to. Also set up alerts on your key topics so you can keep ahead of trends in your field.

- ✔ **Inbound links to your blog:** Inbound links are links to your blog from other Web sites. *Referrers* or *referring sites* is the term used for sites that send readers to your blog. You can see who links to you with your Google Alerts and in the dashboard of your blogging platform as well as with free tools, such as BackType (www.backtype.com); but to track and analyze inbound links, you need to use analytics tools, such as

  - *Google Analytics:* Offers a free service (www.google.com/analytics)

  - *PostRank:* Offers a 30-day trial, but then charges $9 per month (www.postrank.com)

  - *Site Meter:* Offers a free version with limited functionality and a paid version starting at $6.95 per month (http://sitemeter.com)

Figure 13-2 shows the Google Analytics details for a referring site in one month. You can see how many visitors the site sent, the number of posts, and the details for each one. You can also click through and read the original post.

I use Google Analytics, and show you how to get started with it later in this chapter. To use Google Analytics, however, you have to be able to edit the code of your blog. Some hosted blogging platforms may not let you access this, so keep that in mind when choosing your platform. Read more about choosing your blogging platform in Chapter 8.

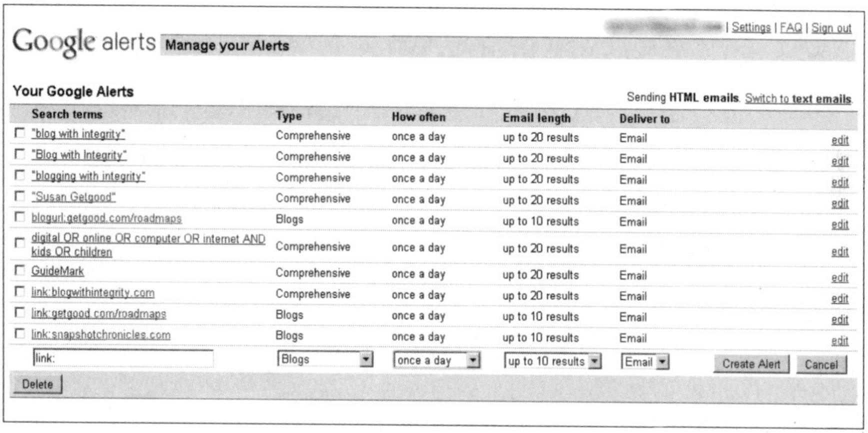

Figure 13-1:
Use Google Alerts to monitor for mentions of your name and blog as well as links to your blog.

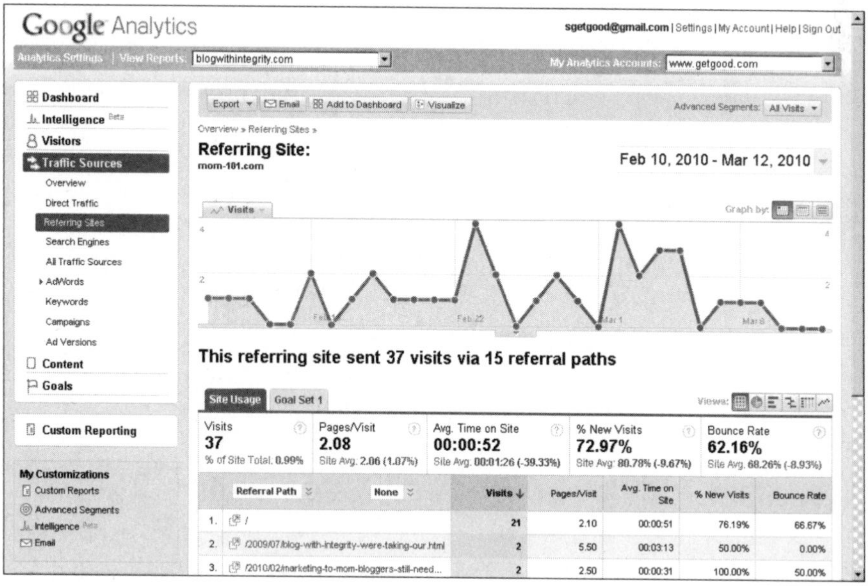

Figure 13-2:
This report from Google Analytics shows the details for one referring site.

✔ **Mentions on Twitter:** These mentions are captured in real time through various free tools:

  • *Twitter Search:* http://search.twitter.com

  • *TweetGrid:* http://tweetgrid.com

  • *TweetDeck:* www.tweetdeck.com

The following services offer free e-mail alerts for Twitter:

  • *TweetBeep:* www.tweetbeep.com

  • *Tweet Scan:* http://tweetscan.com

I also recommend using a tool like Chat Catcher (http://chat catcher.com), also free, to post tweets that link to your posts as comments on your blog. This ensures that you catch the comment for both the ongoing conversation and your monitoring effort.

✔ **Your comments:** Which posts generated the most comments — positive and negative. You can use that information to decide whether to write about the topic in the future.

Measuring

Measurement is the counting side of the metrics equation. Measurement answers specific questions:

✔ What was the result?

✔ Did you achieve your objectives?

But numbers need context for meaning. Your core measurement plan needs to focus on the things that are critical to reach your professional blogging goals — building loyal readership and crafting compelling content. Start by using your analytics program to answer these questions:

✔ How many people read your blog?

✔ How engaged are they with your blog?

✔ How do people find your site?

✔ What keywords are the most common?

> ✔ Where does your blog traffic come from?
>
> ✔ Which sources send the most readers?
>
> ✔ What are your most popular posts?

Also measure your results from your monetization efforts. I get into that in more detail later in this chapter. For more on strategies for monetizing your blog, see Chapter 4.

Understanding Your Readership by Using Analytics

Analytics programs count a lot of things. If you like that sort of stuff, it's all interesting, but only a few things are critically important for understanding your readership and improving your results. The rest? Save them for a rainy day when you feel like digging in deep.

Here I look at how analytics programs can answer the core questions in your measurement plan. My examples use screen shots from *Google Analytics* (www. google.com/analytics) and *FeedBurner* (http://feedburner.google. com), the free tools most commonly used by bloggers in the survey I conducted for this book (see Figure 13-3). All the analytics tools measure the same basic Web activities, so you can apply the general principles to any analytics software.

If you really want to dig into how engaged your audience is with your blog, PostRank (www.postrank.com) shows a consolidated view of how people have engaged with your blog content across the major social networks (Twitter, Facebook, and so on) as well as on blogs. To check out the level of information PostRank provides, use the free Analyze It feature on the PostRank Web site to see the data for any blog, as shown for the blog Mashable in Figure 13-4.

An analytics tool's *dashboard* gives you a snapshot view of the data. From there, you dive into the relevant detail. Figure 13-5 shows the Google Analytics dashboard.

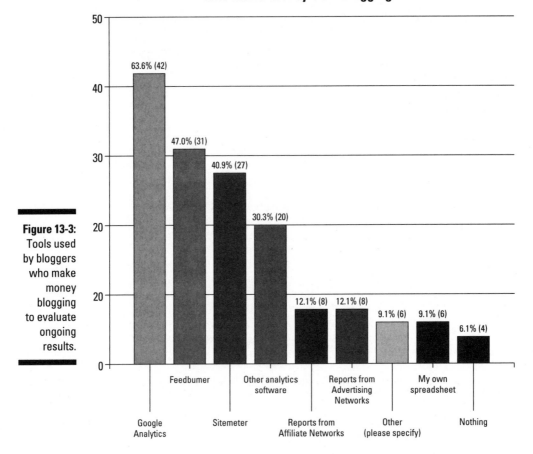

Tools Used to Measure Results by Bloggers Who Make Money from Blogging

Figure 13-3:
Tools used
by bloggers
who make
money
blogging
to evaluate
ongoing
results.

Source: Professional Blogging For Dummies survey, Susan Getgood, 2010

To sign up for Google Analytics, follow these steps:

1. **Sign up for a Google account or log in using your existing Google credentials at www.google.com/analytics.**

2. **On the New Account Signup page, shown in Figure 13-6, type the URL you want to track, enter an account name, and then click the Continue button.**

3. **On the next page, enter your name and select your country; then click Continue.**

4. **Accept the Terms of Service and then click Create New Account.**

   Google generates a tracking code, as shown in Figure 13-7.

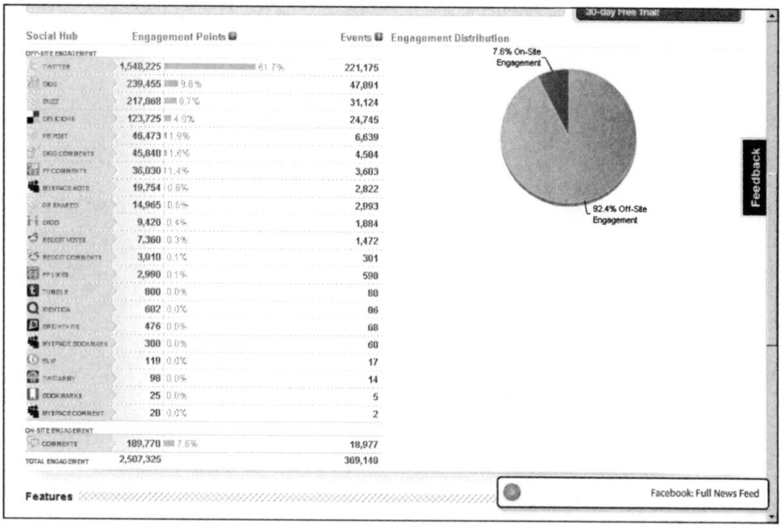

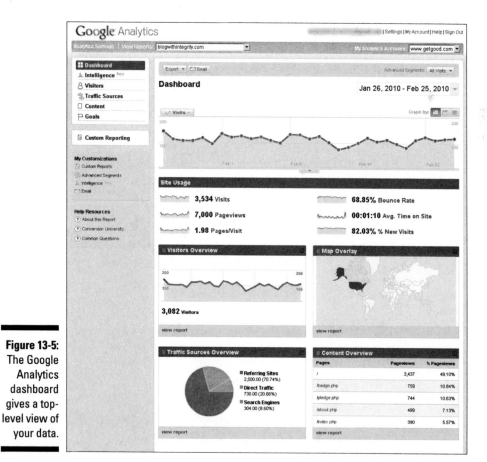

Figure 13-4:
PostRank
delves
deeper into
engagement
with your
blog content
across the
social Web.

Figure 13-5:
The Google
Analytics
dashboard
gives a top-
level view of
your data.

5. **Copy this code and paste it into your blog template.**

   Google says to paste it after the `<body>` tag on every page you want to track, but your blog template will have a specific place within the template to copy the code, often somewhere in the footer code.

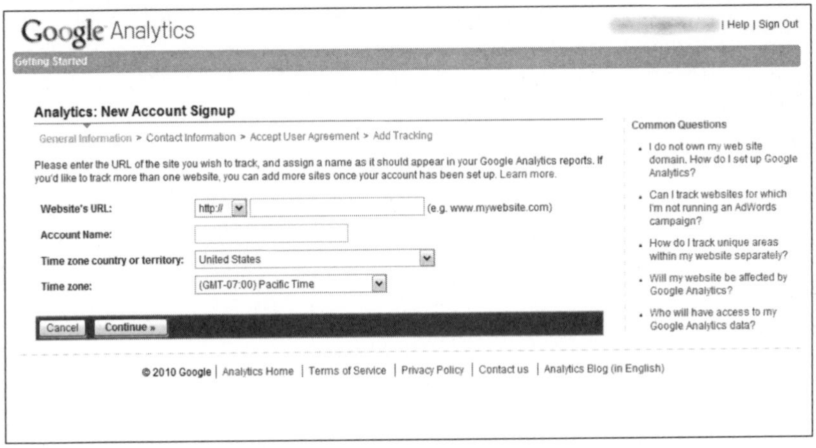

Figure 13-6:
Sign up
for Google
Analytics.

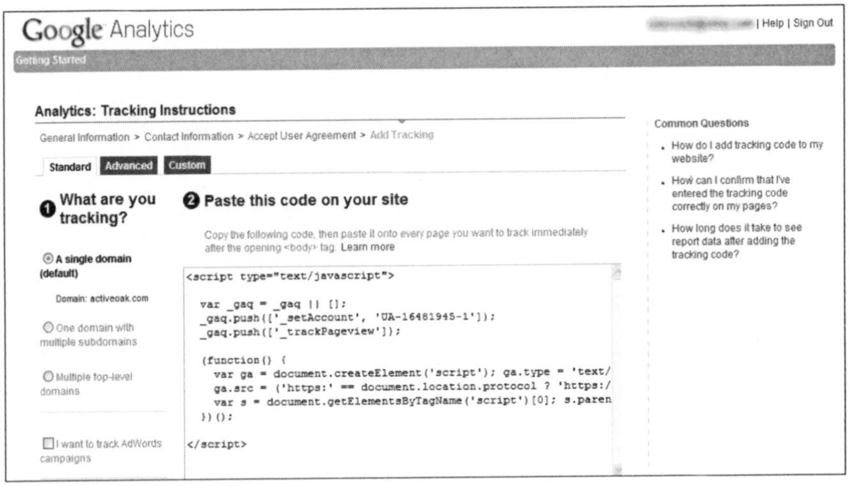

Figure 13-7:
Google
Analytics
tracking
code.

Figuring out how many people read your blog

You never know exactly how many people read your blog. Analytics offers a number of ways, each of which is an *approximation,* to look at your readership. Focus on the three important ones: absolute unique visitors, page views, and Really Simple Syndication (RSS) subscribers. I talk a bit about each in the next few sections.

Absolute unique visitors

The *absolute unique visitors* (see Figure 13-8) number is the number of visitors, tracked by IP address, minus repeat visitors. This is probably the closest approximation to the number of people visiting your site that you'll find with current technology, which makes it a good yardstick for consultants interested in establishing a thought leadership position. However, because absolute unique visitors uses IP addresses to count, it underestimates traffic from multiple people who may be reading your blog from the same computers and double-counts people who log in from multiple networks, such as home and work.

Figure 13-8: Absolute unique visitors is the best estimate of the number of people visiting your site.

Page views

Page views (see Figure 13-9) tell you how many pages of your site have been viewed in a specified time period — a day, week, month, or a range of dates. Although page views are bound to count people more than once, this metric gives an accurate representation of the total reach of your blog content, which is why it's the preferred measure of advertisers. Advertisers are interested in the total number of potential views of their ad. The advertising business model is based on frequency and repetition, so duplicate views are fine.

RSS subscribers

RSS is a format that allows readers to subscribe to your blog and read it in
an application — an *RSS reader,* such as Google Reader. Although most blog
readers still read the original site rather than subscribe to an RSS feed, for a
total picture of your readership, you need to understand how many of your
readers access your content through an RSS feed reader.

The best way to keep track of your RSS subscribers is to replace the RSS feed
created by your blogging platform with a feed from Google's free FeedBurner
service at `http://feedburner.google.com`. This gives you access to the
FeedBurner reports of subscribers (see Figure 13-10) and lets you offer e-mail
subscriptions through FeedBurner.

Follow these steps to create a FeedBurner feed:

1. **Log in to the FeedBurner service at `http://feedburner.google.com` with your Google login.**

2. **Enter your blog URL and then click Next.**

   FeedBurner checks your blog for a feed and then uses the original feed
   to create a FeedBurner feed.

3. **On the next page, click Next.**

   Your FeedBurner feed is now live.

4. **Use the new FeedBurner address in the hyperlink for your Subscribe button or link, not the original one created by your software.**

   Most people use this link to subscribe.

5. **Redirect all requests for an RSS feed to the FeedBurner feed so that the only available feed is the FeedBurner feed.**

   You do this in your blog dashboard, and each blogging platform handles it a little differently. For example, in Blogger's Site Feed menu item, you type in the FeedBurner URL to redirect the feed. In WordPress, many bloggers install the FeedBurner FeedSmith plug-in to redirect all feeds to the FeedBurner feed.

Figure 13-10: FeedBurner gives you details on readers viewing your blog through an RSS reader.

Discovering how engaged readers are with your blog

A number of data points helps you understand how engaged your readers are with your blog. The most important are

- ✔ **Time on site:** How long they stay on your site
- ✔ **Pages per visit:** How many pages they view per visit

✔ **Bounce rate:** The percent of single page visits; that is, the visitor leaves the site from his entrance page

✔ **Loyalty:** New versus repeat visitors

Always view these numbers in the context of your site and your goals. If your blog has lots of deep content beyond the main post — for example, recipes and how-to's — you want a low bounce rate and multiple pages per visit. On the other hand, if you have a loyal readership that comes every day, your pages per visit tend to be low and your bounce rate high. If they come every day, they don't need to explore your site every time. They read the new post and move on.

Figuring out how people find your site

The most important reports for understanding how people find your site are

✔ **Traffic Sources:** This report, from Google Analytics in this case, shows where your traffic comes from. Figure 13-11 shows the overview for a site, and Figure 13-12 shows the detail for all traffic sources for a site. You can this data to fine-tune your strategy. If you don't get much traffic from search engines, perhaps you need to look at your keywords. If your *direct traffic* (people who type in your URL in the browser bar or connect from a previously saved bookmark) is very low, you may want to work on building your community of readers. As I note in the "Monitoring" section earlier in this chapter, your report of referring sites tells who links to you and how much traffic they send.

✔ **Keywords:** Keywords are how search engines find your blog. You want to maximize the use of keywords people already use to make sure that you appear higher on the search results for those terms. (Figure 13-13 shows a Keywords report.) Pay particular attention to how productive keywords are in terms of *engagement* — pages per visit, average time on site, percentage of new visitors, and bounce rate.

Discovering which are your most popular posts

Your most popular posts hit big when you first post them and continue to pull traffic over time. To get a good picture, run the report over a fairly long period of time — at least six months. Figure 13-14 shows the top content on my professional Marketing Roadmaps blog for 2009.

Figure 13-11:
Visitors
come to
your blog
directly,
from refer-
ring sites,
and search
engines.

Figure 13-12:
A detailed
report for
all traffic
sources
from Google
Analytics.

Figure 13-13: A Google Analytics Keywords report for Blog With Integrity.

Figure 13-14: A Top Content report lets you know which posts resonate with readers.

The *root,* or home, page of your blog is always number one because most direct traffic goes to the home page. The *permalinks,* short for permanent links, are the links to each specific post URL and reflect visits to leave comments, from search engines and inbound links; in other words, community and long-term interest.

Topics that generate traffic, inbound links, and comments are all good candidates for repeat posting.

Using Analytics Data to Improve Your Results

The real power of your analytics data is using it to improve your results. That's when you move beyond counting things and actually measure your performance. Identify something you want to change, analyze the different areas that impact it, develop a plan to improve the results, execute the plan, look at the numbers again, fine-tune, and repeat.

Here are three examples of ways to use your analytics data to improve results:

- ✔ **You want to increase your page views.** One way to do this is to get more people to your site. Take a look at your traffic sources. If you don't get many visitors from the search engines, you could improve page views (and visits) by focusing on search engine optimization. Take a look at the list of keywords people use to find your site now. Can you use these keywords more frequently? Could you use other, better keywords? (See Chapter 11 for more tips for optimizing your blog for search.)

- ✔ **You want to get more views from the visitors already coming to your site.** How much of your traffic is *one and done* (in which the visitor reads one page and leaves), and how many readers stick around to read more during their visit? Length of time on site, bounce rate, and pages per visit are all indicators of how "sticky" your blog is. Regular readers form a habit of reading the new post and moving on, so you need to break them of it. Do the following to break this habit:

  - • Link to past posts within your posts.

  - • Include short lists of previous entries on the same topic; many platforms have plug-ins or widgets that do this automatically.

  - • Include a list of your most popular posts in your sidebar to attract new visitors to dig deeper into your content.

✔ **You have lots of page views and visitors, but your loyalty is very low.** You have a small cadre of loyal readers, but most visitors come once and don't return. This usually goes hand in hand with *too much* of your traffic coming from search engines. In this case, improve your other sources of traffic. Convert your search engine visitors to regular visitors, using some of the tactics I mention earlier, and then look at your referring sites. How much of your traffic comes from other blogs? If the traffic's low, comment on and link to relevant blogs to improve your profile in the community.

Don't obsess over your stats. Analytics and measurement are a toolset for improving your results, but they don't replace writing a great blog with unique, compelling content. That's what attracts and keeps readers.

Making Sense of Advertising and Affiliate Marketing Reports

Web analytics help you improve your blog. Your advertising and affiliate reports give you information you can use to improve your revenue.

Unfortunately, although you have standard advertising sizes to go by, there is no single advertising network business model. I can outline four broad categories — pay-per-click, cost-per-thousand impressions (CPM), flat rate, and affiliate, as described in Chapter 6 — but within those categories, each network has its own way of doing business, which means the reports are all different.

Nevertheless, some standard terms let you perform some comparisons among networks and fine-tune your strategy within a network:

✔ **Impressions:** The number of times an ad displays. Impressions don't correspond exactly to page views, but it's fairly close. If a reader has an ad blocker, the ad doesn't render but the rest of the page does. Ad networks include tracking code to count impressions and clicks in ad widgets (and links, in the case of affiliate programs) that you install on your blog.

✔ **Clicks:** The number of times an advertisement is clicked by readers. Some networks report this as *visits,* to indicate that the reader visited the destination site.

✔ **Click-through rate (CTR):** The number of clicks divided by the number of impressions. CTR is a good measure of ad effectiveness.

✔ **Cost-per-thousand impressions (CPM):** In traditional media, CPM corresponds to cost-per-thousand subscribers or viewers. In digital media, CPM represents cost-per-thousand impressions, or page views.

✔ **Effective cost-per-thousand impressions (eCPM):** You may see this on reports from networks that don't set rates on a CPM basis. eCPM represents estimated earnings for every 1,000 impressions. To calculate this: Divide your estimated earnings by total page impressions, and then multiply by 1,000.

Not so standard is how the advertising networks report your earnings. This is different for each network, depending on how it sells ad space on your behalf and the commission or fees it retains.

Affiliate reports are a little more standardized. Regardless of the terms they use, you can find transactions, the number of completed sales, the dollar amount of sales, the earnings per click, and your commission, or earnings, from sales.

Using the Reports to Maximize Your Revenue

You only have so much ad space on your blog. You can use the data in your advertising and affiliate reports to select the channels that are most productive for you. And as long as you have impression data, you can compare the performance of networks that use different business and revenue models with CPM and eCPM to put them on the same footing.

As I noted earlier, CTR is a good measure for ad effectiveness. Use CTR to compare the performance of different ad contents, sizes, and positions on your blog. Advertisers may purchase ads for a flat rate or by CPM, but they come back to the blogs that deliver the ad clicks. Knowing the optimum ad sizes and positions for your blog and your audience improves your chances that your advertisers will come back.

If you participate in affiliate networks, your reports tell you what stores appeal most to your audience. Mir Kamin, author of shopping blog Want Not (`www.wantnot.net`), says that at the beginning, she joined the programs of stores she shopped at, but

> *"As time went on, I grew to know my audience and have a greater understanding of what deals were likely to appeal; now I regularly feature stores I personally shop at, and stores I love to shop at for my kids, but also stores that have proven popular with my readers (like, say, plus-size clothing stores, even though I myself am not a plus size, or stores that carry scrapbooking stuff even though I'm not a scrapper). It doesn't cost me anything to belong to an affiliate program, so if I can join a program and they only have a great, post-worthy deal once a year, well, that's still worth doing."*

Using Analytics and Reporting to Forecast

After your blog is established and earning revenue, your Web analytics and advertising revenue reports are the source data for your revenue forecast. Rather than your best guestimates, as I discuss in Chapter 4, you have real data to base your projections on.

The simplest projection forecasts are based on known monthly earnings, remembering to account for seasonality. The fourth calendar quarter tends to be stronger for ad and affiliate earnings, so you'd be foolish to base your whole year on the month of December.

You can get cleverer about reporting if you layer your Web analytics with sales results to see how your Web traffic correlates to sales and earnings, especially for affiliate and pay-per-click advertising. This gives you a baseline understanding of how shifts in reader numbers affect your revenue. You can use this in your planning. For example, you might decide to invest in a Facebook ad campaign. Knowing how an increase in readership affects your revenue gives you something to evaluate the expense against. This approach isn't perfect, but it's better than guessing when your budget is tight.

Putting Metrics in Perspective

I've said this before, but I'll say it again: Using your analytics and reporting can only help you make your good blog better. They can't make a bad product good. First and foremost, concentrate on writing a unique, compelling blog that attracts readers and makes them want to come back. That's the ice cream and sauce in your sundae. Analytics and revenue reports are the nuts and the cherry.

Many successful bloggers don't pay much attention to analytics at all, for various reasons. If that's you, you're in good company.

Using my ice-cream metaphor, Christine Koh of Boston Mamas (`www.boston mamas.com`) is all about the sundae:

> *"I probably sound like an idealist but I am so not into metrics. At the very beginning, I checked my metrics obsessively and they totally stressed me out. It was a waste of time and energy in my opinion (in the sense that just sitting there fretting about the metrics wasn't going to make them grow). Plus, I don't think they are indicative of the full picture. So I stopped checking them and now only do so when a potential advertiser requests them. Instead I believe in focusing on quality of content, integrity of practice, and connecting with others in the space."*

Edward Hasbrouck, author of The Practical Nomad (`www.hasbrouck.org/blog`), started his blog to support his career as a travel writer and consultant. He says:

> *"I'm not looking primarily for numbers of clicks or direct revenue. Numbers and quality of mentions in the news, in print, and on other Web sites and blogs are important, as are [the] number and quality of invitations to speak, offers (and rates) for consulting work, [and so on]."*

Carla Birnberg of MizFitOnline (`www.MizFitOnline.com`) shares Christine Koh's attitude about metrics for a similar, but not quite the same, reason:

> *"I never check my stats. Until I know I will change anything, I figure why look? Right now, I'm a full-time mom, full-time freelance writer, I and full-time blogger — doing the best that I can at all efforts. At this point, even if I saw I had low traffic, I wouldn't change anything. That said, I know I feel this way in part due to the fact I have an amazing and vocal community. I average 70 comments per post, and many days get 100 or more."*

Beth Blecherman of TechMamas (www.techmamas.com) doesn't focus on page views. Her goal was to build a diversified channel of blog, Twitter, and Facebook. She says:

> *"There are some months when I am active on my blog and get more views. Other times, I am more active on my social networks, such as Facebook and Twitter. I view my Twitter metrics — how many followers I have — as important. I only view blog metrics when I have important posts that I am promoting."*

Understand though, that even a little bit of attention to your metrics can reap big rewards. Just keep the importance of your metrics in perspective. After all, you're a blogger, not a calculator.

Chapter 14

Keeping Your Blog Fresh

· ·

· ·

You've launched your blog. Congratulations. Now the really hard work starts.

Unlike a Web site, which you can pretty much set and forget, your blog needs constant feeding and attention to be successful. And not just at the beginning when you're trying to build your audience. You want to get readers and you want to keep them. That means keeping your blog fresh, compelling, interesting, and relevant to your audience, whether it's 10, 10,000, or 1,000,000.

You also need to think about *how* you want to grow your blog. Over time, you may become interested in other topics — some closely related to your original focus, others not so much. Do you add the new topic to the current blog or start a new one? What about adding additional authors to carry the load? Should you ever walk away and start over?

This chapter shares my thoughts on these topics, but they're only a suggested direction. Your personal objectives and experiences are your truest guide to *your* right answer for *your* blog.

Jump-Starting Your Muse

When you first start writing your blog, you have no shortage of ideas and material to draw from. Over time, however, the bank gets depleted. Most of the time, not having a firm idea is okay. You'll get an idea from the news or read a post that you either strongly agree with or strongly disagree with, and you'll be good to go.

One day, though, you'll sit down at the keyboard and realize that you have nothing. Zip. Zero. Nada. The following sections give you ways to cope when that happens.

Don't panic!

Give yourself permission to not post. One day doesn't matter. One week might, and one month definitely will, but one day? Nope. You can go a day.

Think about why you're blocked. Are other professional or personal issues weighing on your mind? Deal with them first. Sometimes that resolution provides just the inspiration you need for your post.

Mix things up a bit

Have you gotten into a rut, posting about the same topic day after day? Or do you always use the same format or template for your posts? Maybe you need a change. Try these suggestions:

- **Add photos:** Your own or from a royalty-free stock photo house, such as iStockphoto (www.istockphoto.com).
- **Work with videos:** If you don't use video clips very often, pull something interesting off YouTube. I regularly plant earworms in my readers' heads of classics like Shel Silverstein's "The Unicorn Song:"

  > "A long time ago, when the Earth was green
  > There was more kinds of animals than you've ever seen
  > They'd run around free while the Earth was being born
  > And the loveliest of all was the unicorn."

  You're welcome. If you're now desperate to hear the song, and I know you are, my post with the full lyrics and link to The Irish Rovers recording of the song is at

  ```
  http://getgood.com/roadmaps/2007/10/17/the-lines-they-
        are-a-blurring
  ```

  Be respectful of copyrights and fair use when you use online video material. Read more about this in Chapter 3.

- **Experiment with shooting your own videos:** If you have a digital point-and-shoot camera or a mini-handheld like a Flip, use it to start. Better to make sure that you like doing video before you invest in equipment. Follow these tips when shooting video:

- *It doesn't have to be a major production.* Take your readers on a tour of your office or your town. Interview a friend or colleague. Kids and pets make great subjects, even on a business blog; just use them sparingly.

  TV weatherman Al Roker often jokes that his college professor told him he had the perfect face for radio. If you feel that way about yours — you just don't want to be in front of the camera — consider doing an occasional *podcast,* a radio show that can be listened to on demand and syndicated to distribution services like iTunes with Really Simple Syndication (RSS).

- *Keep it short.* Under 15 minutes, if it's just you talking. Focus on a single story or topic. If you have a guest or are doing the show with a partner, you can go a bit longer.

For even more ideas on how to jump-start the muse, check out Chapter 17.

Open your notebook

A writer's best friend is her notebook. When you get an idea or something inspires (or irritates) you, jot it down in your notebook. I use a small, thin 3-x-5 Moleskine one so I can carry it with me wherever I go.

More about using a notebook and nine more tips for jump-starting your creativity can be found in Chapter 17.

Taking a Vacation

No matter how much you love your blog, at some point you need to take a break. Maybe you're taking a family vacation and you don't expect to have the time to write. Perhaps you're going somewhere with spotty (or no) Internet access or work commitments demand a brief hiatus.

Whatever the reason, if you don't want to hang up a Gone Fishing sign, you need a strategy for covering the blog in your absence. Luckily, the popular blogging platforms let you schedule posts for future publication, so you can organize everything in advance.

Here are four commonly used strategies for dealing with your much-deserved time away from your blog:

✔ **Greatest hits:** A roundup of previously published posts from your blog, generally on a single theme. This was what I did when I went to Africa in September 2009 for ten days and knew I wouldn't have the time, inclination, or Internet access to post regularly (see Figure 14-1). You can also use roundups when writer's block strikes.

✔ **Banked posts:** Pick some evergreen topics and write your posts in advance. How-to's and tips are good candidates for saving for later. Stay away from anything that might be impacted by current events. I'd even recommend staying away from case studies, unless you're analyzing something pretty old. You never know what can happen. The last thing you want is to publish a glowing analysis of a company, only to find they were in the headlines during your absence for dumping toxic waste or something equally heinous.

✔ **Favorite reads:** Instead of rounding up your own posts, turn to your blogroll and feature your favorite reads. You can do this by theme and roundup posts by multiple bloggers, or you can feature a single writer in each post and highlight your favorite posts from the blog.

✔ **Guest bloggers:** If you're going to be gone for a long while, such as parental or medical leave, and don't want to shutter your blog, guest bloggers, as shown in Figure 14-2, are probably the way to go. If you're very lucky, you have a few trusted colleagues who will take it on in your absence. Agree on some parameters, hand over the keys, and off you go. More likely, though, you'll ask a larger group of bloggers to contribute one or two posts each, which you upload to your blog. This benefits you and your guests. You get to review the post before it goes on your blog, and your guest doesn't have to be familiar with your blogging software to participate.

Figure 14-1:
Schedule
greatest hits
posts to run
while you're
on vacation.

Figure 14-2:
Inviting
guest blog-
gers is a
common
strategy for
covering an
extended
absence.

almost fearless

Work Wirelessly. Travel the World. Do *Anything.*

What Traveling Has Taught Me About Money

⏱ 16. MAR. 2010 💬 32 COMMENTS

38

Today's guest post is from Kyle at OnOurOwnPath, who has been traveling with his wife for over 2 years with no plans of stopping. If you wonder how they do it, read on...

We're making a documentary!

Like travel videos? Give us a hand to support this project...

Donate

Get New Posts in Your Inbox

Email: [   ] sign up

Ebooks

Guest blogging is a great way to showcase new bloggers whose writing you like. In exchange for helping you, they get exposure to your audience. Be willing to return the favor if asked.

Keeping Your Community Engaged

When you start writing your blog, you really don't know who or how many are reading, and it's best to keep it that way for a bit. In other words, don't obsess over your stats.

However, the best way to get people engaged in your writing is to write for "someone." Beth Blecherman, author of TechMamas (featured in the sidebar, "Reinventing yourself through blogging: Beth Blecherman, TechMamas," later in this chapter), says that when she first started, sometimes she felt like she was talking to herself, but she imagined, and wrote for, a community of tech-savvy, gadget-loving parents — and it paid off; now she has one.

Thinking about your readers as people, not just a demographic or psychographic segment, and creating that tangible picture in your mind helps you connect with them, and they with you. That's part of what makes your blog a conversation: People coming together.

Keeping that picture in firm focus helps you keep your community engaged. You're talking with and writing for your readers, not broadcasting at them. Don't let the picture fade over time.

Comments: The currency of engagement

Comments are the currency of online engagement. All comments are important — on your blog, Facebook, Twitter, LinkedIn, inbound links to you from other blogs, and whatever else is invented next month — but the ones on your blog are the only ones you can manage.

Managing comments isn't controlling them, nor is it simply moderating. You manage comments by what you write, how you choose to encourage (or not encourage) comments, and how you respond to them. Most of the time, you want comments on your posts. The conversation is one of the reasons you started the blog in the first place.

Encouraging comments

Some communities are very comment driven; others aren't. If your community is a taciturn one, do yourself a favor and don't compare your blog comment volume to a more gregarious group.

That said, you can encourage comments, even from the normally silent. Here are some tips:

- ✔ **Take a position on an issue.** Leave room for debate and ask your readers to weigh in with a comment.

- ✔ **Ask for advice.** Ask your audience what they'd do in your position.

- ✔ **Push your posts to your social networks.** Twitter, Facebook, and LinkedIn have mechanisms that allow you to share links with followers. Don't be passive. Ask for opinions.

- ✔ **If you mention other bloggers or link to their posts, don't count on the ego search.** Let them know about your post with an e-mail.

- ✔ **If you know some of your friends are particularly interested in the post topic, e-mail and ask them to comment.** Some communities just need that first comment to open the floodgates. Don't overdo this, but when it matters — when you want that support — ask for it.

- ✔ **When you get comments, respond and use the opportunity to move the discussion along.** If appropriate, ask another question or raise a related point.

From time to time, you may not want comments on a post. Perhaps the topic is personal and although you want to share with your community, you aren't ready for the conversation. You can turn comments off once in a while: It's okay. Just be clear about why, and don't do it too often.

If your blog has comments, the reader assumes that you want to have the conversation with him. Saying that you don't too often sends a mixed message.

If you don't want comments, turn them off on the post before you publish it rather than in the middle of a thread. You can't always call that in advance, but if you can, it sets a better expectation.

A blog without comments? That's a Web site, regardless of the platform used to build it.

Dealing with negative comments

Don't turn off comments simply because you expect, or get, negative comments. You'll find that it's usually much better to deal with the negative issue than to avoid or shut it down. For example, your post is about a customer service problem and you've shared everything you know so far. The temptation is to turn off the comments because you have nothing to add.

That's a mistake. You may have nothing more to say, but your readers probably do. If you shut down the conversation on your blog, they'll just take it somewhere else. On your blog, they're still talking with you, and you can influence the discussion.

The exception is when a troll hijacks your comments to spew negativity and insults. In that case, the conversation is going nowhere. Hopefully, this doesn't happen to you, but it might. Unfortunately, you'll probably have to let things get pretty ugly before you shut it down, or you'll risk the accusation that you acted precipitously. In this case, you're in a lose-lose situation, so cut your losses. Post a comment that you're closing comments and move on to your next post.

The best way to handle a troll is to ignore it. Trolls thrive on the negative attention. Nothing irks them more than to be ignored. If you decide to engage, know what you're getting yourself into and don't take it personally — no matter what the troll says.

Setting a clear comment policy on your blog, as discussed in Chapter 10, helps you manage these situations. If you delete a published comment, you may want to note why it was deleted, such as violation of comment policy or spam. Moderating comments avoids some of these issues because you can review comments before publishing, but be careful. You don't want to delete everyone who disagrees with you. Debate is healthy, and it's better to let it happen on your blog (within reason), where you can respond, rather than let it take place elsewhere.

Blogger spotlight: Kimberly Coleman, Mom in the City

Kimberly Coleman started her Mom in the City blog (www.mominthecity.com, as shown in the following figure) to share information with her offline mother's group. Since then, her blog has become a professional effort and led to additional opportunities, such as speaking events and consulting. She says the most rewarding thing about blogging is helping moms feel more comfortable about their parenting choices: "I am the ultimate middle-of-the-road mom — avoiding extremes at all costs!"

Here's her tip for someone starting a new blog:

"To thine own self be true. As long as you're upfront and honest, do whatever you like with your little piece of the Web. As you change and grow, feel free to have your blog reflect those changes. As people, we are constantly changing and evolving. Personally, I think that it's great to see blogs reflect the authors' interests/passions during the various stages of their life. Don't feel like you have to fit in a box. We are individuals. We were not designed to fit into nice, neat boxes! That would be so boring . . ."

Mom in the *City*

Eyes to the Future: Growing Your Blog

Businesses revisit their marketing plans every year, and you need to do the same with your blog. Is your blog accomplishing what you hoped? Are you? Have things changed, either for you or your audience, that require you to revisit your plan and set new objectives?

When developing a growth plan for your blog, here are a few key things to consider:

- ✔ Is the blog delivering the results, or do you need to adjust or change your focus?
- ✔ Do you need to add one or more authors?
- ✔ Do you have new opportunities for monetization?

Changing your focus

Evolution is to be expected. You change. Your business changes. Slight shifts happen as your interests, and those of your readers, change. Acknowledge them and keep moving forward.

Kimberly Coleman, who blogs at Mom in the City (www.mominthecity.com) and is featured in the "Blogger spotlight: Kimberly Coleman, Mom in the City" sidebar earlier in this chapter, says that's part of what she loves about blogging:

> *"Personally, I think that it's great to see blogs reflect the authors' interests/ passions during the various stages of their life."*

However, if your goals have changed or you aren't achieving the results you expected, you may need to make bigger changes. Start with an honest assessment of your mission, niche, and focus. Do they still fit? What do your readers want? What do you want to achieve with your blog? Do you want to explore an interest, hobby, or passion in greater depth than your current blog allows?

More often than not, the solution is to develop a new blog rather than drastically alter your current one. In the blogger survey I conducted for this book, more than 70 percent write or contribute to two or more blogs (see Figure 14-3).

How Many Blogs Do You Write or Contribute To?

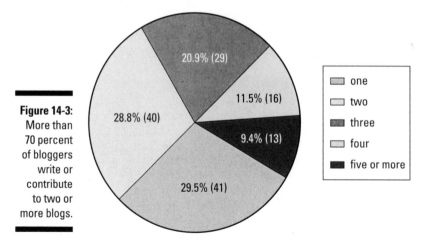

Figure 14-3: More than 70 percent of bloggers write or contribute to two or more blogs.

Source: Professional Blogging For Dummies survey, Susan Getgood, 2010

A few examples of second (or third blogs) written by bloggers featured elsewhere in this book:

- ✔ Liz Gumbinner and Kristen Chase met through their personal blogs (Mom-101 www.mom-101.com and Motherhood Uncensored http://motherhooduncensored.net, respectively), and then partnered to create shopping blog Cool Mom Picks (http://coolmompicks.com).

- ✔ Mir Kamin's shopping blog Want Not (www.wantnot.net) was a spinoff of her personal blog Woulda Coulda Shoulda (www.wouldashoulda.com).

- ✔ The Bad Pitch Blog (www.badpitch.blogspot.com) evolved from, and in some ways has eclipsed, Kevin Dugan's professional blog, Strategic Public Relations (http://prblog.typepad.com/strategic_public_relation).

- ✔ Christine Koh's first blog, Boston Mamas (www.bostonmamas.com) was conceived as a shopping portal for local parents, and she subsequently created a more personal site, Pop Discourse (www.popdiscourse.com).

Sometimes, though, you don't have any other choice to meet your objectives. To accomplish your goals, you have to reframe everything, shut down the old blog, and start a new blog. Think long and hard before you do this, but if it is the right choice for you, do it. Blogger Julie Marsh made this choice in 2009, when she shut down her mom blog MotherGooseMouse (see Figure 14-4), which chronicled her experiences as a parent, and started The Mom Slant, as shown in Figure 14-5 (www.themomslant.com).

Figure 14-4: Marsh shut down her Mother-Goose-Mouse blog and started a new one.

Figure 14-5:
Marsh's The
Mom Slant
blog.

She still writes about her children, but on The Mom Slant, Julie looks at social, economic, and political issues through the lens of parenthood. She described the shift in her final post at MotherGooseMouse:

> *"[Although] I love writing about my children, it's clear that op-ed is my passion, particular from a parent's perspective: Delving into issues, analyzing them through a mother's lens, gaining insights, drawing conclusions, and engaging in discussion with those whose views conflict with mine — these are the high points of blogging for me and what I will focus on at my new site, The Mom Slant."*

Jeff McIntire-Strasburg made a different but equally game-changing shift when he relaunched Sustainablog in 2010. His blog and URL didn't change, but the business model did. His business model went from advertising supported to affiliate marketing in his branded store.

There's no wrong answer to the question of when to create a new blog: There's just *your* right answer after you weigh the pros and cons.

Adding authors

You may find that your problem isn't that your interests have changed or that your readers want something else. Your problem may be that they want more than you can provide on your own. You only have so many hours in a day. For your blog to reach its potential, you may need to add authors.

This can be a difficult transition. If you start your blog as the lone author, on some level, it becomes an extension of you. You may find it hard to let in others. No matter how tightly you write your editorial guidelines, the new writers aren't you, but their personalities become part of your blog.

You certainly can start a new group blog, but if you've built a strong brand and the topic is the same, you probably don't want to start over.

Test the waters by inviting a prospective coauthor to write a guest post. Treat the post like a freelance assignment; invite the blogger to write on a topic of your choosing and offer reasonable compensation.

Finding new ways to make money

The basic business models that I discuss in Part II aren't going to go away. Finding sponsors, selling advertising and products, and providing services will continue to be the principal ways to make money with your blog. But within each of those areas, you'll continue to have innovation: New ways to deliver advertising online and new ways to pay for it.

Reinventing yourself through blogging: Beth Blecherman, TechMamas

Beth Blecherman was a senior manager with a focus on technology projects at an international accounting firm but had to leave full-time employment when her twins were born in 2003. She wanted to keep her job skills relevant, and thought starting a blog would be a good way to stay up-to-date with technology and reinvent her career.

Deciding to focus on the niche of parenting and technology, in 2006, she launched both her blog, as shown in the following figure, and her online social networking presence under the TechMamas brand:

> *"I felt that there were not enough mom voices being represented in the technology discussion — but lots of technology savvy*

moms and moms who are not only power users of technology but also the ones making the technology purchases in their families. I wanted to get my voice heard as a "TechMama" and engage other moms in the discussion."

Initially, Beth focused on establishing the blog and her online TechMamas brand, rather than monetization, because she wanted to give her voice time to settle. However, an important part of her strategy from the beginning was to establish her bonafides with technology companies so she'd be included in their press events.

She's now at the stage in which she's building a monetization strategy, but is proceeding slowly:

"Because I cover all the technology brands, I need to be technology-agnostic. I am focusing on consulting with software companies that are doing outreach to moms. This fits with my online brand and is separate from my coverage of hardware gadgets."

Blogging has led to other opportunities for her, including speaking events, consulting, and participating in marketing programs, but she is very careful and only accepts ones that are relevant to her technology voice or that offer business networking opportunities. She says:

"Keeping with my technology 'mom' niche has opened doors for me and given me a way to get my voice heard while raising my kids. All the major tech companies now reach out to me with press releases and information, and even better, they ask for my feedback as a mom."

Beth generously shared a few tips for new bloggers:

- ✔ Pick a topic you're passionate about so you'll enjoy researching and writing.

- ✔ Define your niche, and then build your blog and social network interaction around it.

- ✔ Network online to build a community to share your voice with.

- ✔ Don't ever forget that community happens in real life, too. Put time into outreach via conferences, meet-ups, and talking to people.

- ✔ Keep up-to-date with information related to your niche. Share that information and your personal voice across your platforms.

New services emerge — like Twitter in 2007, and geo-local services like four-square (www.foursquare.com) and Gowalla (www.gowalla.com) in late 2009, which let users announce where they're using the GPS in their mobile device. Sooner or later, folks will experiment with ways to make money with the service. Some will fly, some will fail, and eventually, some will be applicable to you and your blog.

Other innovations will come within the models themselves. In some cases, business consolidation, partnerships, and joint ventures lead to better integration across different strategies, making it easier for you to manage your business. An example of this now is Google, which is evolving its advertising and analytics acquisitions into a single dashboard. What will that look like? I wish I could gaze into a crystal ball and tell you for sure.

I think innovations in *hyperlocal advertising* — targeting regional and local advertising with greater accuracy — will appear. However, this relies on knowing a great deal about the consumer, which has privacy implications. And if you're trying to find consumers where they are *at the moment,* this also has security implications.

Mobile devices — especially smartphones and e-readers — are bound to offer new monetization options for your blog. Eventually. Today, you can develop apps for phones and offer your blog on an e-reader, such as the Amazon Kindle, but it's still pretty small, if any, money for you. Apple's iPad may (or may not) be the game changer, but eventually there *will* be a game changer, and the innovators will follow with new technologies and models for monetization.

Keep your eye on those areas. And keep your eyes open in general because the next big thing could be something else entirely.

Part V
The Part of Tens

©RICHTENNANT

BUNGCO
BUNGEE CABLE
COMPANY

"Come on Walt — time to freshen up the
company blog."

In this part . . .

In this part, I discuss common mistakes you want to avoid, ten other blogs you can learn from, and tips to jumpstart your creativity.

Chapter 15

Ten Common Mistakes and How to Avoid Them

The first nine mistakes that I discuss in this chapter are some of the most common mistakes of professional bloggers. They're also easily avoided if you plan the work and then work your plan. The last mistake applies to any small business and is probably one of the hardest hurdles for most small businesspeople. Don't worry, though. You can avoid these mistakes, and I give you some tips for doing just that.

Failing to Plan is Planning to Fail

You don't have to have a complicated business plan, with P&Ls and cash flow projections, but you need to at least have an outline of your business objectives (which I tell you how to define in Part I) and a general idea of what you can afford to invest in your venture. And you absolutely should have a plan for the blog development, especially if you're hiring someone to help. The plan doesn't have to be much more than the blog specification (see Chapter 9), an editorial calendar, and a target launch date that everyone aims for.

Without a plan, you're liable to succumb to the next common mistake: shiny object syndrome.

Succumbing to Shiny Object Syndrome

Shiny object syndrome is when you feel compelled to add the latest and greatest widgets, plug-ins, community features, and so on to your blog. In fact, you feel that something is always newer or better. You have to have them all, and you have to have the newest ones. The end result: You never quite finish and you spend far more time on the design of the blog than you should. Design is important, but blogs aren't billboards. Blogging is about content.

I have no concrete proof, but I'm willing to bet that most bloggers spend twice as much time on the design of their blog than they probably need to. That isn't disastrous unless the corresponding happens — they spend half as much time on the content than they should. You've read blogs like that, right? Don't let yours be one.

Overcrowded Sidebars

Don't try to put all the content you want your readers to have access to in the sidebars. Use your navigation to direct readers to important information on secondary inside pages.

The stuff at the top of the page is what people see most often, and unless they're looking for something specific in your sidebars, they generally won't scroll past the end of the post they're reading. That's why advertising tends to be at the top of a site or embedded within the post, usually above the fold. *Above the fold* is a term inherited from the newspaper industry, and originally referred to the top half of the tabloid-size page. The term is now used to refer to the first screen of digital content on a Web site.

Design your blog with simple navigation that includes links to text-heavy reference content, such as your About page, blogroll, and ethics and disclosure information. Reserve your sidebar for things like recent posts, comments, and graphical items such as advertising, buttons, and widgets.

Buried Contact Information

People need to be able to easily contact you. Take advantage of the free e-mail services, such as Gmail and Yahoo! Mail, to set up a contact e-mail address just for your blog and publish the address on your sidebar. In the background, you can forward the e-mails to your regular e-mail account if you want. This makes it easy for people to contact you, but keeps the e-mail spam out of your regular e-mail account. If you prefer, you can set up a Contact page that automatically e-mails you in the background.

Either way, make sure that visitors easily find out how to reach you privately. Otherwise, they may not bother, and you might miss business and personal opportunities that people don't feel comfortable sharing in public comments.

Forgetting to Check Your Design in Multiple Browsers, on Different Operating Systems

Make sure that your design looks good in the common Web browsers on the common operating systems. Even readers who read your blog in a Really Simple Syndication (RSS) reader have to visit the home site to leave a comment, and depending on what you have on your blog and how the reader has his browser configured, your blog may look a little different on each one. That's okay; it can look a little different. You just want to make sure that your blog looks good and functions properly.

Test your blog design based on the following table:

Operating System	Browser
Windows	Firefox, Internet Explorer, Chrome
Linux	Firefox, Chrome
Macintosh	Safari, Firefox, Chrome

If you have an existing site or blog, you can check your Web analytics for the commonly used operating systems and browsers, and optimize for the ones the majority of your readers use. For more about your Web analytics, read Chapter 13.

Browsershots.org (http://browsershots.org) is a great site for checking compatibility across a wide range of browsers, versions, and operating systems.

Neglecting to Add an RSS Feed

RSS is a format that allows readers to subscribe to your blog and read it in an application — an *RSS reader,* such as Google Reader. Even though most folks still read blogs on the blog site and not in an RSS reader, some 11 or 12 percent of readers do subscribe, so don't forget to create *and* promote an RSS feed on your blog with a link or a button.

If you're using one of the popular blogging platforms, your feed is created for you. Many bloggers use the ubiquitous orange button graphic (see the following figure) for their download link to make it easy for readers to spot the feed.

 Subscribe in a reader

A better way is to create a FeedBurner feed at `http://feedburner.google.com` and then promote this URL on your blog instead of the feed created by your blogging platform. More about FeedBurner in the following section.

Not Knowing Your Subscribers

You also want to understand who accesses your RSS feed and what they're using it for. Although most of the uses of your feed are probably legitimate, grabbing RSS feeds is the principal way content thieves steal for their spam-scraper blogs.

Spamscrapers illegally grab your content through your RSS feed to populate a blog that primarily exists to generate ad revenue. For more about this and how you can protect your blog while still offering your content in RSS format, read Chapter 3.

Run your feed through the FeedBurner service at `http://feedburner.google.com` so that you can easily monitor subscribers and other activity on your feed. FeedBurner creates a *FeedBurner feed* that you can use to promote on your site and hyperlink to your Subscribe button or link, not the original one created by your software. See Chapter 13 for details on setting up a FeedBurner feed.

In return, you get stats (as shown in Figure 15-1) about your feed, including subscribers and uncommon uses. You can also offer an e-mail subscription and run Google ads within your feed if you want.

Figure 15-1:
FeedBurner
stats.

Not all uncommon uses are unwelcome. Some search engines and aggregators that you want (or at least don't mind) indexing your feed will be considered "uncommon" by FeedBurner. Use the uncommon uses list, as shown in Figure 15-2, to check them out. Just click the hyperlink. If the uncommon uses are something you don't want, you can take steps to prevent them, as outlined in Chapter 3.

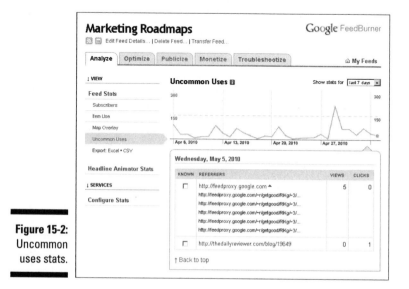

Figure 15-2:
Uncommon
uses stats.

It's All about Me!

Blogging is both an individual and community activity. You write your blog posts as an individual to share your ideas and opinions with the community. In turn, the members of the community comment on your blog and refer to each other's work by linking back to the original in posts or on a blogroll.

Comments and links are an integral part of the blog ecosystem. That's how you talk with others through your blog and share your sources of inspiration with your readers. With your professional blog, you're trying to establish connections with the community, to build readership, or in the case of your customers, to sell products. The best way to do this is to make your blog as much about them as it is about you:

✔ Include links when you can.

✔ Build an interesting blogroll.

✔ Allow reader comments.

✔ Respond to reader comments.

Without these things, you're broadcasting, not communicating. You don't have to link to other blogs in every post, but if you don't do *any* of these things, your blog is nothing more than a Web site.

By the way, blogs in the narrative diary form are a little bit different. Typically, they attract their audience because they offer a glimpse into someone's life. That glimpse is what readers come for. For example, Notes from the Trenches (www.notesfromthetrenches.com) is a well-written narrative of life in a family with seven children. You don't expect links to other blogs in every post. These types of blogs also tend to have fewer outbound links and more comments.

However, it's hard to build an audience for your story — even a brilliantly written one — without some outbound links or a blogroll to help in blog discovery.

If I Build It, They Will Come

Umm, no. This might have been true in the movie *Field of Dreams,* but that's definitely not true in blogging.

If you want readers to find your blog, you have to promote it. That starts with linking to other blogs in posts or on your blogroll. When those bloggers look at their *inbound* links — links to them — they see your blog and hopefully check it out. But unless you're a famous celebrity, you're going to need to do a little bit more to promote your new blog.

Here are just a few ideas to get you started:

- ✔ Announce your blog posts on Facebook, Twitter, and your other communities. If you write frequently, you may not want to promote every post but definitely do it when you have something original or new.

- ✔ Start a Facebook page for your blog and develop some complementary content so your audience visits both.

- ✔ Offer an e-newsletter. Some of the content can be from the blog, but remember to have a little something special, such as an exclusive article or a discount, for the e-newsletter readers in each issue.

Forgetting to Update Your Copyright Date

This is a personal pet peeve. You only have to remember this once a year. If you put a copyright date in your footer or sidebar, update it when the year changes.

There's no legal issue if you don't update this date, and your content is still protected even if you don't assert your copyright. (More on this in Chapter 3.) But, nothing says "I don't pay attention to the details" like an out-of-date date.

Like I said, a pet peeve.

Poor or NonExistent Recordkeeping

I recently asked a Certified Public Accountant (CPA) his most important piece of advice for a small blogging business. The answer: recordkeeping, recordkeeping, recordkeeping.

You need to keep track of

- Your business expenses for the blog
- Any personal expenses you incurred so the business can pay you back
- Taxes paid/owed
- Revenue streams
  - Advertising
  - Affiliate income
  - Sponsorships
  - Consulting fees
  - In kind, or free, products and services

Your accountant can help you set up a simple accounting package like Quicken or Excel spreadsheets to help you manage and track your revenue and expenses. He can also do the recordkeeping for you. That adds to your costs, but it may be a better choice depending on your business and product mix.

Chapter 16

Ten (Or More) Blogs You Can Learn from Simply by Reading

In This Chapter

▶ Looking at blogs that help you improve your own

▶ Identifying blogs that help you market your small business

▶ Looking at blogs that set good examples

This chapter could have easily featured 40 or 50 blogs you can benefit from just by reading, and to be honest, I add a few extra ones at the end.

Three blogs are about blogging and technology. Filled with concrete practical advice and clear explanations about blogging technology and tools, these blogs offer tips and techniques that help you improve your blog.

Because your blog is your business, I also include two blogs focused on marketing and small business.

The other five blogs set good examples. Simply stated, these blogs do blogging right and illustrate important points that I hope you remember when you sit down to create and write your blog.

ProBlogger

www.problogger.net

Professional blogger Darren Rowse started ProBlogger (as shown in Figure 16-1) in 2004, to capture what he was learning about how to make money as a blogger. This blog is now one of the most well known on the planet and has evolved into a book and a subscription-based online community for professional bloggers. However, the core blog is still free, with more than 3,500 articles in the archives, and Rowse continues to share his tips, tricks, and techniques to improve your blog and make a living as a professional blogger.

Common Craft

www.commoncraft.com

Although the Common Craft blog (see Figure 16-2) provides good tips for people who want to incorporate video into their blogging, the main reason I include it here is the Common Craft video series, *In Plain English*. Husband and wife team Lee and Sachi LeFever started making simple videos that explain complex technology subjects with paper cutouts in 2007. Their video about Really Simple Syndication (RSS), one of their first, is just about the best explanation of this technology that I've ever seen.

They're always adding new videos, so as you go down your blogging journey, if you run across a technical subject that you don't understand, check Common Craft to see whether they've explained it "in plain English."

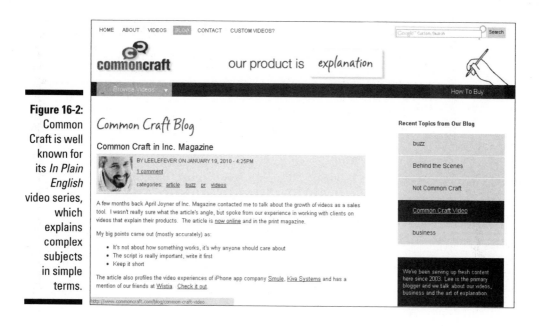

Figure 16-2:
Common Craft is well known for its *In Plain English* video series, which explains complex subjects in simple terms.

Want Not

    http://wantnot.net

Mir Kamin's shopping blog Want Not is all about finding the sales and the deals. Her blog started as a hobby and has evolved into a full-time business. If you're planning a shopping or e-commerce blog, remember these lessons from Want Not:

✔ You need to post regularly to get people in the habit of checking your blog for deals so that they'll use your affiliate links to purchase.

✔ Don't lose sight of your voice; without personality, a shopping blog is a directory.

✔ Take a look at Mir's Disclosure policy and how she identifies affiliate links. Perfection.

The other reason I want you to check out Want Not? This blog just might save you some money.

Copyblogger

www.copyblogger.com

If ProBlogger is about the money and Common Craft is about the technology, Copyblogger (see Figure 16-3) is about the content. Specifically, Copyblogger is about using content marketing strategies to improve your site traffic.

Founded in 2006 by entrepreneur and former attorney Brian Clark, Copyblogger started as a personal blog and has expanded to include an editorial team and multiple authors, all focused on helping bloggers create remarkable Web content that differentiates their blogs and builds loyal readers.

If you want to hone your persuasive writing skills and craft compelling blog posts that drive your readers to action, Copyblogger needs to be on your reading list.

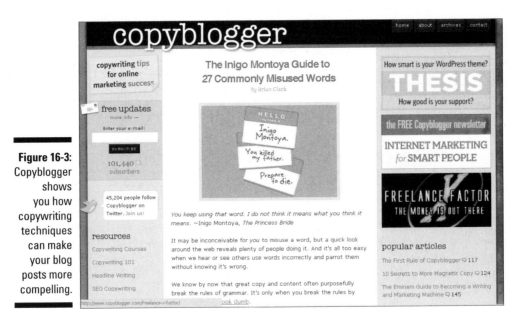

Figure 16-3: Copyblogger shows you how copywriting techniques can make your blog posts more compelling.

AlmostFearless.com

http://almostfearless.com

Christine Gilbert's top-ranked travel blog AlmostFearless.com recounts her adventures about leaving the corporate world to become a full-time traveler and freelance writer. Her voice is fresh and frank, and I love that she shares her knowledge in e-books like *30 Ways in 30 Days to Redesign Your Life and Travel the World* and *Twitter for Travelers.*

Share your knowledge and give back to your readers. Periodically, Christine offers an e-book for free if you subscribe to her blog by e-mail.

Duct Tape Marketing

www.ducttapemarketing.com/blog

Duct Tape Marketing (see Figure 16-4) is a classic in the small-business marketing space. John Jantsch has pretty much covered all the bases in helping small businesses with their marketing strategies — books, e-books, online course, seminars, consulting, and so on. His site has so many resources and products to help the small-business owner, it's actually hard to know where to start.

Make the effort here. This blog has good, affordable marketing information underneath all those tabs and buttons. And although the products aren't free, the blog is; and plenty of good advice about marketing a small business is found here.

Figure 16-4:
Duct Tape
Marketing
is a classic
in small-
business
marketing.

Cake Wrecks

http://cakewrecks.blogspot.com

The tagline for Jen Yates's blog Cake Wrecks says it all: *When Professional Cakes Go Horribly, Hilariously Wrong.* Read this blog for a laugh, enjoy the jokes, and then take a minute to think about why this blog became so successful that the author got a book deal.

Humor is hard. Cake Wrecks achieves that difficult balance of gut-busting funny without being mean spirited because Yates only pokes fun at badly done professional cakes. In other words, people who should know better. She actively involves her readers in seeking out Wrecks, and does a regular feature on beautiful cakes around a theme, also reader submitted, to offset the daily badness of the Cake Wrecks.

Lip-sticking

www.lipsticking.com

The Lip-sticking blog, started by author and entrepreneur Yvonne DiVita, focuses on marketing to women online, but many of the posts are common-sense advice that would apply to any marketing plan.

If you're thinking about doing a group blog, pay special attention to how Yvonne added other smart, successful women authors to the blog without losing the Lip-sticking "voice." For example, in the post shown in Figure 16-5, Yvonne builds upon a post written by a contributing author the day before.

Figure 16-5: Lip-sticking offers common sense guidance about marketing to women online.

Mom-101

www.mom-101.com

Liz Gumbinner's personal blog Mom-101 is full of funny stories about her life, family, and career. An advertising copywriter by profession, Liz can turn a phrase like no one else. She can make you laugh and cry, sometimes in the same post. She's also not afraid to take a stand on issues like BPA, high fructose corn syrup, handmade toys, and integrity in blogging.

Liz makes you care. If you're writing a personal narrative blog, pay attention to how she keeps her voice consistent across a number of very diverse topics.

GlobalVoices

http://globalvoicesonline.org

GlobalVoices (see Figure 16-6) is a citizen journalism project founded in 2005 by Rebecca MacKinnon and Ethan Zuckerman while they were both fellows at the Berkman Center for Internet and Society at Harvard University.

The more than 200 GlobalVoices' bloggers are both reporters and participants in their stories, offering a fresh alternative to the detachment of mainstream media and giving voice to many otherwise silent stories.

Figure 16-6: Global-Voices aims to shine a light on the stories that mainstream media ignore.

This site can be daunting because there's so much to it. I suggest picking an issue or region of the world, and then following it rather than trying to read everything.

Have passion. Don't limit your blog reading to just the things in your immediate circle. Cast a wider net.

Bonus Sites

Because you can't eat just one, and I can't list just ten, here are five other blogs you should check out:

- **Passive Aggressive Notes:** Just for fun

  www.passiveaggressivenotes.com

- **Daily Kos:** A pioneer of political blogging

  www.dailykos.com

- **Cool Mom Picks:** A shopping site for cool moms, and those who love them

  www.coolmompicks.com

- **Notes from the Trenches:** A classic personal blog

  www.notesfromthetrenches.com

- **Diva Marketing:** One of the very first marketing blogs

  http://divamarketingblog.com

Chapter 17

Ten Tips for Jump-Starting Your Creativity

*E*ven if you're passionate about your topic and usually have more ideas than you have time to write, a day will come when you can't get going; you're stalled, and the words just won't come. You need a jump-start.

Try one (or more) of the ten tips in this chapter to relax your mind so that you're ready to write. The first six may also help you come up with an idea for your post. These are just a sampling of the many things you can do to jump-start your creativity.

Capture Ideas in a Notebook

All you need is a small 3-x-5-inch notebook that you can carry wherever you go. Don't forget the pen. When you have an idea or observe something that interests you, jot it down. When you're at a loss for what to write, you can skim through your notebook for inspiration.

I also do this digitally with the social bookmarking site Delicious (`http://delicious.com`). When I read something online that I think I might like to write about, I tag it with a special category. To save a bookmark at Delicious, follow these steps:

1. **Sign up for an account at `http://delicious.com`.**

2. **Navigate to your bookmarks and then click the Save a New Bookmark link in the upper-right corner of the page, as shown in Figure 17-1.**

Figure 17-1:
Save a
bookmark at
Delicious.

3. **Type (or copy and paste) the URL you want to bookmark into the space provided and then click the Next button.**

4. **Fill out the information requested in Figure 17-2.**

   You can use as many tags as you like, but remember to use the same one for items you want to write about each time. I use *forp* to stand for *for post*.

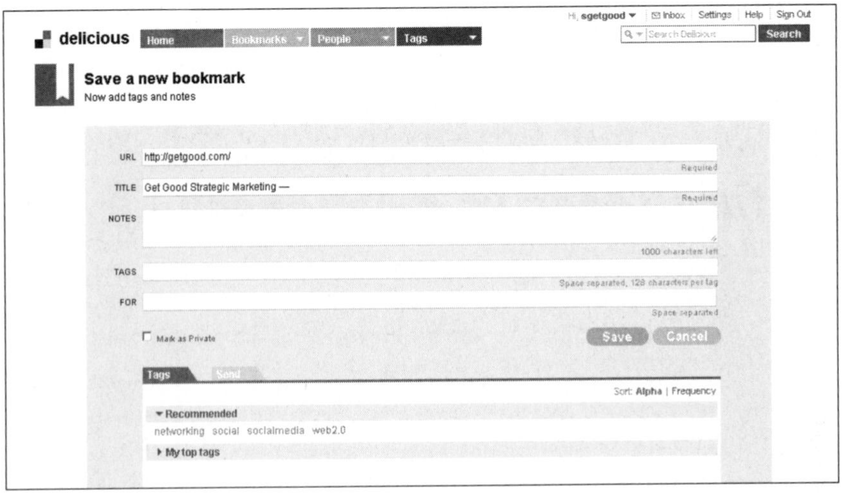

Figure 17-2:
Fill out the
information
for your new
bookmark.

5. **Click the Save button.**

6. **When you're ready to write your post, open the Delicious site and search for items with your special tag.**

   Delicious also has bookmarking tools for the popular browsers, which makes it even easier to bookmark URLs. Just download the one for your browser at `http://delicious.com/help/tools` and follow the instructions to install it on your computer.

If you're the sort of person who wakes up in the middle of the night with brilliant ideas, don't forget to keep a notebook and pen on your bedside table as well. In the light of day, your idea may not sound as good, but you'll never know if you don't capture it.

Read the Paper

Skim the whole paper, page one to the end, including the ads and the sections you don't normally read. You don't have to read every word of every article, but you need to at least look at everything.

This works better with the newsprint version, so you can let your mind wander across the page. As you read, hopefully something jumps off the page and demands to be written, or perhaps an image captures your imagination and leads to an idea.

And even if you don't find your muse in the morning paper, you'll know what's going on in the world.

Reread Your Favorite Posts

Dive into your archives and reread your favorite posts. Pay particular attention to the comments — both yours and readers'. Perhaps a follow-up is just begging to be written, or you've found new information about the topic that merits an update. If all else fails, you can always write a *roundup* — a post that summarizes a collection of previous posts.

If you go the roundup route, try to have a theme or topic — "My Favorite Posts about *Topic*," — rather than the generic — "Posts I've Loved." The generic is okay every once in a (long) while, perhaps once a year; but do it too often, and it becomes somewhat cliché and a bit boring. Following a theme also lets you and your readers see how your thoughts on a subject have changed (or not) over time.

A roundup that has a theme is also a good tactic to cover a vacation or other extended periods in which you won't have time to blog or don't have Internet access. For example, before I left for a ten-day trip to Africa in September 2009, I pulled together thematic roundups of previous posts on customer service, Facebook, and the BlogHer conference and then scheduled them to publish every few days while I was gone.

Read Blogs

Give yourself permission to catch up on your blog reading. And not just the ones written by competitors and close colleagues. Check in on the blogs about your hobbies and personal interests — the ones you usually skip because you don't have enough time.

If you normally read your favorite blogs in a Really Simple Syndication (RSS) reader like Google Reader, make a point of reading at the blog site. Check out some of the other links on the page, particularly the blogroll. Take the time to leave some comments.

If you're lucky, you'll read something that inspires you and gives you the jump-start you need to write your next post. If not, the roundup idea that I mention in the preceding "Reread Your Favorite Posts" section, in this chapter, works nicely here as well but instead of just listing the blogs, write one or two sentences about each one and link to a recent post that you really like.

Surf the 'Net Aimlessly

Don't have a destination in mind. Start at a search engine, aggregator, or portal and just wander where the mouse clicks take you. Here are a few suggestions for starting your journey:

✔ At the Google search page, type in a keyword and then click the I'm Feeling Lucky button, which automatically takes you to the first result for your chosen keyword rather than the results page with multiple links.

✔ Aggregators like Alltop (www.alltop.com, as shown in Figure 17-3) and Yahoo! let you choose from categories and trending topics, and then surf in a pretty traditional manner. Just remember to be a little bit aimless.

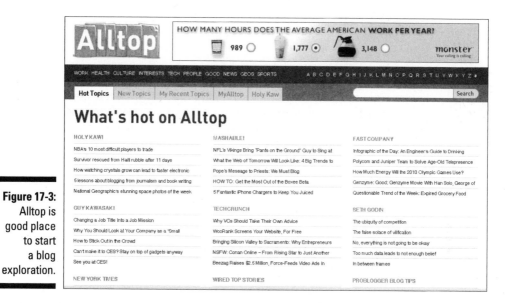

Figure 17-3:
Alltop is
good place
to start
a blog
exploration.

✔ Recommendation community StumbleUpon (`http://stumbleupon.com`) has aimless built right in. After you register and provide a little information about your interests, StumbleUpon takes you to a site. You can give the site a thumbs up or thumbs down, or simply stumble along to the next site from the StumbleUpon toolbar (see the following figure). StumbleUpon uses the information about what you do and don't like to tailor results to your interests.

Spend an Hour on Your Hobby

If your blog is about your hobby, this may not seem like much of a break, but there's a big difference between *doing* something and *writing* about it. Doing something reminds you why you love it, and that's why you started a blog in the first place.

Even if you don't have a hobby, such as stamp collecting, scrapbooking, or bird watching, to which you devote a great deal of time, other activities you enjoy would be worth an hour of your time. For instance, if you like to cook, bake some cookies or a cake. If you enjoy gardening, putter about with your plants. If you like to shop, go window-shopping — online or off. Plan the next family vacation. Grab your camera and take pictures of the cat. Backyard bird watch. Just spend an hour doing something you love.

Play a Game

Truly aimless: Play a game. Word games like Scrabble and Boggle are great ways to take a break while still exercising your verbal skills. You don't even have to own the game or have someone to play with. Online sites like Pogo (www.pogo.com), as shown in Figure 17-4, have more games than you can think of, and many can be played for free.

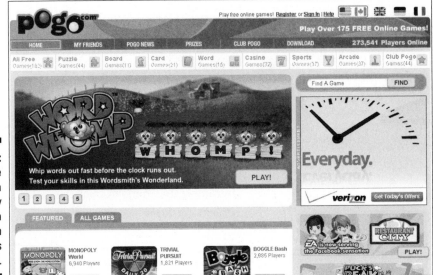

Figure 17-4:
Online game sites are a good way to take a break when your muse is stalled.

Look Up Childhood Friends on Facebook

Yes, this may seem silly, but it's fun to see how people you knew way back when, but have lost touch with, turned out. You may find that it can also be frustrating if you can't find someone you really want to connect with again, but that's part of the game.

Look for someone with an unusual name first, even if that isn't the person you're looking for. She may have already friended other classmates, and you can follow the trail from there.

You can also look for people on LinkedIn, although that's generally better for finding work colleagues than for finding your long-lost best friend from 6th grade.

Take a Walk

Take a walk (and bring your pet if you have one). If you like to take pictures, bring your camera. Don't forget your pen and notebook. If walking isn't your thing or the weather isn't cooperating, any physical exercise works, but make sure that it's something that helps shake off your cobwebs. The exercise needs to also be something you can finish in about an hour. For example, if golf is your activity of choice, don't plan on 18 holes. Instead, go to the driving range for an hour.

The best thing about this? Even if you don't come back inspired, you'll have gotten a little exercise.

Move to a "Different Window"

You can get in a rut, sitting in the same place, looking at the same surroundings, day in and day out. Sometimes all you need is a little change of scenery to shake up things.

Some of the ways you can move to a "different window" are

- ✔ Work in a different room in your home or office.
- ✔ Change your chair.
- ✔ Relocate to a coffee shop or the local library for an hour or two.

The coffee shop or library also allows you to people watch, which can be a good source of material for a blog post.

Index

• J •

Jantsch, John, 331
Jetson Green blog, 70, 176–177
Jordan, Megan, 66
Judy, Jaelithe, SEO expert, 262–264, 266

• K •

Kamin, Mir, 21, 75, 148–149, 300, 312, 329–330
Kane, Erin, 119–120
Kepnes, Matt, 20, 39–40, 87
keywords, 294. *See also* tags
Keywords report, Google Analytics, 294, 296
kirtsy, content aggregator, 27, 36
Kmart, pay-per-post promotion example, 154, 156–157
Koerner, Preston, 70, 176–177
Koh, Christine, 123, 274–275, 301, 312

• L •

legal advisors. *See also* attorneys
  business entities, 57–58
  desirable traits, 59
  existing business blog addition, 59–60
liability protections
  business entities, 55–56
  corporations versus LLC, 56–57
  existing business blog addition, 59–60
libel, 78
like box, Facebook links, 257–258
Like button, Facebook, 258–259
limited liability company (LLC), versus corporations, 56–57
link baiting, avoiding, 245
link farming, 230
LinkedIn, public social network type, 36–37, 251

links
  affiliate marketing, 75, 142
  blog discovery enhancement, 230
  blog enhancement, 324
  blog navigation elements, 206–207
  blogrolls, 39–40, 222–226, 241–244
  category organization methods, 224–226
  versus comments, 250
  exchange request, 244
  existing domain name, 181
  Facebook like box, 257–258
  Flickr photos, 234–235
  Google Alerts, 66
  inbound, 49
  link baiting, 245
  link farming, 230
  post element, 244–246
  professional services, 101–102
  referrers, 284–285
  search engine tracking, 241–242
  trackbacks, 246–247
LinkShare, 143, 145
Linux/Apache/MySQL/PHP (LAMP) environment, 186
Lip-sticking blog, 19, 178, 332
living room doctrine, 228
logos, blog design, 197–198, 204
loyalty, reader engagement, 294

• M •

MacKinnon, Rebecca, 333–334
MailChimp, e-mail marketing software, 71
MamaPop blog, rate card example, 36
marketing campaigns, CAN-SPAM Act compliance, 70–72
marketing programs, 227
Marketing Roadmaps blog, 5, 82
marketing toolkits, blog promotion, 240
Marsh, Julie, 141, 312

• *Q* •

• *R* •

Business/Accounting & Bookkeeping

Bookkeeping For Dummies
978-0-7645-9848-7

eBay Business
All-in-One For Dummies,
2nd Edition
978-0-470-38536-4

Job Interviews
For Dummies,
3rd Edition
978-0-470-17748-8

Resumes For Dummies,
5th Edition
978-0-470-08037-5

Stock Investing
For Dummies,
3rd Edition
978-0-470-40114-9

Successful Time
Management
For Dummies
978-0-470-29034-7

Computer Hardware

BlackBerry For Dummies,
3rd Edition
978-0-470-45762-7

Computers For Seniors
For Dummies
978-0-470-24055-7

iPhone For Dummies,
2nd Edition
978-0-470-42342-4

Laptops For Dummies,
3rd Edition
978-0-470-27759-1

Macs For Dummies,
10th Edition
978-0-470-27817-8

Cooking & Entertaining

Cooking Basics
For Dummies,
3rd Edition
978-0-7645-7206-7

Wine For Dummies,
4th Edition
978-0-470-04579-4

Diet & Nutrition

Dieting For Dummies,
2nd Edition
978-0-7645-4149-0

Nutrition For Dummies,
4th Edition
978-0-471-79868-2

Weight Training
For Dummies,
3rd Edition
978-0-471-76845-6

Digital Photography

Digital Photography
For Dummies,
6th Edition
978-0-470-25074-7

Photoshop Elements 7
For Dummies
978-0-470-39700-8

Gardening

Gardening Basics
For Dummies
978-0-470-03749-2

Organic Gardening
For Dummies,
2nd Edition
978-0-470-43067-5

Green/Sustainable

Green Building
& Remodeling
For Dummies
978-0-470-17559-0

Green Cleaning
For Dummies
978-0-470-39106-8

Green IT For Dummies
978-0-470-38688-0

Health

Diabetes For Dummies,
3rd Edition
978-0-470-27086-8

Food Allergies
For Dummies
978-0-470-09584-3

Living Gluten-Free
For Dummies
978-0-471-77383-2

Hobbies/General

Chess For Dummies,
2nd Edition
978-0-7645-8404-6

Drawing For Dummies
978-0-7645-5476-6

Knitting For Dummies,
2nd Edition
978-0-470-28747-7

Organizing For Dummies
978-0-7645-5300-4

SuDoku For Dummies
978-0-470-01892-7

Home Improvement

Energy Efficient Homes
For Dummies
978-0-470-37602-7

Home Theater
For Dummies,
3rd Edition
978-0-470-41189-6

Living the Country Lifestyle
All-in-One For Dummies
978-0-470-43061-3

Solar Power Your Home
For Dummies
978-0-470-17569-9

Internet
Blogging For Dummies,
2nd Edition
978-0-470-23017-6

eBay For Dummies,
6th Edition
978-0-470-49741-8

Facebook For Dummies
978-0-470-26273-3

Google Blogger
For Dummies
978-0-470-40742-4

Web Marketing
For Dummies,
2nd Edition
978-0-470-37181-7

WordPress For Dummies,
2nd Edition
978-0-470-40296-2

Language & Foreign Language
French For Dummies
978-0-7645-5193-2

Italian Phrases
For Dummies
978-0-7645-7203-6

Spanish For Dummies
978-0-7645-5194-9

Spanish For Dummies,
Audio Set
978-0-470-09585-0

Macintosh
Mac OS X Snow Leopard
For Dummies
978-0-470-43543-4

Math & Science
Algebra I For Dummies,
2nd Edition
978-0-470-55964-2

Biology For Dummies
978-0-7645-5326-4

Calculus For Dummies
978-0-7645-2498-1

Chemistry For Dummies
978-0-7645-5430-8

Microsoft Office
Excel 2007 For Dummies
978-0-470-03737-9

Office 2007 All-in-One
Desk Reference
For Dummies
978-0-471-78279-7

Music
Guitar For Dummies,
2nd Edition
978-0-7645-9904-0

iPod & iTunes
For Dummies,
6th Edition
978-0-470-39062-7

Piano Exercises
For Dummies
978-0-470-38765-8

Parenting & Education
Parenting For Dummies,
2nd Edition
978-0-7645-5418-6

Type 1 Diabetes
For Dummies
978-0-470-17811-9

Pets
Cats For Dummies,
2nd Edition
978-0-7645-5275-5

Dog Training For Dummies,
2nd Edition
978-0-7645-8418-3

Puppies For Dummies,
2nd Edition
978-0-470-03717-1

Religion & Inspiration
The Bible For Dummies
978-0-7645-5296-0

Catholicism For Dummies
978-0-7645-5391-2

Women in the Bible
For Dummies
978-0-7645-8475-6

Self-Help & Relationship
Anger Management
For Dummies
978-0-470-03715-7

Overcoming Anxiety
For Dummies
978-0-7645-5447-6

Sports
Baseball For Dummies,
3rd Edition
978-0-7645-7537-2

Basketball For Dummies,
2nd Edition
978-0-7645-5248-9

Golf For Dummies,
3rd Edition
978-0-471-76871-5

Web Development
Web Design All-in-One
For Dummies
978-0-470-41796-6

Windows Vista
Windows Vista
For Dummies
978-0-471-75421-3

How-to?
How Easy.